Charles University
Karolinum Press

PRAGUE

ITS GARDENS AND PARKS

Božena Pacáková-Hošťálková

Photographs by Věroslav Škrabánek

Translated by David Short

Karolinum Press

Originally published in Czech as *Praha – zahrady a parky*, Prague: Karolinum, 2016
KAROLINUM PRESS, Ovocný trh 560/5, 116 36 Prague 1, Czech Republic
Karolinum Press is a publishing department of Charles University in Prague
www.karolinum.cz

Edited by Milada Motlová (Czech) and Martin Janeček (English)
Cover and graphic design by Zdeněk Ziegler
Typeset by DTP Karolinum
Printed in the Czech Republic by EUROPRINT a.s.
First English edition

ISBN 978-80-246-3422-7

The manuscript was reviewed by Prof. Václav Girsa (Czech Technical University,
Faculty of Architecture, Institute of Heritage) and Dr. Věra Vávrová (The Silva Tarouca
Research Institute for Landscape and Ornamental Gardening)

The Prague series is edited by Milada Motlová

OBSAH

The Art of the Garden Across the Thousand-year History
of Prague   /13

A Guide to the Gardens and Parks of Prague   /45

Hradčany: The Castle – Pohořelec – The Marian Walls   /46
*Stag Moat – The Royal Garden – The Paradise and Rampart Gardens –
The St Wenceslas Vineyard – The Bulwark (Na Baště) Garden – The Černín
Garden – Chotek Gardens – Villa Kramář*

Hradčany: Strahov   /78
The Great Strahov Garden – The Monks' Garden

Malá Strana: Petřín Hill   /85
*The Lobkowicz Garden – The Garden at Three Red Roses House – The
Garden of the Storberg House – The Schönborn Garden – The Wratislaw
(Mitrovitz) Garden – The Vrtba Garden – The Seminary Garden –
Nebozízek Garden – The Park by the Petřín Lookout Tower – The Petřín
Hill Rose Gardens*

Malá Strana: Malá Strana Square – Klárov   /114
*The Leslie Garden – The Wallenstein (Valdštejnská) Garden – The Palace
Gardens on the Southern Slope of Prague Castle – The Ledebour Garden –
The Lesser and Great Pálffy Gardens – The Kolowrat Garden – The Lesser
Fürstenberg Garden - The Great Fürstenberg Garden*

Malá Strana: Kampa Island – Kosárek Embankment   /146
*Kampa Island and The Nostitz Garden – The Maltese Garden – Vojan
Gardens – The Straka Academy*

Prague Old Town (Staré Město)   /158
The Kranner Fontain

Prague New Town (Nové Město)   /162
*The Franciscan Garden – Slavonic (Slovanský) Island – Charles Square
Park (Karlovo Náměstí) - The Amerika Summer House – The Botanical
Garden of Charles University*

Vyšehrad   /179
The Ducal and Royal Acropolis – Karlach Gardens – Štulc Gardens –
Villa Kovařovič

Vinohrady   /190
Rieger Gardens – Svatopluk Čech and Bezruč Gardens – Gröbovka Garden

Vršovice   /200
Svatopluk Čech Square

Nusle   /202
Fidlovačka Park – Jezerka Park

Chodov   /206
Chodov Fort

Smíchov And Košíře   /210
The Kinský Garden – Bertramka – The Na Skalce Gardens – Santoška
Garden – Klamovka Garden – Cibulka Park

Břevnov And Liboc   /228
The Monastic Garden at Břevnov – The Hvězda Game Park and Summer
House

Střešovice (With Part of the Area Belonging to Břevnov)   /238
Villa Müller – Villa Rothmayer

Bubeneč And Troja   /244
The Royal Game Preserve – Stromovka – Troja House (or Villa Šternberk) –
St Clare's Vineyard – Prague Botanical Gardens

Holešovice: Letná   /262
Letná Gardens

Karlín   /266
Karlín Square – Lyčka Square – The Invalidovna – Kaizl Gardens

Prosek   /273
Friendship Park

Connections Through Space   /276
Glossary   /283
Trees and Shrubs   /287
Luminaries in the History of the Gardens of Prague   /306
Where the Gardens Are   /310
Illustrations   /314
Acknowledgements   /317
About the author   /318

THE ART OF THE GARDEN ACROSS THE THOUSAND-YEAR HISTORY OF PRAGUE

The ways in which the parks and gardens of Prague were laid down and have progressively altered in appearance went hand in hand with how human settlement has evolved in the picturesque environment of the Prague basin. From the very outset, Prague spread out along both banks of the River Vltava (Moldau) and gradually expanded along its tributaries. Gardens and, later, parks evolved meanwhile into distinctive topographical entities. The naturally favourable conditions were successfully exploited by their originators and designers whatever the age and prevailing style. The range of gardens began to be enhanced by parks as civil society evolved during the bustling nineteenth century, which was in many senses a turning-point.

The first gardens in Prague are assumed to have been in the twelfth and thirteenth centuries, chiefly in association with monastic houses and burgher dwellings. From the very start there were cultivated gardens and vineyards at the Premonstratensian priory at Strahov, founded in 1140 on the Stráž hilltop. Extensive archaeological research has revealed a unique Romanesque aqueduct, which, exploiting gravity, kept all the lands managed by the priory fed with water. One part of it was a through-flow trapezoidal reservoir in the cloister garth to which was linked the lavatorium, a structure consisting of a well and fountain. The monastery was integrated into the fortifications of Hradčany when these were extended in the mid-14th century. The first written records of a garden at the Bishop's Court in Malá Strana are dated 1336; in 1661, however, the site became home to a community of Discalced Carmelite nuns. Prague's Old Town boasted a model garden at the Convent of St Agnes, founded *c.* 1234 by King Wenceslas I and his sister Agnes for the Poor Clares and shortly after that for the Franciscans. Also in the Old Town there are historical references to gardens attached to burgher dwellings in the Old Town Square, Fruit Market (Ovocný trh), and along three streets: Štupartská, Rytířská and Bartolomějská.

The mediaeval garden had its spiritual context, the sense of which is broadly encapsulated in the familiar symbolic representations of an enclosed garden (*Hortus conclusus*) associated with images of the Madonna. Pictures of her in a garden full of flowers, with a fruit-laden tree, or a basket of pomegranates and spring of life-giving water, are to be found in this country at, say, Duchcov or Litoměřice. These are taken to be their painters' renditions of the story of the Virgin Mary linked, along with a unicorn hunt, to the Annunciation. Motifs from the Song of Songs were also transformed into the symbolism of the security and harmony afforded by an enclosed garden.

THE MASTER OF VYŠŠÍ BROD: *Christ on the Mount of Olives*, tempera on wood, before 1350

A scene from the Passion from the altarpiece in the church of the Vyšší Brod Cistercian convent adds profound symbolism to the eternal theme of the garden. Here, in the Garden of Gethsemane, a place of contemplation and repose, the symbolism is conveyed, not only by the figures of Christ and the apostles Peter, James and John, but also by the trees and birds. The oak marks the boundary between the spiritual and the temporal, while also symbolising the power and steadfastness of faith, ivy its constancy and laurel its triumph. The sleeping apostles are being guarded by their vigilant souls, symbolised by the birds in the trees: a goldfinch, a bullfinch and a hoopoe.

In 1348 Charles IV issued his *Maiestas Carolina,* which covered, among other things, the enlargement of Prague by its New Town and the foundation charter of the university. Both were part of Charles' grand scheme to boost the all-round prosperity of the Kingdom of Bohemia and elevate Prague to the administrative and economic centre of Central Europe and the seat of the ruler of the Holy Roman Empire. In the beginning, most houses were built in the area between to-day's Wenceslas Square and Růžová Street and between Charvátova and Spálená Streets, and gardens were an essential part of them. Charles IV's personal physician, Angelo of Florence, built a house near Růžová Street with a physic garden adjacent. It lay roughly at the intersection of today's Jindřišská and Politických

MASTER OF THE TIBURTINE SIBYL: *Madonna and Child in a Garden*, tempera on wood, 1494.

This image of the Virgin and Child is from Litoměřice and is of the "Hortus conclusus" type. The designation does not just denote the mediaeval enclosed garden, but is one of the titles accorded to the Virgin Mary, expressing the closed condition of her womb, her condition of virgo intacta that endured right from the conception of her son through to his birth. The various motifs (tower, flowers, trees and shrubs, peacock etc.) lend the image its symbolic meaning, all being related to her virginity and motherhood, but also to Christ's immortality and divinity. The depiction also concerns the Church's interpretation of the message of the Song of Songs.

Men Working in an Orchard

Illuminated illustration from the Wenceslas IV Bible (1390–1395), held at the Austrian National Gallery in Vienna, capturing to perfection the essence of the mediaeval garden or orchard. The sense of enclosure and man's need to demarcate and protect a place of security in which to live and work is given material expression in the wicker fence.

vězňů Streets. Angelo grew medicinal herbs, aromatic plants and herbs and spices for the kitchen and to flavour wine. At a later date another Florentine apothecary, Onofrio, had a garden at the spot called Na Slupi.

Charles IV granted quite large lands to all newly founded religious houses. In the northern part of the New Town there were the monasteries of Our Lady of the Snows (Franciscan) and St Ambrose (Benedictine), to the south the 'Na Trávníčku' (On the Lawn) monastery (Servite), St Catherine's convent (Augustinian), the Augustinian Canons' house at Karlov, the Benedictine monastery 'Na Slovanech' and also the College of Canons at St Apollinaris' atop Větrov hill. Imaginary lines joining the main churches still form a discernible cross over the area, expressing the blessed status of the city. The upright runs from Sts Peter and Paul at Vyšehrad through St Mary's on the Lawn, St Apollinaris' and St Catherine's. The cross-beam meets it at St Apollinaris' and runs between the church of the Virgin Mary and the Slav Saints ('Na Slovanech') and that of the Virgin Mary and St Charles the Great at Karlov. Convent and monastery gardens reinforced the visual aspect of their churches and served essentially as basic distinguishing features.

The siting of most Christian churches on an east-west axis is connected with the movement of the Sun and is projected onto the classical cross that underlies all compositions of space and architecture from the Gothic to the Baroque and it is taken up by almost all thoughtful systems of development. Derived from it is also the interior layout of monastic gardens: the position of the church usually determined where the garth would be and the church's length its dimensions. Then it was quite common for the other parts of monastic gardens to be derived from the garth in a modular manner in patterns recalling a cross or regular grid.

In the Middle Ages everything had to have a use. This applied equally to monastic gardens, which were also places for rest, meditation and the winning of knowledge. To this end they were plotted with great care, considerably aided by a plan of the ideal monastery at Sankt Gallen, drafted in the scriptorium of the monastery at Reichenau. Like all mediaeval gardens, monastic gardens were typically enclosed and of sober aspect, with a striking emphasis on the symbolism of life. This was concentrated in the garth, bordered by the cloister and set between the monks' quarters and the church. The garth was the centre of gravity, the very heart of a claustral complex, and life and spiritual purgation were symbolised in it by the water in the well or cistern. Additionally, the presence of water had a practical cleansing significance. Within the garth flowers for the altar were grown, and sometimes medicinal herbs. The structure of a monastery's land stabilised at quite an early date. There would always be an orchard, often a vineyard, and separate areas for growing medicinal plants, herbs and vegetables. With the passage of time the space began to be differentiated according to occupancy of the house: there would often be one garden for the monks and another for the abbot.

Prague New Town, which enjoyed unprecedented numbers of gardens thanks to the grand scale of its planning, took some of the pressure off the Old Town. For their part, the Lesser Town and Hradčany were extended up to the line of the later Hunger Wall. All around the established quadripartite city of Prague a ring of gardens and vineyards sprang up to complete the city's image and reinforce perception of it as home to the official residence of the Holy Roman Emperor. Charles IV ordered and promoted the outward spread of vineyards to a distance of three leagues by two privileges issued in 1358. Prague was able to draw on the land accumulated in New Town, the areas added to the Lesser Town and Hradčany and within the three-league belt for the next five centuries and more.

A 1562 view of Prague, known as the Wroclaw Panorama, was done over two hundred years after Prague New Town was founded and captures the city's transformation at the Renaissance. However, the situation depicted provides an excellent idea of how the city was arranged and structured in its Gothic aspect, including the ring of vineyards. The image is also confirmation of how far ahead of their time such developments were in anticipating the ideals of the Proto-Renaissance.

During the turbulent fifteenth century the Prague conurbation had to cope with the tensions and dissensions that preceded and accompanied the Hussite Wars and went on even after they ended in 1436. The city had to wrestle long and hard with the consequences, which is why there is little point in seeking parallels with the great centres where the Renaissance flourished, most notably Florence. Moreover the application of the rules of linear perspective and the principles of the method of intersection, rediscovered by Fillipo Brunelleschi and reworked after him by Alberti, were only being experimented with in the organisation of actual spaces and many mistakes were made.

PRAGA BOHEMIÆ METROPOLIS,

To the benefit of how people lived in the Old Town the Renaissance left its mark chiefly through restructurings of and remarkable alterations to courtyards. The perception of the tree as a symbol of life, man's lineage, knowledge or Paradise has bequeathed to us a striking repertoire of house signs. The best conditions for new departures were to be found particularly on the southern slopes beneath the Castle and on the slopes of Petřín Hill, which had been joined to the Lesser Town.

The first fully integrated Renaissance innovation in Prague is deemed to be the Royal Gardens including Queen Anne's summer house (the Belvedere) with its quite remarkable and, north of the Alps, unique sculpture and reliefs. The garden was begun in 1534, and the summer house in 1538, by Paolo della Stella and Giovanni Spatio. It was commissioned by Ferdinand I Habsburg, at the time King of Bohemia, Hungary and Germany and Archduke of Austria (Holy Roman Emperor after 1556). Since there was too little space within the Castle's fortifications to install a garden befitting a monarch, it was located on the far side of the ravine of the Brusnice stream, where until then there had been a vineyard. The garden's situation was given plenty of forethought, as indicated not only by how it is laid out in parallel to the east-west axis of St George's Basilica and St Vitus' Cathedral, but also by the location of the summer house and *giardinetto* at the eastern end of the garden in the manner of a choir or presbytery. Given

JAN KOZEL – MICHAEL PETRLE: *Veduta of Prague 1562*, woodcut.

A view of Prague, also known as the Wroclaw Prospect after the place where it is held, capturing it as an enclosed, still Gothic city, but with the first signs of its Renaissance transformation, which was largely delayed owing to the great fire of Malá Strana and Hradčany in 1541. It also reveals the surprising number of gardens, orchards and vineyards with which the city became endowed in the age of Charles IV. They were enclosed by fences and formed a ring round the town.

the period, the local climate and other circumstances, the construction of the garden and summer house is viewed as an extraordinary feat.

Ferdinand I was involved personally in setting up his palace garden. There are ample indications that he himself set down the basic design, which reveals a knowledge of the spacing of intermediate nodal points and the prolongation of specific directions. The garden's deliberate east-west orientation underlay the vertical symbolic link to the Castle and city, which may be taken as a conscious allusion to the St Wenceslas tradition. It takes the form of a cross with its base in Lesser Town Square (Malostranské náměstí) at the spot where the Romanesque rotunda of St Wenceslas once stood (in 1283 the parish church of St Nicholas was built close by, only to be displaced by St Nicholas' church during the Baroque period). The cross's upright ends in the middle of the garden, its cross-beam lying on the east-west axis of St Vitus' Cathedral and St George's Basilica, with the east-west axis of the garden parallel to it. It is conceivable that the basic east-west line was deemed to be one connecting the fountain in the second courtyard and

(21)

The Royal Garden and summer house, copper engraving, 1666.

An illustration from *Historia Coelestis*, a book published in 1666, under the pseudonym Lucius Barrettus, by the German astronomer Albert Curtz, latinised as Albertus Curtius. The disposition of the garden as captured here confirms its division into western and eastern parts, still with the covered walk in the latter. The eastern part is dominated by the summer house, in front of which lies the *giardinetto* with the Singing Fountain. The Royal Garden is seen here still in its Renaissance form with Mannerist touches, which permits us to describe the image as a unique document of its kind.

the well (not visible today) between St Vitus' Cathedral and St George's Basilica; the east-west axis of both buildings runs parallel to this line. It is also possible that the symbolism is based on the principle of the double, that, is archbishop's or patriarch's cross, which could be evidence that the draughtsmanship was rather accurate. An understanding of the principle also explains why the brothers Nicolas and Claudius Reinhardt, no sooner had they reached Prague from Alsace, began altering the square space in the middle of the garden in 1541. Ferdinand I had asked the Prince-Bishop of Strasbourg, Wilhelm III von Hohenstein, to send them to him after he had visited the latter with a view to discovering more about the softly-softly methods he was using in pursuit of the Counter-Reformation involving art and an evolving education system. During his visit, Ferdinand I had seen the Alsatian bishop's palace garden at Saverne, where he was quite taken by its layout and conceived the desire that the garden of his own residence be modelled on it, organised according to the principles of axial and crosswise connections and divided into syntactic compartments alternating both spatially and in terms of their content. Ferdinand also had the time to see the compositionally and ideologically most important *giardinetto* and summer house enclosed by a wall with niches and windows, thus crowning his idea of a having a 'chancel'.

In 1534, the construction of the Royal Garden having started, Ferdinand I also founded the *Nová obora* (New Game Park) at Liboc. It was here that his son, the Archduke Ferdinand of Tyrol, later demonstrated both his imaginative sense of space and his artistic talents: in 1555-58 a summer house was built here to his design, later to be renamed, along with the Game Park, *Hvězda* (Star). Previous to that, in 1547, the Archduke had been designated Vicegerent of the Lands of the Bohemian Crown and gradually he also took on supervision of the works in progress at the Royal Garden, which had been interrupted in 1541 by a great fire in Malá Strana and Hradčany.

Mannerism, into which the late Renaissance had evolved, became an international movement after 1550 and crystallised at the court of Rudolph II into a distinctive late-Renaissance trend. Rudolph II was crowned King of Bohemia and of the Romans (German King) in 1575 and a year later became Holy Roman Emperor. He had long dreamed of relocating to Prague and fulfilled that dream in

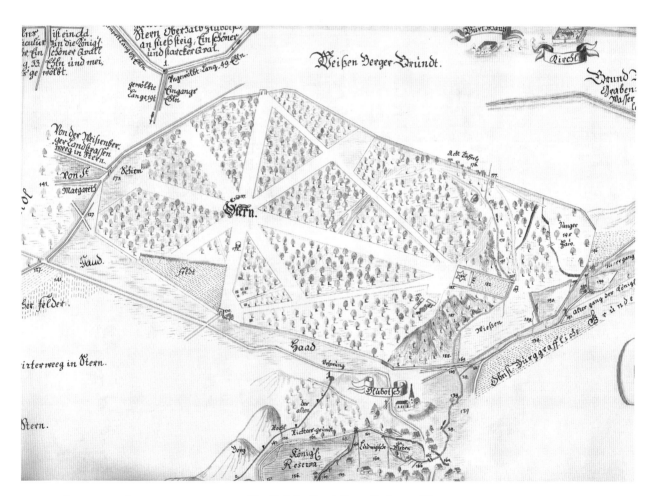

FRANTIŠEK ANTONÍN LEOPOLD KLOSSE: *The Hvězda (Star) Game Park on a Plan of the Castle Water Supply System*, drawing – section of the map, 1723.

The map of the Castle water supply system shows the route of the pipeline with the wider environment, from Hostivice to Prague Castle. Water was drawn from the Litovice Stream, which runs alongside the boundary wall in the lower part of the Park. The depiction of the game park is evidence of its striking star-shaped design and internal structure. Also visible is the park's outer wall and the keeper's lodge by the Liboc Gate.

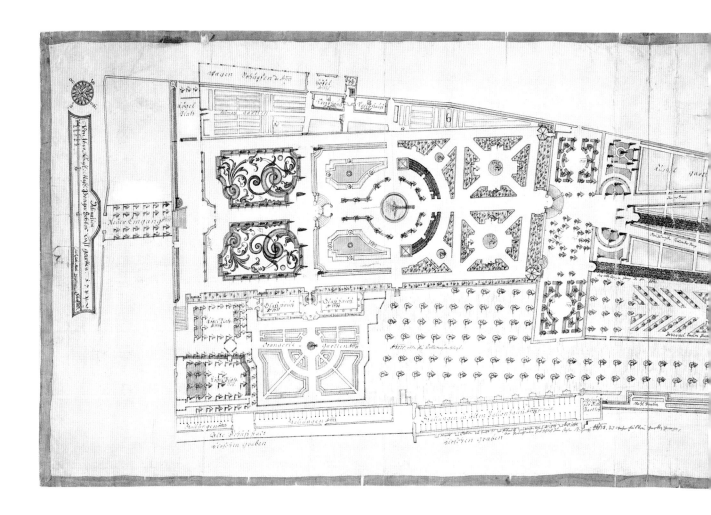

1583. His father, Maximilian II, had completed the second pathway in the Royal Garden, long before, on an east-west axis that reinforced the dominant axial conception. He had also seen the great ball-game hall built, and the figgery on a sheltered terrace beneath the summer house. Rudolph II replaced the wooden menagerie with a brick-built lion yard, which is said to have served as a theatre. Like his father, Rudolph II was not minded to alter the Royal Garden in the spirit of, say, 'mise-en-scène' or any other apotheosis of Mannerism as created in Italy at the Tivoli, the Villa Caprarola or the Villa di Pratolino. He probably settled on the layout of certain areas following drawings sent him by Jan Vredeman de Vries, described as the practical theorist of the Mannerist garden. The Renaissance structure also suited Rudolph when it came to positioning his various quirky elements, such as the cave with mirrors and concealed musical instruments, the topiary statues or the metalwork structures filled with topiary work, climbing shrubs and flowers, one of which was said to express the Lord's Prayer in Latin.

In the Royal Game Preserve at Bubeneč (probably founded by Přemysl Otakar II back in 1268), Rudolph II was quite unstinting in his new departures. After 1582 he enlarged the lake (constructed in 1548 under Ferdinand I) to an area of 20 hectares, and to keep it fed with water from the Vltava he had a tunnel built between 1582 and 1593. This was dug by miners from Kutná Hora; four shafts having been sunk, the men worked towards each other from opposite directions.

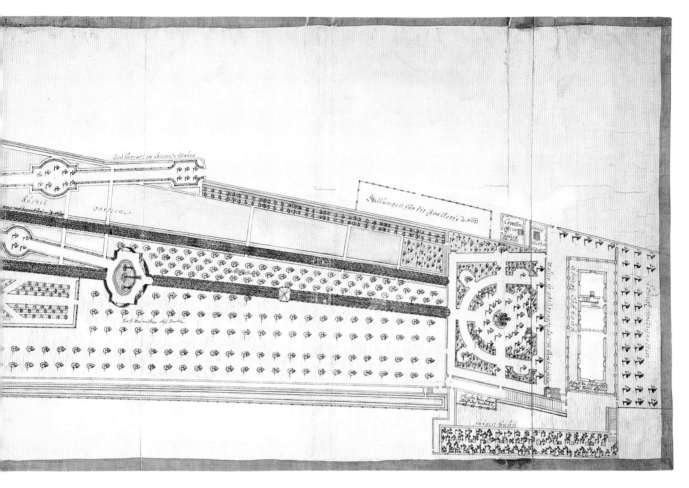

J. M. ZIEGELMAYER: *The Royal Garden*, plan, 1744.

The arrival of the Baroque in the Royal Garden was heralded as early as 1670 by the erection of the Hercules Fountain. The main phase of Baroque adaptations came later, in 1728–1735, with themes attributed to the clerk of works J. H. Dinebierovi, the overall design of the Baroque innovations being worked out by the court gardener František Zinner. Ziegelmayer's plan captures the Royal Garden shortly after the Baroque reworking was completed.

Rudolph's Tunnel is a unique piece of engineering, situated some 45 metres beneath ground level. It can be traversed on foot, and it is 1102 metres long, 0.8 to 2.5 metres wide and 2 to 4 metres from floor to ceiling. The point of entry with the water-gate is on the river bank in a small waterworks building called *Havírna* (the "Miners' Place"). And at the Royal Game Preserve end a portal was completed with a monogram of Rudolph II and the date 1593. The lake, originally linked to the tunnel by a 100-metre-long canal, was drained in the late 18th century, but its banks and an island remain in evidence of it. Rudolph's creativity in the Game Preserve went further: for example, at one point on the lake's shore a vivarium was set up in which the fish needed for daily consumption were kept, while three smaller ponds were dug for raising trout and waterfowl; the western end of the preserve was adapted as a pheasantry, and a small hunting lodge was converted into a summer house. Later plans reveal that the composition aimed for and stabilised under Rudolph II largely remained intact when the preserve was turned into a public park in 1804. The nearby mill and hide were given to Rudolph in 1584 as a gift from the Prague burgraviate; later he started to reconstruct it as his summer retreat. The Mannerist appointments of the Imperial Mill included in particular an arcaded walkway, a fish-pond and a unique grotto. And by permission of the Emperor, Petr Hýbl and Ottavio Misseroni had their workshop for grinding and polishing stones here.

The 1606 panorama of Prague by Philip van den Bossche, known as the Sadeler Panorama, captures the city with the sheer amount of land given over to gardens, and on closer inspection it is even possible to make out the summer house and the greenhouse used for growing pomegranates and figs in the Royal Garden. After Rudolph II's abdication in 1611, pomegranates and figs may well have continued to flourish, but otherwise it was a time of tragedy. The fate of Bohemia for the next three hundred years was sealed by the Battle of the White Mountain on Sunday, 21st June, 1621. The defeat of the army of the Bohemian Estates at the hands of the armies of the Catholic League and the Holy Roman Empire was completed by the execution of twenty-seven Bohemian lords on Old Town Square, where imperial troops were on guard under the command of General Albrecht von Wallenstein.

The late-Renaissance residence of Albrecht Wenzel Eusebius von Wallenstein in Malá Strana was constructed between 1623 and 1630 on the site of 25 houses, gardens, a brickworks, a gateway to the Castle and some unoccupied plots. The "Colonel of Prague", as the then supreme commander of the city, Albrecht von Wallenstein, was called, was quick to enlist Giovanni Pieroni de Galiano, much to the benefit of his palatial seat. Pieroni had come to Prague to modernise its fortifications. This Italian fortification engineer and architect, but also cosmographer and mathematician, had worked out the most propitious moment for the foundation stone to be laid when the wings of the Pitti Palace in Florence were to be reconstructed. Hand in hand with this development was one major stage in the shaping of the Boboli Gardens, whereby the knoll at the back of the Pitti Palace was shaped into a semicircular, six-row garden amphitheatre.

The Wallenstein Garden (Valdštejnská zahrada) in Prague is remarkable for its composition of upward sightlines that reveals, above the vista of the sizeable *sala terrena*, a panorama of Prague Castle. The grotto motif, typical of Mannerist gardens, is rendered here in an unusual planar form. The collection of Mannerist statues is the work of Adriaen de Vries. His teacher had been Giovanni Bologna (Giambologna), who had created, for the Medici Villa di Pratolino in Tuscany, the Appenine Colossus, a huge figure leaning over a pool. The deployment of de Vries' originals was originally governed by a scheme rooted in mythology, though the nodal points and hierarchy have yet to be fully appreciated.

Following Albrecht von Wallenstein's murder in Cheb (Eger) in 1634, Emperor Ferdinand II appointed as supreme commander of the imperial army his own son, who in 1637 became his successor. The prudent and educated Ferdinand III entered peace negotiations, though the Thirty Years' War did not end until the Peace of Westphalia in 1648. The Swedes, who had been laying siege to Prague (actually until November 1st, though the peace had been signed on October 24th),

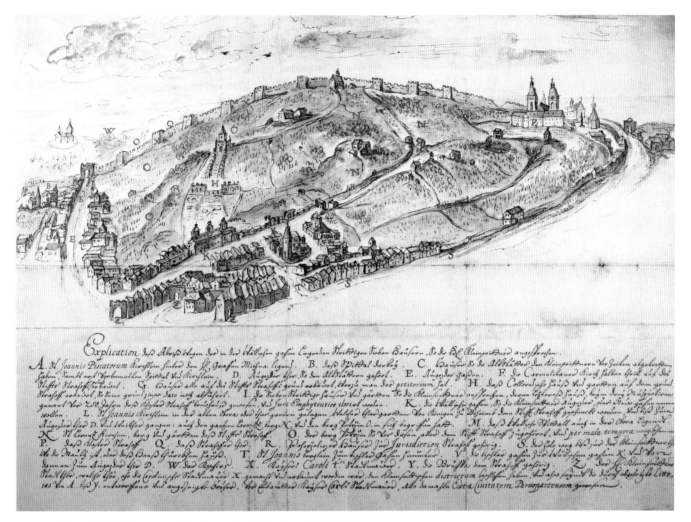

View of Malá Strana and Strahov, tinted drawing, 1659–1665.

This view from Hradčany of unknown authorship captures Strahov and the Malá Strana part of Petřín Hill. Its incorporation in the then Lesser Town was decreed by Charles IV, who also ordered the construction of the fortified Hunger Wall that encloses the area depicted. The drawing confirms the existence of the spectacular early-Baroque Colloredo Garden (marked H), later altered many times over and renamed the Schönborn Garden.

removed and took back with them numerous precious objects from Rudolph II's collection and also the originals of de Vries' statues from the Wallenstein Garden. These are held in the Swedish royal palace of Drottningholm and they have been replaced in the garden by copies.

The changes in aesthetic awareness that signalled the onset of the Baroque came hard on the heels of the Thirty Years' War. Baroque garden art was prolific in Prague, diverse in its expression, but quite specific in its conception and range. Palace gardens became the rage and they were noteworthy for their sheer variety and the ingenuity of their layouts. Dedicated reflexion of the local milieu acknowledged its powerful Gothic heritage, and the development of axial systems also made full use of the knowledge of how arrangements of the various elements were assembled and sequenced during the Renaissance. This was also manifest in the amazing variety of objects that recalled the *casini*, gloriettes and *palazzi* on the topmost terraces of Italian gardens, not to mention the native tradition of a wine press with a view, which within a range of possibilities unheard-of elsewhere – a *theatron*, a *bellaria*, a gloriette, a pavilion, loggias, and a little lookout tower – are all on view in one or other of the palace gardens of Malá Strana.

On the northern slope of Petřín Hill there is a *theatron* on the highest level of the Vrtba Garden, an ingenious edifice that encloses the terraced composition of the garden in the manner of a theatre backdrop. It bulges outwards towards the garden and is decorated with reliefs of marine deities and originally it also had a trompe l'oeil fresco by Václav Vavřinec Reiner that amplified the structure's effect. In the neighbouring Wratislaw Garden there was a *bellaria*, a summer house with an open gallery, whose lightness, openness and airiness (as suggested by the Italian word), became a thing of the past first because of general dilapidation and then because of being reconstructed in modern times as an office building. At the highest point of the Schönborn Garden there is a gloriette with an arcade at ground level and a pavilion-like extension which even today stabilises the north-south orientation of the garden's original Baroque composition.

The *casini*, gloriettes and *palazzi* on the topmost terraces of Italian gardens and the native tradition of wine presses with a view are also brought to mind by the buildings in the Palace Gardens on the Southern Slope below Prague Castle (as they are collectively known). In the Ledebour Garden there is a polygonal pavilion as the furthermost point on the main axis of the terraced composition. A pavilion is usually a smallish free-standing structure, but here it is integrated into the perimeter load-bearing wall, which is given rhythm by its niches and blind arcades and serves as a point that adds stability to the space. For beyond this wall the Rampart Garden takes matters further and the entire composition actually culminates in the Maria Theresa wing of Prague Castle, which works on the *shakkei* principle of "borrowed scenery" in the connecting spatial projection. A unique pair of structural features is to be found at the top end of the Lesser Fürstenberg Garden, where the axial composition of the terraces is surmounted by the *loggetta*, a loggia open to the garden through three arches and supporting an observation point. The other feature is a kind of summer house topped off with a little lookout tower, the whole set at the highest, eastern, extremity of the garden and approached by a staircase that joins the loggia and the viewing terrace. For its part, the terraced composition of the Great Fürstenberg Garden is crowned by an intriguing two-storey pavilion. It is integrated into the boundary wall (behind which are the Old Castle Steps), and the rooms on its two floors are linked by an exterior staircase.

The configuration of Prague's Baroque gardens bears clear evidence of how various fashionable forms were being received, though they were invariably displayed in a distinctive new cast and with due regard to the highly specific environment. One can only marvel at the skill required to create works of genius in conditions of spatial constraint. Given the rugged terrain, there is no gainsaying the inspiration, fired by trends coming from Italy, in the use of systems of terraces, stairways, platforms and water features. Knowledge of linear perspective and projection methods was often put to good use. Prague lacked the optimum

ANTONÍN LANGWEIL: *The Vrtba Garden* –
section of a model, 1826–1837.

This section of the model created by Antonín
Langweil over a hundred years after the Vrtba
Garden was founded perfectly captures the dynamism and gradation of the Baroque system of terraces. It documents the concave and convex lines
of the supporting walls with their inbuilt staircas-
es and also shows the terminal *theatron*, probably
with its original fresco, while the paintwork on
the blank panels of the decoratively articulated
walls is no longer to be seen. We can also see the
changes in the layout of the paths and the use of
vegetation, amounting to Empire and Romantic
implants into the garden's Baroque substance.

conditions for grand-scale Baroque gardens in the French style, yet their influence, too, is manifest to a degree, notably in the enhancement of the axial system
by having an expanded linear network and spatial expansion managed by a
system of transecting lines. A further asset was in the application of knowledge
of how to sculpt vegetation as a substitute for buildings and how water could be
put to use. An interesting attendant phenomenon was the morphological cross-
fertilisation of various styles.

   The Baroque was brilliant at emphasising plasticity, creating depth and achiev-
ing spatial overlapping. In the conglomerate of terraced gardens in Malá Strana
the 'theatre box' effect is employed. Gardens cut into the sloping terrain afford
a progressively wider panorama of the city as one passes up from one level to
the next. For example, the Vrtba Garden presents the view that stretches from
St Nicholas' Cathedral on Malá Strana Square to the church of Our Lady of
Victories in Karmelitská Street, but having ascended to the vantage point on the
theatron at the very top, one is rewarded with a wide, veduta-like panorama in
which Prague Castle is the dominant feature. Taking the downward view from

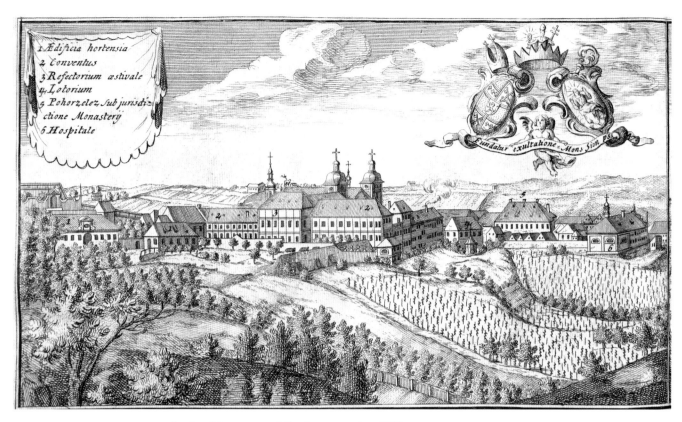

Strahov Monastery and Garden, engraving, 1736.

The engraving is by an unknown hand probably after a 1732 drawing by J. J. Dietzlera, published at Nancy in 1736 by the Premonstratensian historian Ludovicus Hugo in the order's annals, *Sacri et canonici ordinis praemonstratensis annales II*. The view confirms the continuing practical use of the gardens on the slopes to the east of the monastery buildings.

the theatron, one may also take in the Vrtba Garden's entire composition. A mix of rewarding views is also to be had from more palace gardens on the northern slope of Petřín Hill. The principle is analogous to that which applies to those set into the southern slope beneath the Castle above Valdštejnská Street. And here, too, downward views come into play, revealing the adjacent gardens.

Ingenious overlapping that picks up on external nodal points and creates amazing connections across space was put to good effect in many gardens adapted to the Baroque. In the Monks' Garden at Strahov Monastery there is the renowned 'keyhole peep', a full panorama of the city opening up from the eastern terrace. The Černín Garden at Hradčany makes much of an association with the legendary Mount Říp. It is all the more surprising, then, that what its instigator, Humprecht Jan Černín of Chudenice, had available to him was an L-shaped piece of land on which it was tricky to design any kind of ostentatious palatial residence. It took him a while to find the right architect, but Francesco Caratti was able to oblige: he opted for a rectangular ground plan for the palace and raised the grand façade on its longer side, facing Loreta Square and by extension the Castle, as Černín had desired. He designed the garden as an unusual extension of the front façade, but facing the side of the house, to which he gave the stamp of a garden-facing frontage. He achieved both unity and contrast by

*Prospectus Palatii Czerninensis cum Horto accliri Prospect des Gräffl. Tzerninischen Haüßes samt demselben Berg-aüf.
Pragæ in urbe parva. steigenden Garten Zü Prag aüf der Kleinen Seiten.*

F. B. Werner del. *C. P. S. C. Maj.* *Ioh. Georg Ringle fecit.* *Mart. Engelbrecht exc. A.V.*

JOHANN GEORG RINGLE: **Černín Palace and Garden**, engraving, *c.* 1740.

This engraving, probably done by Ringle from a drawing by F. B. Werner, is testimony to
the extraordinary garden creation on the northern slope of Petřín Hill, related axially to the
garden frontage of the palace. The garden's composition is characterised by the broad main
axis and the system of snaking paths.

having the front façade in the style of a *villa urbana*, and the garden side as a *villa
suburbana*. Thus to enter the garden meant entering a different world; in it the
notional link to Mount Říp, so wreathed in legend, was asserted by a connecting
line that amplified the downward view from the Great Hall on the second floor,
taking it compositionally beyond the limits of the garden. Černín himself, the
architect and the actual builder – none of them lived to see the project completed,
and later building works have completely engulfed the spatial connection to Říp.

The compositional outline of the Villa Šternberg (also often known as
Šternberg House or Troja House) and its garden ensured not only an ingenious
conceptual linkage between them, but also the new, Baroque, plan for the entire
area of Troja. The house and garden share the *cardo* axis that determines the
primary composition of the layout as running north-south. Beyond the garden
boundary this axis continues towards Prague Castle, constituting an imaginary
association with it. The transverse *decumanus* axis defines the house's east-west
orientation and extends into the orchard, which is in turn organised in terms of
a star. This basic structure is developed further in the way the garden is divided

Prospect der Pulver Thurms auf dem Hiberner Platz in Prag, von Morgen gegen Mond anzusehen
zu finden bey Johann Balzer in Prag.

LEOPOLD PAUKERT: *The Powder Gate and Old Avenues*, colourised etching, 1790.

The fusion of Prague's Old Town and New Town had been prevented for over four hundred years by a deep defensive ditch. Along the line of today's Na Příkopě Street the ditch was filled in back in 1760, giving way to what came to be called the Old Avenues.

internally, and originally this went further so as to take in the game park (where today Prague Zoo stands).

The Baroque concept behind the Benedictine Monastery at Břevnov goes back to the mid-18th century and is attributed to Kilián Ignác Dientzenhofer, though the possibility is allowed that it could be the work of his father, Kryštof Dientzenhofer, and that Kilián Ignác merely developed it and brought it to fruition. The idea it conveys and the emphasis on its internal integrity is again expressed by a cross. The east-west axis links the Lazarka chapel, the Vojtěška pavilion and the Josefka gloriette and then continues beyond the garden along an imaginary axis through space to St Vitus' Cathedral at Prague Castle, which houses the relics of St Wenceslas, the patron saint of Bohemia, and those of St Adalbert (Vojtěch), the monastery's co-founder. On the north-south axis, which extends in the direction of the high altar of St Margaret's church, lie the garth, the summer refectory and the orangery. Symbolism involving crosses can be seen in other senses and at more than one level. Cross shapes are designed into the garden, in which to work was a lesson in humility and industry, attributes that accord with the order's

FILIP AND FRANTIŠEK HEGER: *The New Avenues*, colourised etching, 1794.

Along the line of today's National Avenue (Národní třída) the deep defensive ditch separating Old Town and New Town was filled in in 1781. In its place came the so-called New Avenues, made up of a roadway and two rows of horse chestnuts. There were marble benches in the New Avenues and later, in 1791, Classicist fountains were installed.

motto, 'Pray and work'. And the Vojtěška pavilion erected over the Brusnice stream has cross vaulting in the oldest surviving part, directly over the spring; it was from here that the foundation of the original monastery followed in 993 A.D.

In the mid-18th century the Baroque peaked, as did, sadly for Prague, the Wars of the Austrian Succession. These had catastrophic consequences especially for the Royal Game Preserve at Bubeneč. It had recovered from the consequences of the Hundred Years' War of a century before, but this time it was so badly ravaged that there was thought of abandoning it completely. Between November 1741 and January 1742 it had served as a Saxon army camp, and in 1744 the Prussian army took up residence. Game animals disappeared as did all the trees, with the exception of the oaks on one small island and part of an avenue of limes along a dyke. The summer house was burnt down and other buildings badly damaged. In 1746 Maria Theresa granted the wish of the Bohemian Estates to have the preserve restored, but no game animals returned.

Some idea of the structure and appearance of Prague as produced in large measure by its Baroque remoulding can be gained from Huber's 1769 plan of the city, done in cavalier perspective. It already captures the first signs of Classicism, the influence of which can be detected on the lower terraces of the Great Pálffy Garden. In 1784, under Joseph II and three years after he had issued the Edict of Tolerance and abolished serfdom, moves instigated by the Emperor demanded the merger of the administration of the four separate towns that made up Prague. It was right after this that Ignác Jan Nepomuk Palliardi designed a by then quite unexpected rococo creation, the Lesser Fürstenberg Garden.

Herget's 1791 map of Prague gives an idea of the planning structure and composition of the city that were the end product of the fertile and formative age of the Baroque. By this stage we have entered the era of Classicism, which was joined, in the early 19th century, by new trends brought in by Romanticism and described as the 'park style'. Space for setting up parks and avenues was initially made available by the scrapping of stretches of defensive ditches and walls within the four towns.

A deep defensive ditch along the line of today's Národní třída and Na Příkopě, which for over four hundred years had been an impediment to the fusion of the Old Town and New Town of Prague, had been filled in along today's Na Příkopě back in 1760, and Huber's 1769 plan captures three or four lines of trees, known as the Old Avenues. The stretch that is today's Národní třída was filled in in 1781 and replaced with avenues of trees complemented with marble benches. These, the New Avenues so-called, consisting of the street and two rows of horse chestnuts, had Classicist stone fountains added at either end in 1791. Increasing traffic soon required the trees to be removed and the promenade to be relocated to the embankment.

Development of the new embankment went hand in hand with the erection of the Emperor Francis I chain bridge in 1839–41, designed by Bedřich Schnirch, at the point where Legions Bridge (Most Legií) stands today. The entire western line of the Francis (today Smetana) Embankment was planted with a line of false acacias. Horse chestnuts reminiscent of the New Avenues did not appear on the Embankment until 1865, over the length of the then Rudolph (today Aleš) Embankment. In connection with the new layout of the Francis Embankment, the years 1844–46 saw the creation of a park in the form of a retreat with a view and including a monument to Emperor Francis I called the Kranner Fountain or Homage of the Bohemian Estates, the model for which was the Schöner Brunnen in Nuremberg. In 1848, to mark the 500th anniversary of the founding of Charles University, the small square that had taken shape between the monastery of the Knights of the Cross with the Red Star and the Bridge Tower at the Old Town end of Charles Bridge saw the erection of a statue of Charles IV by the Dresden sculptor E. J. Höhnel, cast by D. J. Burgschmidt in Nuremberg. The islet next to the Bridge Tower, on which we can see the very acme of the complex symbolism of the court art of Charles IV and Wenceslas IV, recalls the early days when Prague Old Town maintained a very close association with the river. The islet is all that is left of a larger natural island that was still here in the 18th century.

VINCENC MORSTADT: *Prague from Chotek Road (Chotkova silnice)*, colourised drawing, 1832.

Morstadt's drawing, from which C. A. Richter produced an engraving, captures the new, zigzagging Chotek Road that replaced the old hollow way linking Malá Strana and the Marian Walls. It also shows the advancing conversion to gardens around the Baroque fortifications on both the Hradčany and the Letná side, forerunners of the People's Garden, later to be renamed Chotek Gardens, and the park atop Letná Plain.

Classicism and Romanticism evolved in an atmosphere of inspirational trends coming in from the outside world, though with due reflection of the domestic, artistically very powerful milieu, which was the very antithesis of others thanks to the accumulation of Baroque culture in architecture. Changes in expression under the impact of Classicism and Romanticism, essentially contradictory, became entwined within this milieu and in Czech garden art of the last third of the 18th century and the first half of the 19th resulted in a remarkable symbiosis.

In parks and gardens the close tie between contrary styles is seen in the Classicist organisation of space and Romantic ways of filling it, or in the use of Classicist buildings and accessories as landmarks, the furthermost point of vistas, or eye-catching details. Romantic organisation of space is governed by the terrain, while also having a very, often surprisingly, regular order. The principal spatial schema is created by a network of imaginary axes or lines, which are the source of the tie-in between macro and micro views of the scenery, and this gives rise to how blocks of vegetation are organised.

The revelation of the symbiosis of Classicism and Romanticism, synthesised in English landscape garden architecture, is an excellent didactic tool. The most striking samples matching this conception arose in Smíchov and Košíře. The characteristic compositional features of the Klamovka garden in Smíchov, successor to an earlier Rococo garden on the site, have unfortunately been obliterated by

Ansicht des Dianen Tempels im Garten zu Cibulka.

V. GOTTMANN: *A view of the Temple of Diana in the Cibulka Park*, colourised engraving after a drawing by J. Rattay, after 1830.

The engraving was done over a century after the Cibulka park was set up. It records the end product, in its day, of a scene with a little temple of Diana composed in painterly terms. After being badly damaged in a storm, the temple was demolished in 1959, leaving just the statue of Diana with her Dogs, and the overall impression of the space being gradually obliterated.

time. The idea behind the Cibulka park in Košíře has also become very blurred; first conceived as a Romantic park of the *ferme ornée* type, parts of it reflected sentimental Romantic trends, as witness the sheer quantity of views cluttered with buildings and statues. The dwelling of the original farm was rebuilt as an Empire manor house and beside it even Thun's *giardino segreto* was brought into being. The Kinský Garden was founded on conspicuously Classicist lines, which showed chiefly in how ground plan and space were handled in successfully shaping the composition of the sightline with the summer house, including the visual extension to the church of Our Lady Before Týn.

A superb example of Classicist organisation of a Romantic park is the erstwhile People's Garden (Lidová zahrada), today called Chotek Gardens, which also reckoned with how the sightlines were composed, specifically in the clever continuity to the 'borrowed' landmark of the Renaissance summer house in the Royal Garden next door.

Quite worth a pat on the back is the transformation of the Royal Game Preserve into a park after it passed into the public domain in 1804. The transformation took almost a century to complete and, despite all the influences, pressures and the number of people involved in the process, it stuck to the idea of shaping a park-like environment in sections that essentially comport with the structure of the game preserve as it had been stabilised under Rudolph II during the Mannerist period of the Renaissance. In each part they succeeded in expressing whatever purpose it had served originally. For example, in the western salient, which used to be an orchard, the tent lawn set into an arc of taller vegetation can be seen as symbolic of a basket or fruit bowl. And the shaping of the area that was once a pheasantry, to the west of the dyke of the former Rudolph Pond, produced the outline of a wing. The scattered structure of the woodland in the horseshoe-shaped part contiguous with the former pond from the east recalls the wood-clad character of the main game-breeding area, known as Thirgarten. The landmark function of the summer house is obvious in any wide-angled view. The lower summer house, integrated into the promenade area, became a social centre. The former fishpond is still detectable, including the dyke, the bottom and a little oak-decked island. Rudolph's tunnel, dug in 1582-93, began to feed newer, smaller ponds and fountains and bring up water for watering the gardens. This is why a waterworks was built not far from its mouth including, since 1859, a pumping system designed by Romuald Božek, the younger son of the eminent Czech mechanic and design engineer Josef Božek, who in 1815, in the Royal Game Preserve, demonstrated the first steam-powered automobile. The pumping system was driven by a water wheel and the water was collected in a reservoir from where it was delivered to wherever needed by gravity. In 1929 a Francis turbine was installed.

We have reliable evidence of the new parks and gardens created under the influence of Classicism and Romanticism from imperial Austrian cadastral maps. These also reveal clearly the extent of the assimilation of earlier structures to Romantic assumptions, likewise, conversely, the degree to which manifestations of Baroque and pre-Baroque styles were preserved. The land surveying that resulted in printed Imperial Survey maps and sketch copies derived from them took place in Bohemia and Moravia between 1824 and 1843. Most of the ones pertaining to present-day Prague were made in 1840-42. The situation within the boundaries of the four towns is further illuminated by Antonín Langweil's unique 3D model of Prague produced over the period 1826-1837; this gives us a good idea of the transformations undergone by Baroque palace gardens, and not only in Malá Strana.

In the middle of the 19th century, the extent and outward appearance of gardens and parkland and the uses to which they were put were affected not only by newly emerging styles, but also by the critical moment in social conditions wrought by Ferdinand V the Good's imperial decree of 7 September, 1848, by which serfdom was abolished; this brought with it the gradual demise of landed estates, the end of seigneurial administration and the constitution of a new state administration and local self-government. Additional to that, following the defeat at the Battle of Sadova on 3 July 1866, a start was made in the same year on removing the fortifications surrounding the four towns, Franz Joseph I, by an imperial decree issued in October 1866, having abolished the strict status of Prague as a fortified city. By then, half a millennium had passed since the fortifications were put in place and the first gardens came into being. In the hectic period of industrial development and the construction of the railways, Prague had seen, from 1868 onwards, the building of the National Theatre, the creation of the horse-drawn tramway, the beginnings of electrification, the construction of the Rudolfinum and National Museum and the completion of St Vitus' Cathedral. Preparations for the Jubilee Exhibition began at the eastern end of the Royal Game Preserve in Bubeneč, and also to mark that event the lookout tower and funicular were constructed on Petřín Hill.

ANTONÍN LANGWEIL: *The Palace Gardens on the Southern Slope of Prague Castle*, section of a model, 1826–1837.

This part of the Langweil model captures perfectly how arresting these gardens are, an effect in which the Ledebour, Great Pálffy and the Great and Lesser Fürstenberg gardens with their demanding architectural conceptions all play a part, the Lesser Pálffy and Kolowrat gardens having a contrasting soothing, buffer effect.

ANTONÍN LANGWEIL: *The Wallenstein (Valdštejnská) Garden*, section of a model, 1826–1837.

The model captures the Wallenstein Garden with its fairly dense tree cover, thereby also showing how, in contrast to the gardens beneath the Castle, it had begun to fall under the influence of Romanticism very early on. The model also shows, in the part of the garden next to the business wing of the palace, on odd wall spread out like wings; to this day its purpose and execution remain without any satisfactory explanation.

Park-creation in the second half of the nineteenth century continued largely in the previous vein, though there were differences. Romanticism merged with a leaning towards historicism and in the last quarter of the century the Vienna Sezession (Art Nouveau) began to make itself felt. In any event, new departures called for erudition and serious endeavour. One eloquent example is the Grand City Park (its last remnant is today's Vrchlický Gardens by the Main Station), whose creator, František Malý, had worked in the Belvedere and Prater during the 1873 Vienna Exhibition. He had been brought to Prague to take up the position of managing director of the city's parks and gardens. The position was doubtless offered to him on the strength of the work he had done before arriving in Vienna, notably at the Lobkowicz Estate in Velký Chlum, for the Harrachs in Bruck, the Kinskýs in Prague, the Rothschilds at Boulogne sur Seine, at Battersea Park for Queen Victoria, and elsewhere, all of which led to his recognition as an expert in the field. The park was created between 1876 and 1887 and in the early days Malý put himself in charge; for the pond and cascade he enlisted the cooperation of Bedřich Wachsman. For this part of the park's design lydite rocks were brought from Ďáblice, and the pond and cascade were built with Italian labour. The embedding of the rocks was undertaken by the Vienna firm of Gebrüder Klein, Schmoll u. Gärtner, who had been building the Palacký Bridge. Countless trees were transferred to the park from the erstwhile promenades, 250 mature plane trees were imported from Belleville in France and many other trees from other places. A broad promenade went right across the new park, one view on its proportions being subsequently put in a jocular nutshell by Jan Neruda, who called it an 'elephant promenade'. The park was widely seen as unique, with particular admiration reserved for the views of the lake and cascade.

The Classicist and Romantic approaches to parks and gardens, including echoes of them in more historically conservative ones, was matched by a correspondingly different approach to plantings of vegetation. Romanticising assimilations of older formal gardens were often associated with the introduction of huge tree species, such as the London plane. Their use in both new and older foundations is attested by a fivesome of the species, namely the specimens in the Kinský, Maltese and Kampa gardens and in the Charles Square and Jezerka parks. The acquisition of more interesting tree species also drove the gradual introduction of species being tried out for the first time, such as the false acacias planted in rows on the former Francis, today Smetana, Embankment. In all likelihood, these trees came from Lednice, which ever since 1808 had been a source of trees grown from seed imported from North America. Acacias in particular, but also Canadian walnuts, American poplars, Weymouth pines and others were grown from seed collected by an expedition sent to North America in 1802 by the lord of the Lednice-Valtice Estate, Prince Adam I von Liechtenstein.

The historicising tendencies of the late 19th century were joined by new ideas of ornament and decoration arising from the Sezession (Art Nouveau), which are seen quite differently on horizontal planes, let alone in the vast areas of parks and gardens, from how they appear in the perpendicular on façades. This fact can thwart a proper understanding of the essence of certain period creations,

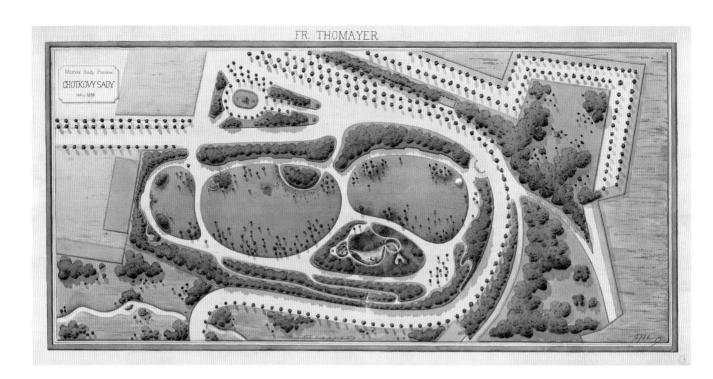

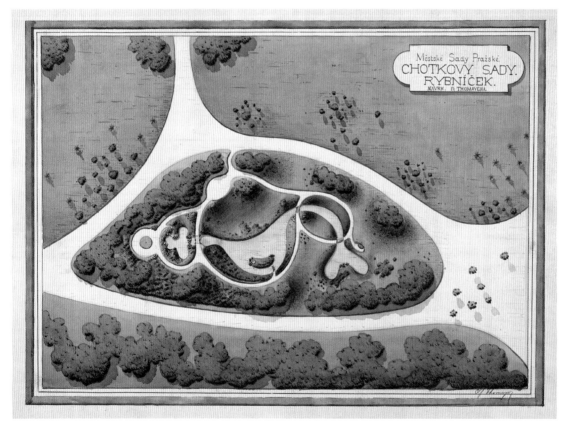

FRANTIŠEK THOMAYER: *Chotek Gardens, The Pond*, colourised diagram, 1889.

When sketched out, the little pond is seen to look like a showy piece of Sezession jewelry, and the composition that embraces it is one of the many garden variants that Thomayer achieved by transposing pendant rings to the horizontal plane. Of note is the way they blend into the silhouette of a fish. This composition was inserted on the fringe of the main sightline through the garden at the end of the 1890s.

especially when they led to the obliteration of what had gone before. Telling examples of how historicising and Sezessionist motifs and forms were featured in parks and gardens are designs by the landscape gardener František Thomayer. For example, in Charles Square he introduced footpaths in loops like the bow of a ribbon knot, an analogue of the pendant rings of Art Nouveau. A kindred view could be taken of the composition of modified circles in the northern part of Slavonic Island, in which from one particular direction the silhouette of a water creature can be seen. The layout involving a small pond in Chotek Gardens is also a variation on the circle theme and looks like a showy Sezession jewel. Thomayer tried to bring the lines and shapes of the Sezession out of the ground plan and up into the landscape, as indicated by the line of vegetation that recalls pipe-smoke. Thomayer's legendary flower gardens and similar parterre and ornamental formations, whose decorative effect was laid out over the underlying historicising ground plan, must have been spectacular in their day. One sample of Sezession playfulness fit to raise a smile is the park on Lyčka Square in Karlín, though this may have been created by Thomayer's followers. The situation today suggests that the creators of their age were well able to cope with snags arising from dependency on a ground plan, while so much else depended on what they had to work from and what they hoped to use for decoration. Some creations are hard to identify chiefly because, irrespective of whether the forms used as the basis were neo-Renaissance, neo-Baroque or neo-Classicist and of the fact that living plants were used for the Sezessionist decoration, the durability of the historicising foundation proved to be the greater. The situation is better in cases where Sezession layouts (especially of paths) are combined with historicising analogues of Romantic or Classicist-Romantic blocks of vegetation and yet total harmony has been achieved.

A transformation in conceptions of layout and the use of space begins to crystallise at the start of the 20th century, fed by a desire to uproot the conventions of the past and the need to dispense with aestheticism and decorativism. The typification of the new age, bewitched as it was with speed and its accompanying dynamism, however manifested, bred new forms of architecture, often lumped together as 'individualistic modernism'. In 1912–13, the Villa Kovařovič was built, beneath Vyšehrad and close to the railway bridge that crosses the Vltava. The house and garden are a unique product of Cubism in architecture, precisely thanks to the garden with its own Cubist morphology. The whimsical aspect here is that the rebellious young Josef Chochol, impaling convention on the spikes of Cubism, sited the house and garden to face the silhouette of Hradčany.

With Czechoslovakia's independence, declared on 28 October, 1918, its first President, Tomáš Garrigue Masaryk, appointed the Slovenian Josip Plečnik from Ljubljana as Castle Architect. His first task was to remould the Paradise and Rampart gardens on the southern rampart of Prague Castle. Plečnik linked the two gardens with a grand promenade accessed from the monumental flight of steps leading down into the Paradise Garden; the vista seen from the steps in quite magnificent. Then throughout the length of the promenade there is an arrangement of vantage points from which the city can be viewed in all its glory.

Plečnik's daring breach of the southern façade of the Castle with his Bull (Býčí) Staircase is extended optically across the garden and points directly, passing a pyramid that serves as anchor point, at the cupola of St Nicholas' Church on Malá Strana Square.

Conscious of the basic thesis of Functionalism, to wit, 'form follows content', we can more readily appreciate how it might penetrate into garden-making. When Josef Gočar was designing the church of St Wenceslas in Vršovice (constructed in 1929-31), he proposed that the square in front of it should be made into a park to match and so give the architecture of the church a kind of pedestal and referential frame. He considered the layout of the footpaths with respect not only to Functionalist form, but also to their own functionality, as routes that worked to the benefit of pedestrians.

Functionalism also made itself felt in the construction of detached houses with gardens, indeed whole areas of them, such as the Baba residential area of Prague, not to mention hotels, banks, schools and colleges, and medical facilities, including spas. The Villa Müller in Střešovice (erected *c.* 1930) was designed by the architect Adolf Loos in cooperation with Karel Lhota, the conception of the garden being a response to both the severity of the house's exterior and to its interior, most notably the salon that makes up its core. Interestingly, the way gardens in general were shaped in the company of the new forms of architecture promoted by Constructivism only exceptionally led to a similarly clear-cut manifestation of style. For this there were several reasons. For one thing, such trends had the lifespan of meteorites, added to which there were conflicting views on what the relationship between a dwelling and its garden should be. The urge to project severity of form from house to garden competed with the very negation of architectural severity through recourse to structurally and chromatically quite elaborate garden compositions, sometimes with motifs inspired by Naturalism or by a fusion of the decorative aspect of the details and the utility aspect of a space.

New ways of organising space, associated with the post-World War II development of standardisation and prefabrication, went hand in hand with new patterns of living and leisure. An interesting example of a park whose design, structure and the rendering of its different spaces and facilities were adapted to the leisure activities of a large slice of the populace is the Friendship Park in the Prosek development. Another is the park around Chodov Fort, which enveloped a freestanding historical object, incorporating it into a totally different environment and giving the whole the aura of an oasis within the vast, anonymous urban sprawl that is Jižní Město ('South Town').

The concept 'garden' is a traditional one and expresses, in full accord with its etymology, a piece of land enclosed by a wall or some other kind of encirclement. The word 'park' came later, initially used for entities based on the Classicist and Romantic conception of landscape. A park would usually flow over into the surrounding countryside, but the term gradually came to be applied to other entities derived or developed from that conception. A park is not usually circumscribed, although today the term frequently includes lands that do have fences or surrounding walls, not to mention the hidden form of barrier that is the ha-ha, though that expedient is not actually attested in Prague.

Gardens and parks were instituted primarily for residential, prestige or social purposes, but their productive importance should also not be overlooked. In the present day, utility areas are most often represented in Prague by fruit gardens, that is to say pomaria, including orchards in the narrow sense, but also vine-yards and, to a degree, even woodland. In earlier times there would also have been areas for growing vegetables, medicinal herbs and spices. It was orchards, or 'fruit gardens' (Cz. *ovocný sad*), that in the late 19th century and the first half of the 20th gave rise to names involving the word 'Gardens' (i.e. *sady*), initially for the newly instituted city parks and then for some of the parks and gardens of the nobility that became open to the public. The early upsurge of names of this kind, with their original orchard associations, was apparently fired by the ideas of Russophilism and Slavophilism (*sad* being 'garden' in Russian), a yen for folksiness and a turning against anything aristocratic.

The typological profile of Prague's gardens and parks is in a way unique and is mostly a matter of the building or buildings with which this or that garden or park makes up an organic, and originally functional, unit. Major types are the gardens of monasteries, palaces (or town houses of the nobility) and burgher dwellings, farms and villas. A special group is made up of castle gardens or parks, which in the case of Prague Castle (the *Hrad*) arose first outside the fortifications and then in their place after they were dismantled; at Vyšehrad they lie predominantly within the fortifications.

Absent from the following account are the gardens and parks that emerged over a long period of time as part of the châteaux that were the residential and showpiece seats of aristocratic estates and mostly also their administrative centres. Given the exclusion of the latter, the inclusion of palace gardens that were inseparable parts of original urban seats, town houses, of the nobility is somewhat of an anomaly. Another exceptional group is undoubtedly that of the city parks and gardens that have no functionally associated building and which were instituted in response to the general expansion of industry, transport and development. Hard on the heels of their establishment, or simultaneous with it, was the opening of original aristocratic and monastery gardens to the public.

The individual entities included in this collection, however akin or disparate as to their nature, are presented according to where they are located physically. Each location or district is described in terms of how it fits into the agglomeration that is Prague and in regard to the kinds or conceptions of gardens or parks that are present within them.

A GUIDE TO THE GARDENS
AND PARKS OF PRAGUE

HRADČANY: THE CASTLE – POHOŘELEC – THE MARIAN WALLS

The monumental silhouette of Prague Castle, dominated by the spires of St Vitus' Cathedral, is widely perceived as a symbol of Czech (and previously Bohemian) statehood, and the entire scene embracing Hradčany and Malá Strana, set between Petřín Hill and Letná Plateau, as the most important and iconic panorama of the city. Its composition is largely down to physical geography, with the high spur on which the castle stands, its steep slopes to the south and the deep ravine to the north with the Brusnice stream running through it.

A major part in how Prague Castle was constituted, gradually expanded and transformed was played by the conversion of a mediaeval stone fortress into a palatial castle residence with its Royal Garden within the northern defensive ditch. The later evolution of the castle gardens was influenced by successive adaptations of the southern rampart, ultimately giving rise to the Paradise (Rajská) Garden and Rampart (Na Valech) Garden. The Hartig Garden, a continuation of the Rampart Garden, belongs organically to the Hartig Palace in Malá Strana, while the St Wenceslas Vineyard recalls the ancient tradition of viticulture on the southern slopes of the spur. The appearance of a garden on part of the erstwhile northern fortifications is attested by the Bulwark (Na Baště) Garden and the cultivation of the once defensive Stag Moat (Jelení příkop). The age of the Baroque saw the collection of Malá Strana palace gardens fan out across the southern slope beneath the Castle.

At Hradčany, which began to evolve in the second quarter of the 14th century within the enclosed outer ward as Prague's third town, there is an eloquent specimen of a prestige palace garden in that of the Černín Palace. The first recorded urban park is Chotek Gardens, originally called the People's Garden (*Volksgarten*). Examples of the gardens of fine dwellings that had been summer houses, but came to be called villas, having been built for permanent occupancy anyway, are the gardens of the Villa Bílek and Villa Kramář.

1A–C/ STAG MOAT

The ditch, or moat, divided into Upper and Lower by the Powder (Prašný) Bridge, is part of the precinct of Prague Castle, open in the tourist season at fixed times. Access from Chotek Street, the Powder Bridge and U Brusnice Street.

The ravine through which the Brusnice stream runs, raised even higher by a bulwark, served originally as a defensive ditch. In the early 17th century red deer were introduced to the site, hence the name Stag Moat. Its split into upper and lower sections came after the original Powder Bridge was replaced in 1771 by a road constructed on top of a new earthwork. The valley looks quite natural, with a fairly haphazard distribution of trees and shrubs and, at the upper end, rather more grassland. Among the woody plants represented the emphasis has been on native species such as small-leaved lime, English oak, ash, field maple, Norway maple and sycamore. There are also some conifers, specifically yew, larch, Norway spruce and Scots pine. In the 1920s a small vineyard was established in the Upper Stag Moat, complete with a semicircular vantage point named after the then President, Tomáš G. Masaryk. The viewpoint is shaded by a small-leaved lime, the Czech national tree.

2A–D/ THE ROYAL GARDEN

This lies within the precinct of the Castle, between Marian Walls Street and the Lower Stag Moat. It is open in the tourist season at fixed times with access from Powder Bridge Street or through a side entrance from Marian Walls Street at a point opposite Queen Anne's Summer House.

Together with the Royal Summer House, also known as Queen Anne's Summer House or the Belvedere, the Royal Garden was constructed during the Renaissance on the far side of the Brusnice ravine at the behest of Ferdinand I Habsburg. There are plenty of indications that the location of the monarch's garden, for which there was not enough space inside the fortifications, was, together with its basic layout, thought through in advance with great care and set up with full awareness of the principles of axis and cross, the interjacent arrangement of nodal points and the extension of defined directions as mastered previously by the builders of Gothic churches and cathedrals and even by such educated monarchs as Charles IV. Ferdinand I seems also to have had this expertise and it is not beyond the bounds of possibility that he selected the site for the garden and did the planimetry for it himself.

Defining features are the east-west orientation of the garden and the location of the giardinetto and summer house at the eastern extremity, a principle shared with the locating of presbyteries. A link from the garden to the most important structures of the Castle and

a conscious expression of allegiance to the St Wenceslas heritage are conveyed by the cruciform connections through space. The foot of the cross is in Malá Strana Square at the spot where the Romanesque rotunda of St Wenceslas once stood, its top end reaching the square space in the middle of the garden. The cross-beam appears to lie on a line from the Second Courtyard through the well (no longer visible on the ground) between St Vitus' Cathedral and the Basilica of St George. Parallel to this are the east-west axes of St George's, St Vitus' and the Royal Garden. It is even possible that the symbolism of the cross is thus expressed by a double, that is, archiepiscopal or patriarchal cross.

Work on the garden and summer house, whose artistic merits and uniqueness north of the Alps are well known and have been frequently highlighted, was begun in 1534, the preparatory stages under the charge of Giovanni Spatio. The summer house itself was begun in 1538 by Paolo della Stella, using Italian stonemasons perhaps from his Genoa workshop, other builders involved being Spatio and, after 1539, Giovanni Mario del Pambio. In 1541 work on both the garden and the summer house was interrupted by the great fire in Malá Strana and Hradčany. However, in that same year the garden project was joined by the brothers Nicolas and Claudius Reinhardt from Alsace, who started on the hugely significant arrangement of the square space in the centre of the garden, for whose demarcation they used a system of fire or smoke signals. The Reinhardt brothers had come to Prague at the request of Ferdinand I, who had been captivated by the garden at the residence of the Bishop of Strasbourg, Wilhelm III von Hohenstein, at Saverne. After 1547, supervision of how the garden was to be shaped gradually passed to Archduke Ferdinand of Tyrol, the son of Ferdinand I, who had been made Vicegerent of the Lands of the Bohemian Crown in that year.

In the final phase, ending in 1564, the completion of the summer house was overseen by Bonifaz Wohlmut with Ferdinand I insisting, in line with the original choir or presbytery idea, on the giardinetto being enclosed by a wall with niches and windows. He did not live to see his Renaissance programme come to full fruition, though his successors did continue with it. Under Maximilian II the Small Ball-Game Hall was completed in 1567 and in the following year the bronze 'Singing' fountain was set in the centre of the giardinetto. This had been cast by the royal bellfounder and gunsmith, Tomáš Jaroš of Brno, to a design by the painter Francesco Terzio from Bergamo. Under the supervision of the architects Bonifaz Wohlmut and Ulrico Aostalli, the Great Ball-Game Hall was constructed in 1567–1570. A figgery was erected beneath the summer house, also designed by Aostalli, in 1572, and fitted, after the manner of the first Italian orangeries, with a detachable roof. The Renaissance age that had shaped the garden so far ended with a Mannerist phase which, during the reign of Rudolph II, involved reconstructing the wooden lion yard in stone and building the orangery by the northern perimeter wall. The Hercules Fountain was set up in 1670, heralding the arrival of the Baroque. Baroque alterations made between 1728 and 1735 with the involvement of Johann Heinrich Dinebier, head of the Royal Office of Works, and the garden designer František Zinner jr., exploited and supplemented the basic axial and syntactic layout of the Renaissance garden by the imposition of Baroque morphology on the interior detail. The western part of the garden saw the appearance of a flame-pattern *parterre de broderie*, some statuary from the workshop of Matyáš Bernard Braun, and to the south of the parterre the court architect, Kilián Ignác Dientzenhofer, began to construct a greenhouse. The rise of Romanticism showed at the turn of the 18th and 19th centuries when Matyáš Jan Weppl became gardener to the imperial court. Under him, but even more so under his successor, Jan František Weppl, the garden's formal character was altered in the spirit of classicist Romantic landscaping. This saw the arrival of more interesting trees, with many others appearing later still.

Thus the Renaissance Royal Garden, together with its summer house as an outpost of the Castle, has seen a stratification of styles superimposed on it, in particular its Mannerist completion in the late Renaissance, the later Baroque elements and finally its classicist Romantic transformation. The original axial plan is still discernible and the form given it by later periods is visible in the various structures, fountains and statues. The giardinetto, which with the summer house and the Singing Fountain is the most powerful element of the original syntax, was reconstructed in the mid-1950s to a design by Pavel Janák. The Romantic-Classicist phase of imitative landscaping – and later developments – are what led to the presence of the many trees and shrubs that are also indicative of patterns of introduction of alien species, of how they were sought by collectors and of a fascination with their intriguing colours and shapes. For example, in the belt above the old orangery there is a ginkgo. Within the two circuits of footpaths east of the summer ball-game hall there are two Turkish hazels, a tulip tree and the torso of a huge false acacia that may date back to the mid-19th century. Magnolias blossom before coming into leaf, and there are two white-flowering kobushi magnolias by the balustrade and a red-flowered saucer magnolia next to the eastern frontage of the garden residence, also known as the president's cottage. Since 1950 or soon thereafter the Royal Garden has been host to a dawn redwood. A second specimen within the Castle precinct is in the Rampart Garden; two more were planted about the same time in the university's Botanical Garden. Until discovered growing in the Szechuan province of China in 1941, this deciduous conifer had only been known as a fossil. In 1948, seeds from it were sent all over the world, probably also arriving at the arboretum at Průhonice. In 1999–2001 a new, 90-metre-long tubular orangery was built on the site of the 1950s greenhouse. It is constructed of crossed metal pipework, the glass panels being fixed to the pipes from the inside. It was designed by Eva Jiřičná with due regard to the Rudolphine wall next to it and to the traces of the old orangery still discernible in the paving.

These two gardens form a belt alongside the southern wing of Prague Castle; they are open in the tourist season at fixed times. Access is via the lookout platform above the top end of the Castle Steps, or at the eastern end from the top of the Old Castle Steps. An additional option is the aproach from the Palace Gardens on the Southern Slope of Prague Castle (the set is treated formally as a unit, hence the capitalisation), specifically from the summer house viewpoint at the top end of the Fürstenberg Garden.

The Paradise and Rampart Gardens were laid out along the line of the southern defensive earthwork, which had been already altered in the past, parts of it several times over. For example, during the Renaissance there had been on the site of the Paradise Garden the private garden of the Archduke Ferdinand of Tyrol, later reworked in the Baroque period. As part of the classicist unification of the south-facing frontage of the Castle the area was levelled throughout its length and, later again, in the 1860s, it saw the emergence of a late landscapist creation by the court gardener, František Ritschl.

In 1921–24, after a design by Josip Plečnik, the Castle Architect, and at the behest of the first President of the Czechoslovak Republic, Tomáš G. Masaryk, both Castle gardens were given the form of promenades.

Plečnik conceived the Paradise Garden as a spacious, trapezoidal, lawn-covered parterre, readily surveyed from the monumental flight

of steps leading down to it and enhanced by the huge granite bowl at its core. The panoramic view over the city is framed by vegetation. The left half of the green backdrop is supplied by a spreading pagoda tree, planted in front of the southern wing of the New Palace. On the side next to the New Castle Steps there is a mixed body of trees, including a catalpa, a weeping ash and some Turkish hazels. They contrast with the dark green foliage of a yew, possibly the oldest tree of all in the Castle gardens at an estimated 400 years. Before going though into the Rampart Garden we find, running south to north: the Matyáš gazebo (1614), a Baroque trough fountain and Kalvoda's statue of the Good Shepherd (1922), while the actual boundary is suggested by a line of seven pyramidal hornbeams.

In the Rampart Garden Plečnik cleverly exploited the principle of axial composition, creating a longitudinal promenade along the spine line with gentle, or even blunt hints as to where the successive sections begin. He used the transverse optical axis from the Bull (Býčí) Staircase to the obelisk as a guideline affording a view towards St Nicholas' church on Malá Strana Square. The promenade has a wealth of views across the city to enjoy, not only from the viewpoint next to Plečnik's cone, but others, too, especially from opposite the Little Bellevue pavilion and from the Moravia Bastion, incorporated into the side of the promenade. The plots lining the promenade are spangled with trees that add the dynamics of light and shade to the site, as well as having their own particular charm in terms of shape, colour or the way they change with the seasons. The atmosphere of warmer climes is evoked in particular by a Turner's oak, *f.* 'Pseudoturneri' tucked away next to the Bull Staircase and other trees such as perhaps the largest paulownia in Prague (and possibly the wider Czech Republic), which stands in a plot by the southern wing of the New Palace. Close to it is the Castle's second dawn redwood from China and another pagoda tree from Japan; a weeping form of pagoda tree is also to be found in the Rampart Garden near the Maria Theresa wing. In a plot adjacent to the promenade and opposite the same wing is another interesting thermophilic species, a catalpa, and hard by the entry to the rock garden there is a Kentucky coffeetree. Next to the gardener's hut a magnolia presents a fine annual display of white flowers before the leaves burst in spring. And in the strip above the vineyard a weeping beech stands out and not far from it a Turkish hazel.

4/ THE HARTIG GARDEN

Organically it belongs to the Hartig Palace, house no. 184/III at 20 Thunovská St, though functionally it has been part of the precinct of Prague Castle since the 1960s. It is open to the public at set times, and the only access is via the steps from the Rampart Garden.

This small palace garden, Baroque in origin, interesting for its link to the upper storey of the Hartig Palace and entered across a *sala terrena*, was joined to the Rampart Garden by a flight of steps in the 1960s. The garden consists of one largish and one very small terrace, with some steps and a trough fountain between them. The upper, larger, terrace is dominated by a pavilion dating back to the garden's foundation *c.* 1720 and is home to a set of five statues of classical deities created in the 1730s by Antonín Braun, possibly from the workshop of his renowned uncle, Matyáš Bernard Braun, but intended for the garden of the château at Štiřín. The statues stand in contrast to the dark green foliage of a large yew, and a particular atmosphere is evoked by the fragile blooms on the climbing roses entwined about a set of eight metal structures. This garden is also home to one of Prague's finer examples of wisteria.

5/ THE ST WENCESLAS VINEYARD

It stretches from the Old Castle Steps, Na Opyši Street and Stag Moat, and is accessible in line with the opening hours applicable to the whole Castle precinct. Entry points are at the upper and lower ends of the Old Castle Steps.

The restored vineyard was commissioned in 2008 to recall the viticultural tradition on the site. There was a vineyard called Opyš back in the Middle Ages (1375) and the site has associations with the

St Wenceslas legend. The main strains grown here, by the
Guyot system, are Rhein Riesling and Ruland Blue. The Villa
Richter, originally a summer house, was built here in the 1830s.
It is one of the main Classicist sights in Prague and carries the
name of its original owner. It is now part of the grounds of Prague
Castle.

6/ THE BULWARK (NA BAŠTĚ) GARDEN

Accessible in line with the opening hours applicable to the whole Castle precinct.
It can be entered either from the Fourth Courtyard or from the steps leading
to the route connecting to Powder (Prašný) Bridge.

The garden was set up on a former bulwark in 1932 to a design
by Josip Plečnik. It is linked to the fourth castle courtyard by a
circular staircase leading to an area covered in white chippings
that contrast sharply with the dark green columnar 'Malonyana'
form of eastern arborvitae (northern white cedar) dotted across
the surface. Then comes an oblong grassy area with solitaire trees
and small shrubberies skirted by footpaths, one of which passes
under a portico above an entrance to the Spanish Hall. Next to the
portico is a pergola draped in wisteria and pipevine (*Aristolochia
macrophylla*). This motif and the other trees present – Turner's oak,
f. 'Pseudoturneri' with its overwintering leaves, a fastigiate oak and a
Colorado white fir, trimmed to shape – are meant to evoke the aura
of a Japanese garden. Serving the same end are the flat stones set in
the grass to give a stepping-stone effect.

The palace and garden no. 101/IV at 5 Loretta Square is the seat of the Ministry of Foreign Affairs of the Czech Republic. The garden is not ordinarily accessible.

The palace garden, Baroque in origin, filled in after 1851 with soil and builder's rubble to a depth of 1-2 metres, was uncovered in the 1930s and partially restored using whatever components had survived, such as the underground substructure. At the same time the newer part came into being. During the period 1994–97 both parts were renovated to designs by architects Zdeněk Kuna, Jaroslav Zdražil and the garden designer Vítězslava Ondřejová and their collaborators. The site and the main spatial parameters of the Baroque garden were set in 1668 by the architect Francesco Caratti within the draft plan of a palatial residence for Count Humprecht Jan Černín of Chudenice. The task was somewhat impeded by the strip shape of the construction sites. This led Caratti to design the garden as an extension of the frontal axis of the palace and he adapted the side of the house to include two loggias, arcades and pillars. By designing the front façade in the style of a grand *villa urbana* and the garden side as a *villa suburbana* he highlighted the contrast but also the unity of the conception, which took the north-south *cardo* axis the length of the garden and developed the transverse axis at right-angles to it on the east-west *decumanus* principle. By so extending the main axis he was also mooting a connection through space to the legend-wreathed hill called Říp, a connection that came into its own if one looked out of the windows of the grand hall on the second floor of the palace, which permitted the fullest appreciation the grand composition from above.

The garden was founded in the period 1692–95 by the new builder Heřman Jakub Černín. The design, by Domenico Egidio Rossi, the architect in charge of finalising the house, respected the principles adopted by Caratti. The layout, developed in dependency on the north-south axis, was closed off in 1747–49 with a pavilion designed by Anselmo Lurago. The garden drops away from the palace in gently stepped terraces and the basic ground plan forms a double cross. At the two intersections there are a four-lobed pool and a fountain with tiny cascades. The structure of the composition is enhanced by the double box hedging, while flower beds complete each border between the trees. The plasticity of the overall impression gains from the freestanding yews trimmed into spheres or cones. Half-cone yews cleave to the perimeter wall along Černín Street. The countervailing bosquet on the west side is hedged with hornbeam, with limes filling the space between.

Beyond the line that extends north from the rear edge of the original palace lies the new garden, the boundary between the old and new gardens being marked by a row of mop-head maples. In the square central patch outlined by footpaths there are groups of trees in which beeches and tulip trees stand out. A London plane features as a solitaire.

8/ CHOTEK GARDENS

The park, which lies within the arc formed by Chotek Street (Chotkova ulice) and Marian Walls Street (ulice Mariánské hradby), is open to the public. Access is from Marian Walls Street or from Letná by crossing the bridge over Chotek Street.

The first urban park in Prague, originally called The People's Garden or, in its day, the Volksgarten, came into being in 1831–33 on the initiative of the burgrave, Count Karel Chotek, the site having been earmarked during preparations for the construction of Chotek Street in 1831–32. The Classicist-Romantic composition of its sightlines cleverly picks up the Renaissance Queen Anne's Summer House in the neighbouring Royal Garden on an extension of the east-west axis.

The system of footpaths is created on the principle of conjoined circles. The outline plan was probably the work of Josef Fuchs, while the choice of trees and shrubs came from Jiří Braul, who oversaw the work and was to become court gardener at the Castle in 1834. The neo-Romantic and Sezession section with its little pond, tucked in on the fringe in 1887–90, was designed by František Thomayer. Later, it acquired the 1913 statue of the writer Julius Zeyer by Josef Maudr.

The sightline to the summer house is secured by a pair of mighty London planes and framed by blocks of vegetation whose inward aspect is keyed by trees conspicuous for their shapes and colours. The southern arm is marked by some impressive durmast oaks, of which the largest has a girth of 332 cm. The counterweight opposite is a Weymouth pine, sole survivor of the original five, in combination with Norway spruces and red buckeyes. The enclosing vegetation to the east consists of a voluminous black poplar, a fastigiate oak and some English oaks and silver-leaved limes. Close to the Zeyer statue in the parts surrounding the pond there are some fine examples of Canadian poplar, the largest having a girth of 465 cm.

9/ VILLA BÍLEK

The house and garden no. 233/IV at 1 Mickiewicz Street serves as a museum of the works of the sculptor František Bílek and is run by the Prague City Art Gallery; it is open to the public all year round at set times.

The garden here was originally conceived in Sezessionist terms as a tiara, most probably the kind that goes with a folk costume, the point where it rises in the centre being taken up by the sculptural group 'Comenius Bidding Farewell to his Homeland'. František Bílek had the house built in 1922 to his own design with a unique arching ground plan. The garden was designed to conform with the house and he specifically counted on having the statue, his own work, placed at this point. To achieve a colourfulness as befits the Sezession, the planting of the garden reckoned with a motley assortment of trees and shrubs, though it proved impossible to sustain the plants in the right Sezessionist proportions. The ground plan of the house, the way the pillars are contrived, the design of the garden and the surviving black pines and field maple in front of the house might jointly suggest that the form of a beetle, most likely a scarab, could be abstracted from the design, and it is within the bounds of possibility that other games are being played here, underpinned by variations suggested by the Sezessionist approach.

10A–C/ VILLA KRAMÁŘ

The house and garden 1/212 Gogol Street is in use by the Cabinet Office
of the Czech Republic. The garden is not normally open to the public.

The garden of the eye-catching family home of the top lawyer Karel
Kramář was created in 1913, rendered with historicising echoes of the
Vienna Sezession. The Neo-Baroque organisation followed the north-
south axis of the house and was marked out by the avenue of mop-
head maples along the approach to the house and by the quasi cour
d'honneur with its oval parterre, in which a pair of Pacific red cedars,
f. 'Aurea' have been planted, replacing the original pair of northern
white cedars. The Sezessionist tone of the courtyard was originally
set by formations of flowerbeds. Outside the frontage facing the river
and the city there are, following the same axis, two terraces joined
by two opposing flights of steps let into the retaining wall. From the
terrace there is a glorious view of the Vltava and the city beyond.

Loosely following on from this composition is the eastern part
of the garden, in the form of an historicising, Classicist-Romantic
picture-postcard scene, shaped in large measure by some remarkable
trees. There are common and copper beeches, English oaks,
including their fastigiate form, Turkish hazel, whitebeam, including

its 'Magnifica' cultivar, and, on the conifer side, cedar of Lebanon, European larch, Colorado white fir and Oregon fir. The Sezessionist tone of the scene is also intimated by the bow-like outlining of the blocks of vegetation and the fine detail of the original colour schemes provided by smaller flowering trees and shrubs such as ornamental apples (*Arnoldiana*, Japanese flowering crabapple, purple crabapple and Its cultivars, and red sentinel crabapple) and an assortment of lilacs (common, nodding, Chinese, Persian and Preston).

To construct his house and garden Kramář had acquired land on the St Magdalena bastion and adjacent to it. He was keen to acquire it because of the location vis-à-vis the Castle and the river, which is beautifully visible lengthwise and the bridges crosswise. The house was designed by the Vienna architect Friedrich Ohmann and construction began in 1911. The garden was landscaped by František Thomayer, who laid it out in 1913. He structured it with respect to the entertainment and day-to-day living needs of the owner while also responding to the shape and differences in elevation of the terrain and to the architectural character of the house. Dr Kramář later became the first prime minister of the young Czechoslovak Republic.

HRADČANY: STRAHOV

The Strahov Monastery is perched in the saddle between Prague Castle and Petřín Hill, with which it contributes to the familiar outline of the panorama of Prague. It was founded in 1140 on the flat area of Pohořelec as an initiative by the Bishop of Olomouc, Jindřich Zdík. Duke Vladislav II granted the monastery vast swathes of land including the hill called Stráž ('Guard') and the eastern slope facing the city, including the foothill as far as the old St John's game preserve, remembered to this day in the toponym *Svatojánský vršek* (St John's Knoll). The monastery's name was originally given in Latin as Mons Sion, later replaced by the Czech Strahov. The derivation of the latter from Stráž hill is explained as connected to the watch (*ostraha*) securing the approach to the Castle, but there is also a suggestion that it relates to Mount Sion in Jerusalem, on whose flank stood the seat of King David. The monastery's position allegedly reminded Bishop Zdík of that biblical elevation. In the mid-14th century, as Hradčany came to be expanded by Charles IV, the monastery complex was included within the Castle's enceinte, though previously it had constituted an entity outside the ward.

Until almost the end of the 16th century the structure of the monastery's lands kept changing. In 1420, during the Hussite Wars, the monastery lost almost all its property and its very existence hung by a thread. A stabilisation of the structure of the monastery's gardens and vineyards in relation to its buildings is known to have taken place after 1586. We know that the then abbot, Jan Lohelius, brought order to the gardens and vineyards, which flourished the better following the reconstruction of the Romanesque water pipeline and the unclogging of the springs on the eastern slopes, the water being captured in new underground channels.

In the 1670s a number of objects were built in the Strahov gardens, designed by the important early Baroque architect Giovanni Domenico Orsi. The structure of the various parts of the gardens gradually stabilised both in terms of content and in relation to the monastery's occupancy. Besides the clearly demarcated space of the garth there was, in the immediate vicinity of the buildings, the Abbot's Garden and the Monks' Garden. And probably also a small garden for the use of the *infirmarius*, who cared for the sick. It is deduced, from correlations with the monastery at Steinfeld, that the prior, as the abbot's deputy, and the superior may have had their own gardens as well. The areas further away from the buildings can be identified as having been pomaria, fruit gardens including orchards, vineyards, vegetable plots and plots for herbs and spices, fishponds and a game preserve. In the 19th century, the productive part of the monks' garden, which probably started as the *infirmarius'* physic garden, was integrated with the other growing areas, as were the vineyards, previously part of the Abbot's Garden. At the same time, the fishponds were removed from the slope beneath the track that was to be merged in the 1950s into the scenic trail that passes from Strahov through the Petřín gardens all the way to Smíchov.

The most significant garden space at the monastery is the garth, which conceals the remains of a sophisticated water supply system beneath modern alterations. The Abbot's Garden, by the eastern frontage of the monks' lodgings, was founded in association with the construction of the new abbey in 1625. In its original form it had a trough fountain surrounded by flowerbeds and trees. A Turkish hazel that allegedly dated back to the garden's foundation grew to monumental proportions and survived into the 1990s. The renovation of the Abbot's Garden, commenced in 1991, included replacing the original hazel, though the renewal programme has not been completed and at the present time [2016] the garden is used for commercial catering purposes. Hence the Strahov Monastery Gardens are presently represented by the Monks' Garden and the Great Strahov Garden, which includes the vineyard and a lookout created in 1991–95 from the eastern side of the Abbot's garden.

11A–B/ THE GREAT STRAHOV GARDEN

It lies between Úvoz and the Hunger Wall and most of it is open to the public; this includes the vineyard and lookout south of the path that leads from Úvoz to Strahovské nádvoří. Entrances are from Strahovské nádvoří, Úvoz, Vlašská Street, the Lobkowicz Garden, or from Strahov Street taking the path that passes through the Hunger Wall.

The garden has always had, and still retains, its utility aspect, presently represented primarily by the pomarium and the wooded upper parts. Fruit trees, chiefly apples, pears, cherries and plums, grow in simple rows, whether on the slopes beneath the Scenic Walk, parallel to Úvoz or on the flat area alongside the Hunger Wall. In the orchard area beneath the Scenic Walk, on the site of a former pond, there is an imposing ash tree, estimated to be around 200 years old. It is one of the tallest in the country and its trunk, thanks to the ideal conditions of its location and its rapid natural growth rate, has reached impressive dimensions, including a girth of 512 cm. Above the Scenic Walk, between the nursery, the Hunger Wall and the Petřín Steps, the backbone of the wooded area is provided by oaks and hornbeams. On the same contour line as the gardener's cottage and dating from the Baroque age when the monastery was expanding, a hermitage has survived, and up by the Hunger Wall an outdoor pulpit.

Viticulture is represented by the vineyard, designed by the architect Otakar Kuča and created along with a lookout platform in the 1990s, just east of the Abbot's Garden. In the orchards that were once part of the Monks' Garden there is presently a nursery and the gardener's cottage, which was originally a fruit-drying kiln. Next to the cottage stands a sturdy weeping willow. In 1994 the lookout platform below the nursery was graced with a statue of the Virgin Mary out of Exile, a gift from expatriates living in the United States and Canada. An east-west projection taken from Vlašská Street affords an excellent view of it. The area above the Scenic Walk underwent a revitalisation in 1996–98 to a design by the garden designers Milan Bubenek and Luboš Gaudník. And in 2009, thanks to the efforts of Jindřich Pavliš, a start was made on the gradual renewal of the fruit tree plantings in the area below the Scenic Walk. Here the design was by another garden designer, Přemysl Krejčiřík, under the guidance of the fruit-grower and pomologist Josef Sus. The first part to be completed was the area round the spring, newly named the Sir Nicholas Winton Spring in honour of the man who rescued 669 children just before the outbreak of World War II.

12/ THE MONKS' GARDEN
Part of Strahov Monastery (1/132 Strahovské nádvoří) serving the purposes
of the Premonstratensian Order. Not normally open to the public.

The enclosed garden alongside the southern frontage of the monks'
lodgings is the product of its Renaissance and Baroque origins,
the contraction that followed, and continuing modifications right
up to the present. It took shape as a separate garden intended for
the use of the resident monks during the 17th century, when it still
included a pomarium. During the Renaissance stage the central
part became a sundial garden, which was then lowered during the
Baroque reconstruction of the monks' lodgings to be on a level
with the summer refectory, and the whole acquired a new, Baroque
composition in 1698–1700. Its conception was down to the author
of the monastery's overall Baroque new look, the French architect
Jean Baptiste Mathey, who linked the lower area outside the refectory
to the higher Renaissance levels with flights of steps. Between 1682
and 1698 a summer house was built by the south-east wing of the
lodgings, named after the Pohořelec reeve and architect Jiří Gottwiek
and adorned with frescos by Antonius Stevens of Steinfels. The
pomarium on the southward slope was separated from the Monks'
Garden and made one with the other growing areas. This proceeding
also gave rise to the high Classicist wall that encloses the garden on
its southern side.

The area by the *sala terrena* of what is known as the Lohel prelature, with its simple 1970s design, has a stone well and a magnolia set in a trapezoidal area under grass; it merges into the lower central section with its stone trough fountain and decorative box hedging. The division of the garden into three parts is reasserted by two pairs of fastigiate oaks and the terrace effect is enhanced by step-trimmed hornbeam hedges. The view through the gaps in the hornbeam is like looking through a keyhole. This refinement was widely used in Roman Baroque gardens, and in the Monks' Garden it is exploited to frame the view of the copula of St Nicholas' church on Malá Strana Square. The eastern end is a terrace with Gottwiek's summer house and offers a wide-angle panoramic view across the city.

MALÁ STRANA: PETŘÍN HILL

Petřín Hill in the middle of Prague is a curious, even extraordinary spot thanks to the many individual gardens, diverse in both their area and aspect, that jointly constitute a unique conglomerate. The hill is traversed by the mediaeval fortification known as the Hunger Wall, constructed in 1360–62 by order of Charles IV and giving more land area to Hradčany and Malá Strana. The Hunger Wall added fortification to both the complex of Strahov monastery and the little church of St Lawrence. It descends towards Újezd, where it originally met the Carthusian Gate, and in the 17th and 18th centuries was complemented by a Baroque bailie.

The name Petřín may be derived from the Latin *petra* (rock, boulder, cliff), but the hill has also been called St Lawrence Height, or Laurenziberg in German, after the place of pilgrimage that is now the Old Catholic cathedral church of St Lawrence, rebuilt in the Baroque period, with the Chapel of the Holy Sepulchre and the Calvary Chapel, at which pilgrims would arrive via the fourteen Stations of the Cross (the original ones were replaced in the 1830s).

During the age of the Baroque, the northern slopes of Petřín Hill that fall away towards Vlašská and Tržiště streets became the site of many gardens belonging to the nobility or the burgher class. These are the spectacular Lobkowicz, Schönborn, Wratislaw and Vrtba palace gardens, and the daintier gardens of the Štorberg house and the house at the sign of Three Red Roses. The adjacent eastern slopes were long home to vineyards, though records show their gradual mutation into an orchard from the 17th century onwards. The pomarium tradition survives in the Seminary Garden, while the Nebozízek garden evinces the next stage of development – into a city garden. During the 1830s, the top of Petřín Hill with St Lawrence's Church, the Calvary Chapel, the Chapel of the Holy Sepulchre and the modern Way of the Cross were brought together as a park in the Romantic spirit, undergoing further changes when the lookout tower came to be erected in the late 1880s and early 1890s. This gave rise to the area's official designation as the Park by the Lookout Tower on Petřín Hill. The tower was built to mark the 1891 Jubilee Exhibition, and the same event led to the construction of the Petřín cable railway that follows the line separating the Seminary Garden and the Nebozízek garden. After the railway was electrified, its upper station moved up beyond the Hunger Wall, and some military premises having been converted into an observatory, the area between the Hunger Wall and the remnants of the Baroque fortifications became a new city park known as the Rose Garden.

The palace at 347/19 Vlašská Street along with the parterre section of its garden constitutes the Embassy of the German Federal Republic. The greater part of the garden is open to the public and can be accessed from Vlašská Street or the adjacent Seminary Garden, the Great Strahov Garden or the Park by the Lookout Tower on Petřín Hill.

Only a remnant of the Baroque core of the palace garden, founded as part of the palace complex of František Karel Přehořovský of Kvasejovice in 1703–08, has survived. The architect of the palace, Giovanni B. Alliprandi, was probably also involved in designing the garden with its axial link to the rear façade of the building and its system of typically S-shaped footpaths. Generally credited with the creation of the garden is the landscape gardener of Italian descent Jan Jiří de Capauli, known as Kapula. When between 1753 and 1769 a second storey was being added to the palace, by then the property of the Lobkowicz family, the garden was also modified, under the guidance of Ignác Jan Nepomuk Palliardi, but in keeping with the Baroque core. At the start of the 19th century, under Prince Antonín Isidor Lobkowicz, the Baroque garden underwent a transformation in the spirit of the English school of landscaping. Involved in that project was Antonín Skalník, son of the renowned Václav Skalník, both of them landscape gardeners; Václav later became Lord Mayor of Mariánské Lázně (Marienbad). The Romantic landscaping accelerated the destruction of the garden's Baroque forms and saw, conversely, the introduction of numerous exotic conifers and broad-leafed species from America. This kind of alteration probably also fired the use of several species of yew as well as stimulating the foundation of the first ever rock garden in Prague.

The composition of the lower end of the garden carries echoes of the garden frontage of the palace. The parterre is decked with miniature box hedging, while along its sides the arboreal framework was kept; the western side includes a magnificent weeping beech. In the sloping section of the garden, separated in modern times by a grille, the system of S-shaped footpaths – lined with horse chestnuts – remains visible and the ramped area culminating in a viewing terrace also survives. The original effect of the disposition based on the letter S was achieved by how the horse chestnuts were handled. There is pictorial evidence of just how splendid it used to look, and we have learned much from valuable finds on the ground, including, beside the footpath system and the profile of the terrain, the remains of two reservoirs, some pillars and geological formations with caves in the vast wooded part of the garden. Today the parts at the top look entirely natural, with oaks and hornbeams playing a major part in the species composition.

14/ THE GARDEN AT THREE RED ROSES HOUSE
Those wishing to visit the garden of the house at 9/355 Vlašská Street, home to
the Institute for Contemporary History of the Czech Academy of Sciences, may
join guided tours during the tourist season, but on Saturdays and Sundays only.

The compact terraced garden, shaped during the late Baroque
and renovated in 2012 (to a design by the architect Ivan Březina
in collaboration with others, including the garden designer Jiřina
Švamberková) using surviving elements and a unifying cruciform
disposition underpinned by the box edging, is held together with
flights of projecting semicircular steps. The posts are adorned
with statues, vases and mascarons, the abutment with balustrades.
Of interest is the dainty fountain at one corner.

15/ THE GARDEN OF THE STORBERG HOUSE

Those wishing to visit the garden of the house at 3/362 Vlašská Street, used by the Police Service of the Czech Republic, may join guided tours during the tourist season, but on Saturdays and Sundays only.

The delectable terraced garden with a pavilion was laid out at the turn of the 19th century, conceived as a very late echo of the Baroque. It would appear that with the Classicist reconstruction of the house in 1844 one of the four terraces was lost, while the remaining three were linked by new flights of steps. The composition, developed from the north-south axis on three levels, was renewed in 2012. The design was prepared by the architect Ivan Březina in collaboration with the garden designer Jiřina Švamberková and others. The garden's focal point is the cruciform middle terrace with a well, and the layout is accentuated by trimmed box edging; the composition is completed by the pavilion on the third terrace. This was originally thought to have been a Chapel of the Holy Family, though the most recent research suggests that the chapel was actually next door.

16/ THE SCHÖNBORN GARDEN

The palace and garden at 15/365-III Tržiště Street is the seat of the Embassy
of the United States of America. The garden is not normally open to the public.

The Baroque shape of this terraced palace garden was reached in
two stages. The early-Baroque garden came into being between 1643
and 1656 as part of the palace complex of the Grand Prior of the
Order of the Knights of Malta, Rudolph Count Colloredo-Wallsee,
the construction of which was overseen by Carlo Lurago. The
unique early-Baroque creation is attested by a view of Malá Strana
and Strahov dated somewhere between 1659 and 1665. The High-
Baroque treatment of 1715–18 was associated with the reconstruction
of the palace for Jeroným Colloredo-Walsee. The design was by Jan
Blažej Santini-Aichel, though Giovanni Battista Alliprandi has been
suggested as a possible alternative source. In 1795 the complex
passed into the hands of the Schönborns and the garden began to
exhibit a morphology having shades of English landscape gardening,
along with associated changes to the vegetation.

The Schönborn Garden has retained its original Baroque components, which include the main retaining wall of the terrace with its central ramp and arcs set into the slope, the retaining wall of the second terrace with its central semicircular niche, and the small building housing a staircase that provides a covered way through to the upper part of the garden. The eastern wall with window-like arched apertures, flanked by stone frames, belongs to the adjacent Wratislaw Garden. The upper level of the garden is dominated by a gloriette, arcaded at ground level and topped with a small, square, pavilion-like tower and viewing platform. The gloriette stabilises the north-south orientation of the original Baroque composition of the terraces and is one of the objects scattered about the palace gardens of Malá Strana that recall the *casini*, gloriettes and *palazzi* to be found on the upper terraces of Italian gardens and the native tradition of the winepress with a view.

The Classicist-Romantic phase and the later alterations inspired by it are visible in the network of 'footpaths in a landscape' that reduced the scale of the sweeping pathways to the proportions of a formal palace garden, and in the deployment and selection of the trees that survive, which actually includes species that grow to considerable heights. Above all, this refers to the sturdy copper beech on the terrace adjacent to the garden frontage of the palace and to other large trees such as oak, ash, horse chestnut and Norway maple. The smaller-scale trees include magnolia, white dogwood, common lilac, Catawba rhododendron and other species whose attraction lies in their shape, colour or ornate blossom. The upper, wider level of the garden, segmented into narrow terraces, serves as an orchard in which apples, pears, plums and to a lesser extent apricots and almonds are grown.

The Wratislaw Palace and garden at 13/366-III Tržiště is leased by Aiga
Investments. The garden is not normally open to the public.

The terraced palace garden, whose early-Baroque core came into
being after 1670, was enhanced, but not substantially altered, by
the Baroque modifications carried out between 1700 and 1712. The
cruciform axial composition forms a unitary whole, complete with a
flight of steps, a structure housing a spring and including a grotto,
and originally also a bellaria at the far, higher, end. Between this
whole and the house there is a terrace. The well housing and grotto
are hidden beneath the head of the forward-shifted double flight of
steps, all of which goes back to the early Baroque phase, while the
window-like arched apertures set into the western wall belong to
the Baroque proper. These apertures contribute to the dynamics of
the garden through the effects of shadows, which change with the
position of the sun as the day progresses.

In the 1980s work began on a major renovation of the entire
palace complex, to designs by Ivan Březina and others, including,
where the garden was concerned, the garden designer Václav
Weinfurter. On the upper, slightly sloping, terrace the new cruciform
layout centred on a quadrilobal trough fountain with a central water
spout. The four quarter plots had concave cut-outs at the corners
facing the middle and were edged with box hedging broken up
by box bushes trimmed into perfect spheres. The cruciform layout
was further highlighted by pairs of columnar hornbeams set in the
widened endpoints of the cross-shaped footpath. Considerable work
went on in the garden during 1992–94, this time to a design by
the Vienna architect Theo Gabler, who, while respecting the basic
conception of his predecessors, also catered for the demands that
followed from the palace's new intended use as a place of business.
Where the bellaria had once stood – one of those structures that
typify the palace gardens of Malá Strana and recall the *casini*,
gloriettes and *palazzi* to be found on the upper terraces of Italian
gardens and the native tradition of the winepress with a view – an
office building went up, and between the palace and the wall with
the jutting-out flights of steps that conceal the grotto and spring, an
underground car park was put in.

The garden of the Vrtba Palace at 25/373-III Carmelite (Karmelitská) Street is managed by Casus Direct Mail a.s. It is open to the public at set times.

This exceptional Baroque terraced palace garden was laid out over the period 1715–20 at a time when the palace was being reconstructed. The work was commissioned by the house's owner, Count Jan Josef Vrtba, chief burgrave of Prague Castle, who entrusted the entire task to the local Prague architect and builder František Maxmilián Kaňka, who had trained in Italy but also had a fine sense for the local ambience. The latest renovation, guided by the findings of a survey of the palace's structural history and the need for restoration, was carried out between 1990 and 1998 once it had been made structurally secure. The design was by the architect Ivan Březina and the garden designer Václav Weinfurter in cooperation with other specialists.

The garden, on an irregularly shaped plot, rises steeply in three stages and a remarkable effect is achieved in it by the gradation of the parts and the convex and concave profiles of the retaining walls. The composition evolves from the axis that is tangential to the short axis of the giardinetto between the sala terrena and the aviary and culminates at the opposite end in a rounded theatron at the highest point of the garden. Its approach via two ramped paths recalls the links, by steps or ramps, leading to the palazzi, casini or gloriettes on the top terraces of Italian gardens or to a wine press with a view in the native tradition. Ascending to the uppermost parts of the garden, we see unfolding before us unique views of the city, its churches, the surrounding gardens and a picturesque patchwork of the tiled roofs

of Malá Strana and Hradčany. From the theatron, especially from the viewing platform on its roof created during alterations done in 1825–35, a sweeping panorama of the city unfolds, dominated by Hradčany, the cupola of St Nicholas' church and the spire of the Church of Our Lady Victorious.

Kaňka's compelling interpretation of the style is intensified by the ornamental statuary by Matyáš Bernard Braun and the frescoes by Václav Vavřinec Reiner. The ensemble along the top of the wall across the middle of the garden consists of relief vases and classical deities: Apollo with a bow, Mercury, Diana with a dog, Juno and a peacock, Minerva carrying a shield, Jupiter with an eagle and Vulkan wielding a hammer (all are now copies). The theatron is adorned with raised reliefs of marine deities and mermaids. The plasticity of the aviary is amplified by illusory paintings of windows, and the retaining wall has also been given the colour treatment (but it proved impossible to reconstruct Reiner's fresco on the front face of the theatron when the garden was renovated over the period 1990–1998). The garden's vegetal décor is the product of substitution based on historical memory, the edging of the beds and the formal flame-patterned parterre being of trimmed box, with additional spheres and cones trimmed from box, European yew and the paler Japanese yew, and cubes and arcades of trimmed hornbeam. Next to the steps up to the middle part of the garden there are two surviving northern white cedars or eastern arborvitae. Colour is supplied by annuals, biennials, roses and perennials.

19A–C/ THE SEMINARY GARDEN

The Seminary Garden rises up Petřín Hill to above Carmelite (Karmelitská) Street. It is open to the public, entered from Helich Street, from the lower station of the funicular railway or along the Scenic Walk, also from the Lobkowicz and Nebozízek gardens.

The Seminary Garden as a pomarium preserves the tradition of the Petřín orchards and vineyards and affords the unique experience of glimpsing the city through fruit trees. The garden's name is derived from the archiepiscopal seminary, which acquired it back in 1793. Previous to that, since 1623, the vineyards and later the orchard had been improved by the order of Discalced Carmelites. Surviving from those Carmelite times are some little caves cut into the sandstone in the uppermost parts, the Classicist refectory (later the Black Eagle tavern, today the Petřín Terrace Restaurant) and the early-Classicist chapel of St Theresa with its bell-shaped roof. During 1912–14 new paths were made and, to a design by Svatopluk Mocker, the fruit trees were replaced. The Prague municipality bought the garden in 1927 and three years later opened it to the public, while retaining the orchard. The replacement of the fruit trees, which was carried out in blocks over a twenty-year period from 1980 without the garden's being closed to the public, was to a project by the garden designer Václav Weifurter under the direction of Karel Červenka, a pomologist. The work was carried out with the assistance of Jindřich

Pavliš, who oversaw the task, did some of it himself and also gave a chance to become involved to the world-renowned traveller, writer and journalist Jiří Hanzelka. While the fruit trees were all renewed, one tree to survive was an outstanding specimen of field maple with a girth of 278 cm, growing next to the small pond beneath the Petřín Terraces restaurant, likewise some valuable ancient pears and selected other fruit trees and some sweet chestnuts, which had self-seeded in the stands of trees growing in the upper sections above the Scenic Walk; these were left almost untouched by the renovation. The new plantings consisted of apple, plum and morello cherry trees and, on the southern, 'American', slope that descends from the wall of the Schönborn Garden, also almonds. Hollows and breaks in the terrain saw the return of walnut and hazel.

20A–C/ NEBOZÍZEK GARDEN

A garden on the side of Petřín Hill above Újezd, in the area between the Hunger Wall and the Petřín funicular railway; it is open to the public and accessible from the Nebozízek station and from the Kinský Garden through gateways in the Hunger Wall.

In 1891–95 this municipal garden acquired its historicising Classicist-Romantic aspect following a design by František Thomayer. The considerable difference in elevation from top to bottom is overcome by a system of paths that cut diagonally across the contour lines. The stands of trees running obliquely between the Hunger Wall and the funicular become less compact and form simulated inlets that offer views over the city, their fascinating plasticity acting as an accompaniment to the funicular. Thomayer's design retained residual elements of the changes brought about by Jiří Braul during 1832–42 and the area around the Haasenburg restaurant, which the municipality acquired in 1883, renaming it Nebozízek after the original mediaeval vineyard and making a proper vantage point of it. The sandstone outcrops in the uppermost parts survived untouched.

The orchard on the site of the original vineyard had been bought by the municipality back in 1822 and after Jiří Braul's 1832–42 partial assimilation to a country park opened it to the public. Thomayer's alterations were triggered by the 1891 Jubilee Exhibition and the associated construction of the lookout tower and funicular railway. Given how much needed to be done, Thomayer's treatment was not completed until after the Exhibition was over; the Exhibition itself is recalled by sculptor Celda Klouček's vase, decorated with garlands and putti and set in the first enclave above the lower station of the funicular. The groups of vegetation clustered along the Hunger Wall thin out towards the railway, leaving some splendid solitaires in the form of a group of eastern hemlocks and specimens of copper beech, fastigiate oak and horse chestnut. The wooded sections above the Scenic Walk, consisting largely of English oaks and Norway maples, saw the arrival in 1895 of the Vojta Náprstek monument, designed by Josef Fanta, in the form of a stone table bearing an inscription attesting to the benefactor's generosity. At the later completion of the municipal garden, a 1910-12 statue of the poet Karel Hynek Mácha sculpted by Josef Václav Myslbek was installed in the third gap in the vegetation above the lower station of the railway, and nearby, a 1950 bust of the composer Vítězslav Novák by Jan Kodeta, their deployment within the site having been suggested by the architect Josef Gočár. The Dahlia Garden, set up on the site of the demolished Újezd barracks as a public works project during the early 1930s slump, was renovated in 2000 to a design by Zdeněk Sendler and Václav Babka. As part of the restoration a line of Japanese cherry trees was included. And in 2002, on the slope along the projection of Vítězná (Victory) Street, a Memorial to the Victims of Communism was installed, the statues created by Olbram Zoubek.

21/ THE PARK BY THE PETŘÍN LOOKOUT TOWER

The park on the summit of Petřín Hill is open to the public. From the top station of the funicular railway in the Rose Garden it can be entered through a gateway in the Hunger Wall. There are other ways in from the Great Strahov Garden, the Lobkowicz Garden and the Seminary Garden.

A municipal park, whose romantic ambience embraces both the Baroque pilgrimage buildings and the fourteen new Stations of the Cross, instigated and designed by Jiří Braul and installed in 1834 by Josef Kranner. The prime mover had been the energetic burgrave Karel Chotek, also responsible for the foundation of the People's Garden (today's Chotek Gardens) in 1833. The park consolidated the Baroque pilgrimage site consisting of the Church of St Lawrence (Baroque rebuilding of 1740–45 to a design by Ignác Palliardi), the Chapel of the Holy Sepulchre (1732), the Calvary Chapel (1735) with its staircase and pulpit and the new Way of the Cross that leads up to them.

   Completion of the park at the turn of the 1880s and 1890s was a response to the new situation at the top of the hill arising from the erection of the lookout tower in connection with the 1891 Jubilee Exhibition. When the Exhibition was over, the Pavilion of Bohemian Tourists was relocated to a spot close to the tower, its

notable feature being the diorama 'Praguers Battling the Swedes on Charles Bridge During the Thirty-years' War'. To serve the ends of the Exhibition, Antonín Wiehl, its architect, had styled the pavilion in imitation of the Gothic 'Špička' gateway at Vyšehrad; the pavilion acquired its mirror maze only after being relocated to Petřín. In the 1930s the park was provided with a way through to the Seminary Garden and in order to achieve access to the Rose Gardens as well two passageways were knocked through the Hunger Wall. The main burden of the alterations made in 1933–34 was the work on plantings, which were to integrate the disparate buildings into a neat whole.

The park exhibits in the footpath design plain evidence of the morphology typical of a period dominated by historical styles. There is a suggestion of an oval parterre, and between the tower and the maze a pattern can be identified matching the divisions of the Czech flag. The predominant oaks, hornbeams and small-leaved limes are supplemented with other trees, notably Norway maples. The horse chestnuts, deployed in a grid, add an interesting effect of colour and shape to the park, most apparent in the spring months when viewed from the lookout tower. Two rows of limes follow the line of the Hunger Wall from the cathedral church of St Lawrence westwards.

22A–C/ THE PETŘÍN HILL ROSE GARDENS

These gardens are open to the public. The top end of the funicular railway from Úvoz lies adjacent to them. Access is also possible from Strahov Street or via passageways through the Hunger Wall from the park by the lookout tower or the Nebozízek garden.

This municipal park between the Hunger Wall and the Baroque fortifications was conceived in the 1930s. It emerged by stages, the first parts to be converted being the Rosarium and the Flower Garden, the western section being done later.

The Rosarium was laid down in a fan shape to a design by Josef Kumpán during 1932–34, while the younger section has a circular disposition, organised radially. Eight thousand different species and forms of roses were planted, gifts from various rose-growing companies, and pairs of hornbeams trimmed into cylinder shapes act as highlights within the circular section. Between the two sections stands the Štefánik Observatory.

The Flower Garden, designed by Zdeněk Profous, began at the same time as the Rosarium in 1932, but took three years longer. It is characterised by its grid-like plan, consisting of oblongs and squares, and brings together a profuse assortment of perennials, bulbs and marshland species that contrast with that striking conifer, the eastern hemlock.

The layout of the western part of the park (1938) recalls the shape of a kite. The shape and the trimmed hornbeam hedging permit the inference that it was intended as another theme-based creation.

MALÁ STRANA: MALÁ STRANA SQUARE – KLÁROV

The rugged terrain between Malá Strana Square and Klárov is due in part to the slopes of the Hradčany spur, which drop steeply down to the level of the left bank of the riverside belt. Along the fall line of the spur there used to be a fortification constructed under Přemysl Otakar II and enclosing Malá Strana from the east. A remnant of this fortification is the massive wall between the Kolowrat and Great Pálffy gardens. Opposite the mediaeval wall, on the line of today's Valdštejnská (Wallenstein) Street was the Písek Gate, approached across Pětikostelní (Five-Church) Square by a track leading down from the southern entrance to the Castle towards the ford at the point where the approach to Mánes Bridge is today. In the context of the construction of the Baroque fortifications, the boundary of Malá Strana was moved to become level with Pod Bruskou Street.

The character of the area was conspicuously altered by the construction of the palatial residence of Albrecht von Wallenstein in the 1620s, which took over the site of a gateway in the defences, twenty-five houses, some gardens, a brickworks, lime works and some vacant lots. The area between Malá Strana Square and Klárov is conspicuous today for its extraordinary concentration of palace gardens, varying in style from the Mannerist through Baroque and Rococo to Classicist and Romantic. The Leslie Garden is set into the slope above Thunovská and Sněmovní streets. The Wallenstein Garden lies behind the buildings of the Wallenstein Palace, its non-residential wing and riding hall. In the same stretch, i.e. from Wallenstein Square to Klárov, Valdštejnská Street is demarcated from the north by the street frontages of several other palaces, behind which gardens rise up the hillside and constitute the corpus known jointly as the Palace Gardens on the Southern Slope of Prague Castle.

THE LESLIE GARDEN

The Leslie Palace and garden at 14/180-III Thunovská Street is home to the
Embassy of the United Kingdom. The garden is not normally accessible,
but the main part of it is visible from the Rampart (Na Valech) Garden.

The garden of the Leslie, later Thun, Palace, is the end product of
a stratification of styles from the Renaissance on, with the Baroque
treatment associated with the reconstruction of the palace in 1710–12
being of particular significance. Surviving from the formal garden
phases are the retaining and perimeter walls, the trough fountain
with its statue of an angel, the garden shed, grotto, the statue of
Aphrodite and a stone table. The garden's internal organisation
was transformed after 1864 on the basis of planar and spatial forms
derived from the English school of landscaping. Paths laid out in
arcs and curves were joined up into a perimeter circuit with trees
installed along and within it. Near the fountain with its statue of
an angel, at the garden's focal point lying on an extension of the
north-south axis of the palace, these were a Norway maple and two
weeping ashes. Within the centre circuit there is a group of three
saucer magnolias and a solitaire specimen of fastigiate oak. The
new proportions and patterns of light and colour also arise from
the effect of other trees, such as ginkgo, small-leaved lime, ash and,
by the retreat in the eastern part of the garden, a false acacia in its
globose 'Dicidens' form. All around the perimeter walls there is an
amazingly rich assortment of flowering shrubs, including forsythia –
both border and weeping varieties, common lilac, kerria, deutzia,
mock orange, purple-leaf plum, shrubby peonies and Catawba
rhododendron.

24A–C/ THE WALLENSTEIN (VALDŠTEJNSKÁ) GARDEN

This palace and garden at 4/17·III Valdštejnské Square, belong to the Senate of the Czech Republic. It is open to the public at set times during the tourist season. Access is via the palace courtyard, from Letenská Street and from Klárov. The garden court of the Wallenstein Riding Hall is open all year round.

The garden, dating from the dying days of Mannerism, came into being as part of Albrecht von Wallenstein's monumental palace complex constructed in the period 1620–30. The works were managed by Giovanni Pieroni, who was also largely responsible for the design of the palace itself and of the sala terrena, as we know from plans kept at the Uffizi Gallery in Florence and the library of the University of Bologna. The connection between the garden and the main palace building is down to the vast sala terrena, whose vaulted ceiling is decorated with frescoes on the theme of Olympus. The front of the sala terrena opens onto the garden through three arches, while its southern side affords access to a circular grotto with a stone, shell-shaped water feature. The view of the sala terrena from the garden reveals it as part of a magnificent composition that shifts attention from ground level up to the silhouette of Prague castle beyond the garden's confines. The typically enclosed nature of a garden is jointly assured by the main palace building, its non-residential wing and riding hall, and a 10- to 12-metre-high perimeter wall. Major survivals among the original Mannerist accessories are the huge grotto and the aviary. The design to which an overall renovation of the garden was carried out in 2000–01 was by architect Pavel Dvořák and garden designer Zdeněk Sendler in

collaboration with other specialists. This facelift saw the restoration
of all the main components, including the aviary, which began
to serve its original purpose, now as home to an eagle owl. The
renovation retained the half-cones shaped from hornbeams that
add rhythm to the garden frontage of the riding hall, as well as the
magnolias lining the enclosing wall and in the riding hall section.
Fig trees were put back in the strip alongside the eastern façade of
the various non-residential buildings. During the catastrophic flood
of 2002, that is, only a year after the restoration was completed, the
entire garden was under water that reached a depth of *c.* 80 cm in
the area of the raised parterre and the adjacent hornbeam hedges.

The various parts of the garden are axially conjoined on
the principle of sequencing, the main syntactic sections being
represented by the square parterre outside the sala terrena and
the lagoon next to the riding hall that repeats the square theme.
Interlocking with them are three other sections: the area next to the
grotto and aviary, the elevated parterre and the bosquet. The ground
plan lineation, the organisation of the spaces and the extension
of connections across space are all governed by an axial system
featuring several crosses, but also a star and a trident. The lineation
is underpinned by box broderie edging; box trees also provide
pinpoint highlights. The overall effect is aided by the hornbeam
espaliers round the bosquet and the archways leading into it, the
characteristic aspect of which is rounded off by the trees. By the
grotto and aviary there is a group consisting of two English oaks,
a hornbeam, two red buckeyes, a small-leaved lime, a honey locust
and a field maple and a line-up of six, one and two fivesomes of
horse chestnuts. Opposite the entrance from Letenská Street, the
front-facing hornbeam bosquet is dominated by a ginkgo, while the
lateral bosquet is dominated by a London plane. At the boundary
between the bosquet area, whose central section is sunken and forms

four plots hedged with box, and the water parterre next to the riding hall there are two red buckeyes. The façade of the riding hall gains added rhythm from hornbeams trimmed into half-cones. And in the strip running alongside the southern section of the perimeter wall there are specimens of saucer magnolia. The overall composition is enhanced by varous kinds of water feature and statuary. Within the cruciform disposition of the parterre outside the sala terrena there is a central fountain made of marble with a bronze statue of

Venus and Cupid set in the middle. The original was created by the
sculptor and metal founder Benedikt Wurzelbauer of Nuremberg for
Kryštof Popel von Lobkowicz, and it was erected on this site in the
Wallenstein Garden in 1630 (now kept in the Prague Castle Gallery).
In the area outside the grotto there is a sandstone trough with a
fish-shaped fountain, while standing in one bed there is a sandstone
pine cone-shape with a sandstone statue of Hercules by its edge. The
raised parterre and bosquet section are linked compositionally by a

concave-convex profiled sandstone trough fountain. In counterposed aedicules, whose connecting line through space runs along the boundary between the bosquet section with the lower centre point and the water parterre in front of the riding hall, there are sandstone statues of Apollo and Diana.

An important part in the composition is played by copies of statues by Adriaen de Vries, a Dutch sculptor who had been through the Florentine school of sculpture (his teacher was Giovanni Bologna [Giambologna], author of the gigantic Appenino statue in the Pratolino), and had worked previously in Prague for the imperial court of Rudolph II. De Vries' originals were seized in 1648 by the Swedes and are kept at the royal palace of Drottningholm. The collection, on mythological themes, and present in the garden as copies, consists of an avenue of bronze statues on the raised parterre, linked axially to the sala terrena. The first pair of statues as we proceed away from the sala terrena is a horse with a serpent and a horse passant, the second is Adonis and Venus, the third Neptune and Laocoon and his sons, and the fourth pair is Apollo and Bacchus. The collection of bronze statues also includes Hercules and the Centaur at the focal point of the lower central part of the adjacent bosquet, a nymph struggling against a satyr opposite the Letná Street entrance, and on an island in the lagoon in front of the riding hall there is a quartet of naiads and a statue of Hercules wrestling a dragon.

In 1630, the layout of the riding hall yard was planned so as to tie in with the garden and riding hall itself, which was later to serve other non-residential purposes; records show it has even been a wood store. The exhibition hall built in 1947 was redeveloped in 1973 in connection with the construction of the A line of Prague metro. The erstwhile riding hall yard was subsequently converted in 1978 into a courtyard garden serving both the Wallenstein riding hall and the metro station. It was co-designed by Otakar Kuča and Zdeněk Drobný among other specialists. Their basic conception was duly respected by the general renovation carried out in 1999–2000, though shortly thereafter it had to be repaired again because of the floods of 2002. In essence, it is a roof garden over the vestibule and associated spaces of the metro station. The plan's outline is carried in part by a wall of clipped hornbeam running parallel to the riding hall and along the wall leading from Valdštejnská Street and in part along the wall from Klárov. The sunken central section is occupied by a pool with water spouts. Leading away from the Valdštejnská Street entrance there are two symmetrically placed groups of six red-leaved crab apples, the eastern row extending along the sunken section of the court. The statues on mythological themes, of which six are on a narrow terrace next to the riding hall and one against the far perimeter wall leading from Klárov, were reproduced from Antonín Braun's original Baroque statues at Valeč.

25/ THE PALACE GARDENS ON THE SOUTHERN SLOPE OF PRAGUE CASTLE

All these gardens are open to the public during the tourist season at set times. Access to the Ledebour, Lesser and Great Pálffy gardens, the Kolowrat and Lesser Fürstenberg gardens is from 14 Valdštejnská Street or from 3 Valdštejnské Square, through the Ledebour Palace, which houses the Czech National Trust. Access is also possible from the Rampart Garden (Na Valech) through the Lesser Fürstenberg Garden. The terraced part of the Great Fürstenberg Garden can be accessed from 8 Valdštejnská Street along a communicating corridor; its lower part is in use by the Polish Embassy with its seat in the Fürstenberg Palace and is not normally accessible.

The collection of gardens that lie beneath the Castle jointly constitutes a world of previously strictly private properties that is the product of a unique synthesis of rational and sensual creativity, typologically Italianate, but at the same time evincing a complementary, thought-provoking relationship to the domestic Czech environment. Their entirely warranted veneration is only reinforced by the views they afford across the palace rooftops of Malá Strana and the wider panoramas of Malá Strana including the cupola of St Nicholas', Petřín Hill and contiguous parts of the cityscape.

The gardens were shaped by all the phases of the Baroque with a run-on into the rococo, Classicism and Romanticism. The more architecturally demanding are the Ledebour, Great Pálffy, Lesser Fürstenberg and Great Fürstenberg gardens. The Lesser Pálffy and Kolowrat gardens recall the utility aspect of the previous generation of gardens and vineyards.

25.1A–B/ THE LEDEBOUR GARDEN

This terraced palace garden's development was spread over two
phases of the Baroque. The first began before 1710 and during that
phase the giardinetto, conceived in association with the sala terrena,
came into being. The terraced part of the garden was made during
the second phase dated to 1787–97, the time by when Classicism and
Romanticism had begun to make themselves felt, though the solution
adopted was carried out in the spirit of the late Baroque.

The giardinetto was constructed at the behest of Marie Karolína
and Leopold Antonín of Trauttmansdorf, its authorship being linked
to that of the sala terrena; those possibly involved, according to the
records, included Santini-Aichl, Alliprandi and Kaňka. The instigator
of the terraced part was Josef Krakovský of Kolovraty, the design
having being worked up by Ignác Jan Palliardi. Over the years
since, the garden has been refurbished and altered many times over,
most recently in 1988–95, this time to a design by Josef Lešetický,
Václav Pína, Marie Pospíšilová and the garden designers Božena
Mackovičová and Jana Pyšková.

The composition of this garden was architecturally demanding
and required a bold approach to managing a site with a 25 metre
height differential. The lower level of the terraced part is stabilised by
a robust retaining wall, which also secured the perimeter enclosing
the parterre outside the sala terrena. In this way, that part acquired
the form of a spacious 'hall' without a ceiling. Originally the wall

bore a fresco by Václav Vavřinec Reiner, *Battle with the Turks*, but it was destroyed, then replaced in 1797 with a copy by Antonín Machek towards the end of Palliardi's reconstruction. Even that is now lost owing to the collapse of the main retaining wall after an air raid on Prague in 1940. The wall was renovated in 1942 and eventually, in 1958, the painter and graphic artist Adolf Zábranský, in cooperation with the artist Josef Holub, adorned it with a sgraffito, *My Homeland*. The Sala terrena on the western front of the garden wing of the Ledebour Palace opens onto the giardinetto through a pillared arcade, its counterweight being a monumental backdrop in the shape of a wall with a branched flight of steps and the Hercules fountain. The parterre of the giardinetto is of a cruciform disposition accentuated by a trough with a fountain, and the four plots of grass have an exterior border of clipped box. The retaining wall and its massive pillars are swathed in riverbank grape and crimson glory vine, while the trelliswork on the adjoining stretch of the retaining wall, originally decorated with a fresco, is adorned with trumpet vine and honeysuckle. A link between the giardinetto and the terraced part is provided by the left branch of the steps incorporated in the backdrop wall with its statue of Hercules battling Cerberus.

In the terraced part the difference in elevation was first overcome by a double flight of steps, then by a pair of terraces with a flight of steps along the axis and a new double flight leading up to the upper terrace. The terraced composition is crowned by a polygonal pavilion incorporated into the perimeter and retaining walls, the latter furnished with niches and blind arcades. The impact of the terraced composition is reinforced by climbers and shrubs and trimmed box hedging; the uppermost terrace is shaded by four round-topped morello cherry trees, the product of grafting the cultivar on a rootstock. Other contributors to the garden's atmosphere are varieties of climbing roses, namely Sympathie, Coral Dawn, Casino and Schwanensee, also 'Edulis supena' and 'Festiva maxima' peonies, English lavender, bushy St Johnswort, lemon trees, hibiscus and pelargoniums in containers.

25.2A–G/ THE LESSER AND GREAT PÁLFFY GARDENS

The two Pálffy gardens exemplify the late-Baroque interpretation of a palace garden combined with a pomarium. The Lesser Pálffy Garden is accordingly divided by simple retaining walls. On the terraces, which are linked by a lateral flight of steps, we find bosc pears, Florina and Primula apples and late Morella cherries, with vines growing on the upper retaining wall. Behind the steps, opposite the penultimate terrace, there is a nook filled with perennials and medicinal herbs.

The architecturally exacting Great Pálffy Garden is divided into eight levels. The distinctive structure of the terrace walls becomes apparent from the spacious terrace second from the bottom, with its solid retaining wall and buttresses and an ancient horse chestnut growing beside it. The retaining wall incorporates an access to the flight of steps which, with all the finesse of the Baroque, are now spiral, now straight, now covered, now open to the sky. The access is framed by a Baroque gateway bearing a sundial and chronogram.

The year 1751 indicates when the garden was commissioned by its founder, Marie Anna von Fürstenberg, and is given in Roman numerals conveyed by letters picked out in red in the text. The gateway is framed in wisteria growing on a trellis. The lawn features Rose of Sharon (*Hibiscus syriacus*) bushes. The upper terraces are graced with climbers and other plants needing the support of trellises, namely Himalayan and alpine clematis, figs, almonds and grapevines. The tops of the retaining walls are decked with belts of shrub rose, common broom, flowering almond and dyer's greenweed. Black chokeberry can be seen growing in containers. The most recent restoration of the Lesser Pálffy Garden took place at the same time as that of the Ledebour Garden, in 1988–95 to designs by the same team. The Great Pálffy Garden was renovated in 1995–97 to a design by Václav Girsa, Miloslav Hanzl and Irena Bartošová.

This is a pomarium whose eastern side is set into the zwinger (outer courtyard) of the surviving defensive wall of the 13th-century fortifications of Malá Strana. It is divided by retaining walls and growing on its terraces there are medlars, some unusual Callery pear trees and apricots. On the bottommost terrace, shaded by a horse chestnut, there is a Baroque corner trough with a gargoyle. The system of terraces was reconstructed during renovations carried out in 1995–97 to a design by Václav Girsa, Miloslav Hanzl and Irena Bartošová, taking the findings of an archaeological survey into account. In 1858 Prince Maxmilian Egon von Fürstenberg had had two houses in Valdštejnská Street demolished, and at the restoration a new approach to the gardens below the Castle from that street was created in the vacant space; it is shaded by one long and two shorter rows of catalpas.

25.4A–D/ THE LESSER FÜRSTENBERG GARDEN

During the period 1784–88 the rococo terraced garden of the Czernin palazzetto replaced an earlier Baroque garden on the same site. The design was drawn up for Marie Barbora Czernin by Ignác Jan Nepomuk Palliardi, whose task it was to create an architecturally uniform palazzetto out of one or perhaps two older houses and devise the garden at the same time. The conspicuously axial composition of the Czernin, later Lesser Fürstenberg Garden unfolds from the main axis laid almost along the fall-line of the narrow, steep plot. At right angles to the main axis the garden is divided by a system of retaining walls and the terraces they support. The main axis is given material form by a straight flight of steps. In spatial

terms the axis is anchored at the bottom end by a gloriette and at
the upper end by an arcaded loggia with an observation deck. The
wine-press tradition is recalled by a gazebo with a slim little turret set
within a salient of the highest level of the garden.

This rococo creation chimes with the life story of the benefactor
and noblewoman, Marie Barbora Czernin, which itself passed from a
period of Baroque dynamism to one of rococo lyricism. She caused
to be set in the place of honour the conjoined crests of the family of
which both she and her first husband, František de Paula Gotthard
Schaffgotsch, were scions, and that from which her second husband,
Heřman Jakub Czernin of Chudenice, the holder of the Šťáhlavy

estate, came. The combined crest of the Schaffgotsch's and Czernins is set in the tympanum of the arcaded loggia.

All parts of the garden and its ornamentation were subject to a thorough renovation in 1997–2000, to a design by Václav Girsa, Miloslav Hanzl and Irena Bartošová. The terraces were planted with, in particular, vines and climbing roses. Two magnificent yew trees were added to the composition, placed symmetrically either side of the axial stairway on the third pair of terraces beneath the loggia. On the basis of an archaeological survey, two orangeries were reconstructed on the second terrace, one on each side of the axial stairway.

The manner in which the vast garden of the Fürstenberg Palace was constituted reflects the complex process of changes in ownership and style through the ages of the Baroque, Classicism and Romanticism. One part is on the level, the other is terraced, and each exhibits a quite different character.

The appearance of the lower, level, section largely corresponds to the late Classicist-Romantic alterations designed by the Fürstenbergs' architect, Josef Liebl, and carried out in 1860, though alterations made in the 1920s and 1930s are also discernible. This section, subdivided into two by an area conceived as a parterre, has footpaths that go in circles and around and within them there are a number of interesting trees. Of particular note in the eastern part is a majestic English oak that stands out against the paler shades of some larches. The circuit of footpaths in this eastern part goes together with the stylisation of the area around the circular fountain and its statue of a boy with a swan, the whole having spheres and cones of clipped yew trees as the key features. The ensemble also includes a magnolia and, along the fence separating it from Valdštejnská Street, climbing roses on arched trellises. The western part is notable chiefly for its awesome copper beech.

The central parterre section, end-on to the rear of the palace, lies on a compositional axis developed during the late Baroque and directed towards the terrace section of the garden, where it culminates in a pavilion. The character of the upper part of the garden is determined by a sophisticated system of terraces, the main axis being given material form in a straight flight of steps; cutting across this axis is a system of terraces supported by retaining walls and joined by ramps and flights of steps. The terracing of the upper garden was done at the same time as the late-Baroque reconstruction

of the palace after 1743. It was all initiated by the then owner,
Kazimír Netolický von Eisenburg, though he did not see it through
to completion. The two-storey pavilion had to wait until the end of
the 18th century to be completed. After 1822 the palace complex was
owned by Karel Egon von Fürstenberg, who oversaw the restoration
of the vineyard on the terraces and the introduction of cast iron
steps.

The terraced part of the garden was renovated in 2006–08 to
a design by the architect Ivan Březina and the garden designer
Václav Weinfurter respecting the late-Baroque treatment and
retaining such survivals as the pavilion and the cast iron stairways.
Other contributors to the overall impression are two reconstructed
orangeries in the centre of the top garden. The repertoire of

plants includes trees, flowers and vines that serve as reminders
of the renewal. For topiary, hornbeams and yews were used, and
as standards field maple and its 'Schwerinii' form with its typical
red autumn colouring, also Norway maple, red buckeye, sweet
chestnut, walnut, gean, Turkey oak, English oak, silver-leaved lime,
small-leaved lime in its more modest 'Rancho' form, and common
hackberry or nettletree. The fruit aspect is sustained by some almost
forgotten species such as cornelian cherry and medlar, but also by an
apricot and a pear. Vines and climbing roses are grown on trellises
and metal supporting structures next to the retaining walls, and
the huge range of flowers is made even richer with shrubby roses,
pelargoniums and beds of perennials, incorporating, inter alia, such
species as lavender, achilleas and sticky catchfly.

MALÁ STRANA: KAMPA ISLAND – KOSÁREK EMBANKMENT
The stretch along the left bank of the Vltava between Kampa Island
and Kosárek Embankment is a fascinating, photogenic area, its allure
magnified by Charles Bridge and the picturesque quality of the
island itself, the millstream called Čertovka, the Great Priory Mill
with its preserved waterwheel and Prague's own 'Little Venice'.

This is a hugely diverse area where past and present are
intertwined. The southern part of the island is taken up by Kampa
Park, joined by a footbridge over the Čertovka to the Nostitz
Garden. Integrated into the park is the building known as the Sova
Mills (Sovovy mlýny, previously known as the Odkolek Mills), today
the Kampa Museum, between which and the Liechtenstein Palace
once lay the Odkolek Garden. During the period 1945–1980, the
upper floor of the house originally called Ohrada, north of the park,
was home to the famous Czech actor Jan Werich, and between 1948
and 1968 the poet Vladimír Holan lived there on the ground floor.
Before them, the house had been inhabited, from 1929 to 1940, by
the historian Zdeněk Wirth. Originally, though, it had belonged to
the Counts Nostitz, and from 1798 to 1803 Josef Dobrovský lived
here. This leading Czech philologist and writer, who had been tutor
to the Nostitz household, is remembered by a monument, sculpted
by Tomáš Seidan and Václav Žďárský in 1891 and situated by the
entrance to the park from Kampa Square.

One part of the Great Priory Palace is the Maltese Garden, closed
off from Great Priory Square (Velkopřevorské náměstí) and the river
by a wall known as the Wailing Wall or Lennon Wall, in memory
of John Lennon of the Beatles. The footpath beneath the pillars of
Charles Bridge carries on along the Lusatian Seminary (U Lužického
semináře) Street, from which an entrance leads into Vojan Gardens.
In the connecting curve of Brickworks (Cihelná) Street is the Herget
Brickworks and nearby the marginal shelf that recalls the original
river bank. The Klárov crossroads, onto which the Mánes Bridge
debouches, is named after the founder of the Institute for the Blind,
the humanist Alois Klar. The garden of the Straka Academy lies
between Edward Beneš Embankment and Kosárek Embankment.

26A–C/ KAMPA ISLAND AND THE NOSTITZ GARDEN

Kampa park in the southern part of Kampa Island and Nostitz Garden to the east of Nostitz Palace at 1 Maltézské Square, the seat of the Ministry of Culture, are joined by a footbridge over the Čertovka and are open to the public. Access is from Kampa Square, the crossroads of Malá Strana Embankment and Říční Street, and from Maltézské Square.

The Kampa municipal park was created in 1947–48 and is thus one of the first new parks in post-war Prague. The area used embraced the former aristocratic gardens of the Michnas, the Liebsteins of Kolovraty and the eastern part of the Nostitz Garden. The remainder of the Nostitz Garden, the other side of the Čertovka, was converted into a municipal park shortly after, in 1950, and kept its original name.

The conception of Kampa Park was derived from forms characteristic of the Classicist-Romantic composition of parks. The basis of the spatial organisation of the park is a broad sightline developed on an imaginary north-south axis and delimited by lateral

arboreal masses. They include those lining the bank of the Čertovka and consisting mostly of alders and ashes. Also used to create the composition were trees preserved from earlier gardens, including a fastigiate oak near the Sova Mills and a yew and an exceptional London plane at the northern edge of the park. The composition is supplemented with groups of pagoda trees and horse chestnuts. The paths go in three circuits that together share in forming the path round the periphery. Between the Sova Mills and the Liechtenstein Palace, where the Odkolek gardens once were, at a spot shaded by the crowns of – mostly – horse chestnuts and maples, there is a view of the river and the opposite bank of the Vltava.

The Nostitz Garden, connected to the park by a footbridge over the Čertovka, forms a simple rectangle, repeated by the perimeter path, with trees framing it on three sides. These are primarily horse chestnuts with an understory of snowberry, lilac and philadelphus. The western side is dominated by a weeping form of ginkgo. In the oblong central space there is an eyecatching Kentucky yellow-wood, the successor to an example of the same species that had been left in place until it completely disintegrated.

27/ THE MALTESE GARDEN

The Maltese Garden belongs to the Great Priory Palace at 4/485-III Velkopřevorské Square, the seat of the Order of the Knights of Malta. It is accessible, provided the summer coffee house is open, through a side entrance from Great Priory Square.

The Maltese Garden is part of the Great Priory Palace, which has a rich structural history. The garden attaches to the sala terrena in the eastern frontage of the palace, and set in the opposite perimeter wall there is a niche with the arms of Gundakar Poppo von Dietrichstein, Grand Prior of the Order of the Knights of Malta. It is more like a giardinetto, but growing in it there is an astonishingly monumental London plane with a girth of 715 cm and the name 'Beethoven's Plane' set beside it. The plasticity and colourfulness of the perimeter flower bed is due in part to the various species of shrubs, notably rhododendrons, wild hydrangeas and scarlet firethorns. These are combined with perennials and roses, including climbers. The present area of the Maltese Garden is only about one-eighth of the spectacular garden recorded on a plan drawn up by Bartolomeo Scotti in 1725 to document its condition before work began on the radical Baroque reconstruction of the palace in the early 18th century.

28A–D/ VOJAN GARDENS
The gardens are is open to the public at advertised times and entry is from
17 Lusatian Seminary Street (U Lužického semináře).

Originally the garden of a convent, it was opened to the public
in 1954 and named after the Czech actor Eduard Vojan (he lived
nearby). Its existence is linked to the construction of the Discalced
Carmelite convent by St Joseph's church, founded on an initiative
by Ferdinand III and begun in 1661. Following the dissolution of
the Carmelite house by a decree of Joseph II in 1782, the convent
was re-occupied by sisters of the Congregation of Jesus. In 1921 the
site was bought from them by the Ministry of Finance, which had a
new building constructed in the southern part of the garden a year
later. It had the original northern fruit and vegetable garden loosely
redeveloped, including a little lake, to a design by an architect
lost to the historical record and today known only by his surname,
Chlustina. The trees brought in at that stage include striking
specimens of Nootka cypress, ginkgo, copper beech and weeping
willow.

The changes of ownership and use, the overbuilding of the southern part with adjacent areas taken over for tennis courts and the establishment of a large company offering garden services to the public – all this has had an effect on the character of the site, though without obliterating it completely. It is still surrounded by a perimeter wall and there are fruit trees growing in the main section; among the plum and apple trees some ancient cherry trees stand out in particular. The basic outline of the original network of paths has survived, and with it the structure established shortly after the convent was founded and sustained throughout the waves of change during the Baroque, as extant records reveal. Integral to the garden are three original chapels: that of St Theresa of Ávila (from 1715 or 1745), half-encircled by small-leaved limes, the grotto Chapel of St Elmo, and the niche Chapel of St John Nepomucene, both of which probably go back to the early days of the convent's constitution.

29/ THE STRAKA ACADEMY

The Straka Academy and its garden at 4/128-III Edvard Beneš Embankment is the seat of the Cabinet Office of the Czech Republic. It is not normally open to the public. A view of it can be had through the railings along Kosárek Embankment.

This prestigious garden matches the Neo-Baroque building of the Straka Academy, built between 1891 and 1896 to a design by Václav Roštlapil. The project was financed by the Imperial privy councillor Jan Petr Straka, Count of Nedabylice, whose will, dated 1710, stated that his property was to be used for setting up an institute for teaching and training young members of the impoverished nobility. The Straka Academy met the terms of his legacy from 1897 up until 1920, when all aristocratic titles and family privileges were abolished, after which it was converted into the Academic House for University Students.

The garden extends the length of the building and is wrapped round its central projection, the link to the building being given by the transverse axis which passes through both the entrance to it from the house and the garden gate, cutting right across the garden in the direction of Kosárek Embankment and the river. The proportions of the projection are replicated in the breadth of the focal point of the parterre, whose circular centre is doubly ringed with clipped box hedging with crushed brick between. On both sides of the entrance from the house there are sunken rectangular plots, lined with box on the house side. The lengthwise path parallel to the house, likewise complemented with box, this time as rounded shrubs, is more akin to a promenade. For its part, the path parallel to the railings along Kosárek Embankment, lined on both sides with Glenleven limes, is like an avenue. At the tree-clad northern end of the garden a London plane survives from the original arrangement, while also here are a Norway maple, sycamore, hackberry and ginkgo.

PRAGUE OLD TOWN (STARÉ MĚSTO)

The oldest cultural 'horizon' of today's Old Town lies at a depth of 6–12 metres beneath its streets. The magnificent Romanesque agglomeration that marked the end of the earlier pre-relocation settlement was followed by its smooth transformation into a Gothic city. The evolution of the outline of the Old Town was, like Avignon, which was built in the 1340s by Pope Klement VI, a friend of the Luxemburgs, basically complete by the mid-14th century, when the breweries, drying kilns, blacksmiths and wheelwrights all relocated to the area of the New Town, whose foundation had already been decided on.

Gardens already existed within the mediaeval Old Town, in the form of a number of small graveyards, the domestic gardens of vicarages and burgher houses, but above all the gardens of the religious houses founded by King Wenceslas I and his sister Princess Agnes for the Poor Clares and Franciscans. As things stand today, the layout of the garden areas within the precincts of St Agnes' Convent is as they are known to have been since the 18th century. The most beautiful part lay between the southern perimeter wall and the two churches. On Huber's 1769 map of Prague even some volutes, circles and ellipses can be made out. By the beginning of the 19th century only the outer garden south of the presbyteries was being maintained. Today the total area of the gardens and courtyards of the Convent of St Agnes equates to roughly two-thirds of the original.

The connection between the St Castulus (Haštal) vicarage garden and the gardens at St Agnes' Convent was interrupted by Agnes (Anežská) and Řásnovka streets. The gardens of the neighbouring Brothers Hospitallers' monastery of Sts Simon and Jude were completely overwhelmed by the pressures of redevelopment; one had been enclosed between the hospital buildings, the other, larger one originally stretched all the way to the river bank. The demolition of the Augustinian monastery and Church of the Greater Holy Cross happened before 1890, and the whole block of the monks' lodgings and garden and surrounding houses disappeared with the total redevelopment of Josefov. In the 19th century, the nearby Pauline Church of St Saviour still had a garth with a cistern on the site of today's Štenc House.

The garden of the Franciscan monastery of St James flourished in the 18th century, and up to the mid-19th century the axial pathway in the northern part was still edged with flowerbeds; and in the section between the butchery and the garden hut there were still clipped and trimmed plantings in patterns of flames and crosses. There used also to be a small ornamental garden behind the chapel (today's vestry).

Within the Clementinum, where the tradition of university-level theological studies was picked up by the Jesuits in the mid-16th century, a vast complex of buildings came into being between 1653 and 1770 with five courtyards and gardens. Their appearance is captured in a Baroque engraving of 1750. In our own day only the western courtyard is maintained as a garden.

The finest palace gardens in the Old Town used to be clustered round the Powder Tower. Clearly visible on Huber's 1769 map is the disposition of the gardens of the former Royal Court and the archiepiscopal seminary, while on Antonín Groll's 1856 photograph all that can be seen is houses and paving. More palace gardens were located south-west of the Powder Tower; they included the garden of the Mint with cadastral number 587/I and that of the Kolowrat Palace, No. 579/I, which even into the 1830s had a handsome centre-focussed design and longitudinal axis. All that remains to offer an idea of what the Baroque gardens of the Old Town were like is the torso of the Šrámek or Manhart house At the Sign of the Goat, today No. 595/I between Štupartská and Celetná Street. It was built in 1700 and in the 1750s and 1760s its garden served as an outdoor 'reading room' for students at the Piarist college.

Faced with all the maps, pictures and Langweil's 19th-century model we can but dream of the countless beautiful Old Town gardens lost to acts of 19th-century utilitarianism. A major event after 1882 was the large-scale redevelopment of Josefov and adjacent parts of the Old Town, which brought with it the loss of part of the Old Jewish Cemetery in Josefov. The urge to keep alive memories of the deceased is accompanied at the cemetery by the ancient custom of venerating trees as cult objects. Yet no tree here reaches more than a hundred years of age, given that since the first burials in 1425 thousands of tombstones have piled up across the site.

Many of the new developments were accompanied by the notion of compensation. That is one way of looking at the replacement of the house and palace gardens adjoining the scrapped defensive ditch by the Old and New Avenues. The ditch along the line of today's Na Příkopě (On the Ditch) Street was filled in as early as 1760 and the stretch along today's Národní (National) Avenue in 1781. When it came to constructing a new embankment and the Chain Bridge during 1839–41 the New Avenue [of trees] along the line of today's Národní Avenue [road] were removed, to be made up for by avenues on the Rudolf (today's Aleš) Embankment. On the František (Francis, today's Smetana) Embankment a park was established including a monument to Emperor Francis I known as the Kranner Fountain.

This public park is set in an enclave between Smetana Embankment
and Theatre (Divadelní) Street.

This exquisite municipal park is a Sezessionist and romanticising
creation dominated by the neo-Gothic monument to Francis I known
as the Kranner Fountain or as A Homage of the Bohemian Estates.
The monument dates from 1844 and the model for it was the Schöner
Brunnen in Nuremberg. The park was originally conceived as a lodge
with a view, but it was altered in the 1880s to one of the designs by
František Thomayer. His principles were also respected during the
renovation of 1992–93 designed by the garden architect Jan Šteflíček.
The Kranner Fountain with its equestrian statue of Francis I
(designed by architect Josef Ondřej Kranner and stone sculptor
Karel Svoboda, with figurative decoration sculpted by Emanuel
and Josef Max, aided by Josef Kamil Böhm) stands on an oval lawn
encompassed by footpaths whose ends are looped into circles. The
backdrop vegetation includes such species as Norway maple, small-
leaved lime, mahaleb cherry and trees typical of the embankment
and the age, namely a pagoda tree and a false acacia. The park was
originally linked into the embankment promenade, but the sheer
volume of traffic this way, including trams, led to the connection's
being broken.

PRAGUE NEW TOWN (NOVÉ MĚSTO)

The grand design of Prague's New Town, founded by Charles IV in 1348, took half a millennium's development of the area to realise. Throughout that time, life within the city's precincts was enhanced by a multiplicity of different kinds of gardens. The most significant ones belonged to monasteries, conspicuously adding to their visibility. The Baroque wrought exquisite transformations of some New Town gardens, most notably those of the Wernier and Piccolomini palaces on Na Příkopě Street. The abolition of the defensive ditches and ramparts had already made itself felt back in the second half of the 18th century. From 1827 onwards the ramparts of the New Town, from Žitná Street to Poříčí, gave way to tree-lined promenades.

Development of the area grew in intensity up to the mid-19th century and the aspect of the New Town slowly changed thanks to large-scale clearance, redevelopment and construction associated with the transport network. For example, the gardens between Florenc and Hybernská Street disappeared under what was at the time the largest railway station in Europe, today's Masaryk Station. When the Palacký Bridge was erected in 1876–78 the old settlement of Podskalí with its houses and gardens simply went. As a response to some of the losses through redevelopment there were at least moves to replace some of the lost gardens with new municipal parks. What typically happened then was that they had hardly come into being when they were altered as newer configurations arose. The most eloquent example of this was the fate of the promenades constructed on the ramparts between Florenc and Žitná Street in 1827–31, where, after 1873, with the gradual liquidation of the ramparts along the extension towards Ke Karlovu Street, a set of four municipal parks was created (today the remnants of Šverma Gardens, Vrchlický Gardens, Čelakovský Gardens and Karlov park). The largest park, Vrchlický Gardens, then known as the Great Park, was founded in 1876 in association with the construction of the railway line and Franz Joseph I Railway Station. Enlisted to model the new park was the landscape gardener and garden artist Ferdinand Malý, who was already managing director of Prague's parks and had gained considerable experience from working at the Prater and Belvedere in Vienna and before that for the Lobkowicz's at Velký Chlum, the Harrachs at Bruck, the Kinskýs in Prague, the

Rothschilds at Boulogne sur Seine, for Queen Victoria in Battersea, Napoleon III at Versailles and again for the Rothschilds at the Château de Ferrières. The special character of the park that he designed for outside the station in Prague resided in the impressive scene it presented including a pond and waterfall against a rocky background inspired by the paintings of Bedřich Wachsman. The lydite rocks were brought in from Ďáblice on a number of wagons drawn by pairs of horses. In 1913 the park was renamed Vrchlický Gardens and since then it has seen numerous changes. In the period 1972–77 most of it fell to the station's new concourse and ticket hall, another part to the north-south arterial road, and its destruction was further compounded by the ventilation shafts of the metro, whose line C runs right beneath it. This time around, the new aspect was no compensation for what had been lost. The remnant of the park speaks for many other parks and gardens around the New Town that suffered a similar fate.

The gardens and parks still extant within the New Town say very little as to their erstwhile richness and the only ones really worthy of note today are the Franciscan garden, once the garden of a Franciscan monastery, the municipal parks of Slavonic (Slovanský) Island and that on Charles Square. The garden of the Amerika summer house is only a remnant, but still worthy of note. Didactically important is the Botanical Garden of Charles University.

31A–B/ THE FRANCISCAN GARDEN

This garden lies between Jungmann Square and Wenceslas Square and is open to the public. Access from the former is along a connecting corridor, from the latter through the passage U Stýblů, from Vodička Street along the Světozor passage and from Palacký Street via the polyclinic. Originally a Carmelite garden after 1348, it passed to the Franciscans in 1604 and was opened to the public in 1950. At the time of its foundation it reached as far as today's Spálená Street, Vodička Street and Wenceslas Square. During the period 1985–95 it was restored on the anamnesis principle, using the identifiable early-Baroque layout and such surviving elements as the late 17th- or early 18th-century gazebo, possibly once a chapel. The project was designed by Otakar Kuča and Ivana Tichá and their collaborators.

The garden remains an organic component of the monastery complex by the church of Our Lady of the Snows, as confirmed by the cruciform link to the east-west axis of the church, the expression of which is a connecting line that runs from the southern entrance

to the monks' lodgings to the aedicule in the southern sector of
the perimeter wall. This line deviated from the ideal north-south
axis during the early Baroque age, which determined the ground
plan of the renewed syntactic composition. Within this composition
an important part is played by the section containing an early-
Baroque chapel, enclosed by a wrought iron grille and evocative
of a herb garden on the "garden within a garden" principle. The
southern sections are delimited by clipped yew hedging, while
the former orchard here is recalled by apple trees. In parts under
particular stress there are trellises supporting roses, and on the wall
that separates the private area alongside the lodgings of the Lesser
Brothers, Franciscans, grapevines are put to good effect. The trees
that form the backdrop are small-leaved limes. At its restoration the
garden was enhanced by a well, named Francis after the figure of a
boy with a shell, and a statue of Aesop (both sculpted by Stanislav
Hanzík) and by another well with a scene of dancing fairies (sculptor
Josef Klimeš). Finally, in 1992 the entrance from the Alfa Passage
saw gates installed, decorated with scenes from the life of St Francis
(sculpted by Karel Císařovský).

An island in the Vltava, south of the Legions' Bridge. It is joined to Masaryk Embankment by a footbridge and is open to the public.

The island, originally called Šítkovský, then at the start of the 19th century Dyers' (Barvířský) Island after a colony of dyers, began to change its aspect in the 1830s, when the miller Antonín Novotný had not only a family home built, but also a single-storey restaurant. After the island was opened to the public in 1836, he supplemented the restaurant with a Classicist-Romantic park. The island grew in importance as a centre of social and political activities, even being visited by the Archduke Franz Karl in 1838, when, in honour of the Archduke's wife, the Archduchess Sofia, mother of the Emperor Franz Foseph, it was renamed Žofín. Only ten years later, in 1848, Žofín witnessed the opening of the Slav Congress, and that eventually led in turn to its being renamed Slavonic Island in 1925.

The urban park on the island consists of two parts, with the Žofín Palace function rooms between them; the current appearance of the Palace is the outcome of the Neo-Renaissance reconstruction of the Classicist restaurant after 1885 as designed by the architect Jindřich Fialka. Before that came about, the old central hall of the Žofín had hosted the premiere of Smetana's *Má vlast* (My Homeland) on 5 November 1882. The northern part of the park constitutes a grand historicising Classicist-Romantic composition with Sezession overtones, whose sightline ends in a viewpoint from which a panorama of the city opens up with Prague Castle as the dominant feature. The garden was designed by František Thomayer, and it was laid out after 1885 in association with the reconstruction of the original restaurant as function rooms. Thomayer based his composition on connections derived from the preceding Classicist-Romantic phase, though he added shape to the stands of vegetation and intensified their tonality with a Sezession finesse based on contrasting pale and dark greens and a floral effect. This modelling is still recalled by the horse chestnuts, yews and a London plane. Thomayer employed palm trees in vases and flowerbeds in order to bolster this Sezession playfulness and he secured the entire composition with an interesting layout of footpaths, which look like classically linked circuits, but in addition depict a Sezessionist silhouette of an aquatic animal. Over time, details of the layout have been altered, but it is still detectable; the flowerbeds have gone. The stands round the perimeter include Norway maples, ashes and horse chestnuts. The island's characteristic period silhouette is recalled by a number of Lombardy poplars. After the Second World War, in 1946, the statue 'Song of Bohemia' (by Ladislav Šaloun, probably from 1927) was relocated outside the front façade of the palace, and later the sightline to the northern façade had set into it a statue of the writer Božena Němcová (by Karel Pokorný, 1955, on a plinth created by the architect Jaroslav Fragner). The southern part of this island park is cut out for social gatherings and games. The southern frontage of the function rooms leads onto a terrace that links onwards to a gazebo, and in the pointed end there is a children's playground. The whole is enveloped in trees, mostly round the outermost edge, consisting largely of black, pyramidal white, balsam and Canadian poplars, some of which have grown to impressive proportions. Along with the renovation of the function rooms in 1991-94 the park was also restored (to a design by architect Tomáš Šantavý and garden designer Veronika Strnadová).

The park takes up most of Charles Square and is open to the public.

The Square, originally called Cattle Market, was conceived within the framework of the New Town founded by Charles IV in 1348 as the core space in the development of the upper New Town and also as the largest public square in the Europe of its day. At its centre stood the Gothic chapel of Corpus Christi (actually of the Most Holy Body and Blood of Our Lord and of the Virgin Mary and of Sts Felix and Auductus), erected during the period 1382–93, but lost after 1789. In the early 19th century there were efforts to give the square more grace and there are records of moves towards breaking it up, though this was prevented at the instigation of the burgrave, Karel Chotek, whose initiative was accompanied by the planting of the first trees in the southern part of the square and a succession of later developments.

The uniform arrangement of the square, to plans by Bedřich Wünscher, was settled once the old armoury had been removed in 1863, and it came to fruition, under the direction of Josef Fiala, during the period 1870–76. The great merit of Wünscher's conception was the handling of trees, which were distributed in such a way that the square could still be crossed on foot from any direction. Wünscher enhanced the impact of the square's huge space by a triple avenue around the perimeter.

Not long after Wünscher's working of the square itself, a municipal park was instituted within it in 1884–85 to a design by František Thomayer. It is characterised by the bath-shaped modelling of the terrain, the Sezession pattern of its walkways and the neo-landscapist system of sightlines through the vegetation, with Sezessionist finishing touches. To form the lateral vegetal backdrops Thomayer used tree species known to be resistant to the urban environment; in the foreground he placed species whose interest lies in colour and shape, and he supplemented the inevitable floridity of the Sezession with a rich array of flowering shrubs. The period assortment is attested by the recurrent use of pagoda trees and the presence of such other interesting species as silver maple, burr oak and catalpa. Then there is the honey locust close by the statue of the writer Eliška Krásnohorská, a late-budding Kentucky coffee tree by the children's playground and the golden rain tree or Pride of India hard by the statue of another writer, Karolina Světlá. There are also several London planes, the impressive specimen in the centre of the park surviving from the earlier, 1870s, version of the square. The use of shrubs brought colourful blossom to the park while also supporting the sense of enclosure within the perimeter achieved by the bath-shaped modelling of the terrain. The perimeter underplanting consists largely of such native species as European spindle, privet and alpine currant, but also weeping forsythia, laburnum, fuzzy deutzia, snowberry, scalloped spiraea and bridal wreath spiraea.

The park is divided by the westward projections of Ječná and Žitná streets into three parts. In the southernmost the layout of paths forms Thomayer's typical bow shape, clasped in the middle by a circular pool; in essence we have here Sezession-style rings or hoops laid out on the flat. In the central section the path layout consists of three interlocking circles, the middle one originally endowed with a Sezession emblem- or brooch-like creation which, following the removal of the Sezession floral décor and some other details, was

converted to Neo-Baroque and today is well past its best. Surviving outside the New Town town-hall in the northern part of the park is an older trough fountain with a 1698 pillar of St Joseph by Matěj Václav Jäckl and a monument to the poet, prose-writer, dramatist and journalist Vítězslav Hálek with a niche, trough and stone benches created in 1891 by the sculptor Bohuslav Schnirch.

With the passage of time several more monuments and statues appeared in the park. In 1898 the southern part saw installed a monument to the botanist and traveller Benedikt Roezl, sculpted by Gustav Zoula and Čeněk Vosmík on a plinth designed by the architect Edvard Sochor. Then in 1910, on the corner facing Ressl Street, came the statue of Karolina Světlá, sculpted by Gustav Zoula, on a plinth created to a design by the architect Josef Fanta. The monument to Eliška Krásnohorská by the sculptress Karla Vobišová-Žáková was set up on the opposite corner in the middle section of the park in 1931. In the southern section, at the point where the footpath bow is drawn together, a monument was erected in 1961 to the physiologist, neurologist, poet and philosopher Jan Evangelista Purkyně, the work of the sculptors Oskar Kozák and Vladimír Štrunc. In the 1980s, exits from the Charles Square station of metro line B appeared on the two corners facing Ressl Street, with their statues of Eliška Krásnohorská and Karolina Světlá.

In the course of the 1998 improvement to the parlous state of the park's northern section (as designed by the architects Magdalena Dandová and Jaromír Kosnar in collaboration with the garden architect Helena Fünsterlová) the Vítězslav Hálek monument and the trough fountain with its central column were successfully re-installed outside the New Town town-hall. Other elements of the planned renovation were never implemented.

34/ THE AMERIKA SUMMER HOUSE

The garden of the Amerika summer house, today the Antonín Dvořák Museum, is open to the public at set times. Access is through No. 20 in Ke Karlovu Street.

The remnant of the garden of this Baroque summer house, the main part of which consisted of a parterre framed like a picture, is all that is left of the older Baroque garden created as part of the summer residence of Jan Václav Michna of Vacínov. The Baroque summer house was built between 1715 and 1720, probably to a design by Kilián Ignác Dienzenhofer.

The plan of the Neo-Baroque design is a sample of the creative thoroughness of the age of historicism that has been the subject of such wide-ranging debate. It was designed František Thomayer and materialised in the period 1884–86 immediately after most of the previous garden had been built over.

The Neo-Baroque design incorporated statues taken from the Baroque garden. Statues of the titans Cacus and Hercules stand in front of the summer house and two vases with putti and two sculptural groups – Spring-Summer and Autumn-Winter – are at the back. They date from *c.* 1750 and are attributed to Antonín Braun, the nephew of the famous sculptor Matyáš Bernard Braun. The Emperor bust of *c.* 1800 has a different provenance.

The Neo-Baroque torso of the garden with its surviving Baroque statues is framed by a vegetal backdrop that includes pre-eminently broad-leaved and silver-leaved limes. Standing out on the same level as the summer house there is a fine horse chestnut.

35A–C/ THE BOTANICAL GARDEN OF CHARLES UNIVERSITY
Open to the public at set times. Entrance via 16-433/II Na Slupi Street.

The Botanical Garden at Na Slupi documents the transition from
plant-gathering by collectors to collecting for the purposes of
education, research and satisfying the needs and interests of the
general public. It arose on the site of the Communal Garden set up
by the Society for the Improvement of Horticulture; the even earlier
occupant of the site had been the garden sanatorium of the Brothers
Hospitallers. Construction of the present garden began in 1897
with the terracing of the steep slopes, levelling the flat top area and
correcting the fracture in the terrain below. At roughly the same time,
a start was made on relocating the plant collections from the first
university garden at Smíchov, founded in 1775 approximately where

the Dientzenhofer Gardens lie today. Of some interest, and typically
for the period, the garden was initially divided into two sections
by a fence, the lower intended to serve the city's Czech university,
the upper the German. The university botanical gardens were
formally brought into service in 1898 and their mature appearance
was largely attributable to the roughly fifty-year-old trees preserved
from the Communal Garden; these include a 'Praga' ginkgo cultivar,
which along with the ginkgo in the Royal Game Preserve and
the columnar ginkgo cultivar at Klamovka, is one the three most
important ginkgos in Prague. At the botanical garden it has been
integrated into the flora of the groves beside the main entrance to
the greenhouses. This area leads on to the sections containing in turn
thermophilic, subtropical, aquatic and bog plants, conifers and the
rose garden. Many further displays were built up gradually, including

those in glasshouses. Today the most significant are the collections of succulents, aquatic plants, bromeliads, orchids and tropical plants. Noteworthy among the outdoor collections are the rhododendrons and azaleas. Like the Royal Garden at Prague Castle, the Botanical Gardens at Na Slupi are host to two dawn redwoods, planted in 1950 following the 1941 discovery of the species in Szechuan; previously it had only been known in fossil form. The visitor will find a host of other fascinating tree species, including a Kentucky yellow-wood, one of the three finest specimens in Prague along with the one in the Royal Game Preserve planted probably in 1844, and the young one sprung from the decaying remains of its ancestor in the Nostitz Garden. Other interesting trees to be found here are a Kentucky coffee-tree and a huge, triple-trunked Caucasian wingnut.

VYŠEHRAD

Human settlement of the Vyšehrad spur that looms over the confluence of the Vltava and the Botič goes back to primeval times and the early stages of the Slav settlement of Vyšehrad fell between the second third of the 10th century and the mid-14th century, as archaeological surveys have revealed. The first stages in the evolution of the seat of the dukes and, later, kings of Bohemia have been illuminated by the discovery of four main palace buildings on the site of the ducal and royal demesne. Many parts of the oppidum and the later mediaeval castle were lost during the construction of the Vyšehrad citadel between 1653 and 1850, when the enceinte with the palace buildings was hemmed in by the still detectable Baroque bastions of St Ludmila and St Wenceslas and dominated by a Baroque armoury (destroyed by fire in 1927). Pieces of one of the four palace buildings are incorporated in the Old Burgrave's Residence, renovated at the same time as when the exterior parts of the Ducal and Royal Acropolis were being laid out.

Vyšehrad existed as a self-governing town until 1884, when it was merged with Prague. The Prague military fortress had been closed back in 1866, but the surviving structures and fortifications remained under army control until the end of 1911. The closure of the fortress enabled the Vyšehrad Chapter, represented by the enlightened provost Václav Štulc and a later successor Mikuláš Karlach, to bring to fruition the idea of building a national necropolis, with its Slavín tomb of major national figures, and reconstructing the collegiate church of Sts Peter and Paul as a Neo-Gothic basilica. Thanks to these activities, the last two decades of the 19th century saw a surge in the cultivation of the fortified area, with the planting of trees along the ramparts and bastions and the construction of promenades and viewing platforms, while in 1893, on the western slope beneath the ramparts, the municipality embarked on the foundation of a scenic park to a design by František Thomayer. On the north-western defences the Štulc Gardens came into being, and adjacent to the necropolis the Karlach Gardens. As at numerous other sites, at Vyšehrad, too, interesting introduced tree species played a part.

From the end of the 19th century there was much new development of the area around the Vyšehrad citadel and the start of the 20th century saw the emergence of a unique area of Cubist tenement blocks and private houses at the foot of the Vyšehrad cliff. There is also an isolated example of the transfer of Cubist morphology into horticulture in the garden of the Villa Kovařovič.

36A–E/ THE DUCAL AND ROYAL ACROPOLIS

This lies between the Basilica of Sts Peter and Paul, the Basilica of St Lawrence and the bastion of Sts Ludmila and Wenceslas. The area is open to the public.

The Ducal and Royal Acropolis is a unique historical site. For its consolidation in terms of layout and the use of space, as for its presentation and functional adaptations, such means and methods as are applied to the creation of parks and gardens were brought to bear. The Acropolis is part of the wider ducal and royal demesne cut off from the north by the Basilica of St Peter, with fragments of the earlier collegiate church. In association with the renovation of the Old Burgrave's Residence, which incorporates pieces from one of the four palace buildings of the ducal and royal seat uncovered by archaeologists, steps were taken to adapt the outdoor parts of the Acropolis. The new arrangement materialised in large measure during 2002–06. The design was by Otakar Kuča, the architect who also drew up plans for the completion of the project.

The resulting visual aspect of the environment of the Acropolis testifies to its well considered conception, which evinces due respect for the survivals from the past and the findings of archaeology. It

(180)

had also been responsive to other results of the archaeological survey relating to how the lie of the defensive ditch to the north and west and the position of the four main palace buildings of the demesne lying in the south-western and western part of the site were identified or inferred. The opening-up of the space right up to the castle wall by the gallery has made it easier to envision the palace buildings, and it leads back the other way to points that offer exceptional views of the river and the city, while also bringing up associations triggered by the dramatic relief of the Vyšehrad cliff, including Libuše's bath-house (actually the remnants of a 14th-century guardhouse erected to overlook the river traffic below), and perhaps even the recollection of the legend of Šemík, the horse who saved his master Horymír's life by leaping off the rock at this point and conveying him safely home to Neumětely.

By sensitive application of the "per purgo" principle the space was cleared of all that was redundant or confusing, and so a meaning shift was achieved in how certain components were perceived. Just how effective the principle is can be appreciated in the neighbourhood of the four sculptural groups by Josef

Václav Myslbek that give material form to stories from the Czechs'
legendary pre-history and are duly named "Ctirad and Šárka",
"Přemysl and Libuše", "Lumír and his Song" and "Záboj and Slavoj".
The statues, made during the period 1889–97, were relocated to
Vyšehrad after the Second World War from the damaged Palacký
Bridge ("Přemysl and Libuše" is a copy made to complete the set
in 1977). With the removal of the historicising oblong parterre
replicating the ground plan of the burned-out Baroque armoury, the
statues shed their role of mere on-looking extras, their symbolism
now able to engage fully with the environment of the Acropolis.
Historical memory suffered no loss thereby, because the position and
areal dimensions of the armoury can still be inferred from where the
statues have been sited. An additional asset is that, following the
changes, Myslbek's statues are amenable to close scrutiny from all
sides.

   The foundation of the sober and disciplined arrangement of the
Acropolis are its trees, lawns and footpaths. Their own mark has
been made, above the Gothic cellar and along the strip behind the

Old Burgrave's Residence, by delicate vines, supported by traditional acacia-wood stakes. The vine varieties grown here are Bianca, Marlen and Festival.

The handling of the vegetation at the Acropolis has ended with an imaginative use of trees right across the space: they have been used to "enwrap" the whole area and to add definition to the spaces outside the Old Burgrave's Residence and where the Myslbek statues stand, while preserving the site's integrity, as achieved by the uncluttered views from ground level, throughout. Contributors to the net effect are the surviving trees, in an assortment dominated by ashes and pagoda trees. There are also small- and broad-leaved limes, Norway maples, sycamores and false acacias. The range is given a special extra quality by the presence of two green ashes, a silver-leaved lime and a 'Purpurascens' sycamore. Later plantings increased the ratio of small- and broad-leaved limes and ashes, and behind the Old Burgrave's Residence two fastigiate oaks were put in.

37/ KARLACH GARDENS
A park lying between the streets K Rotundě and V Pevnosti
and Vyšehrad cemetery. It is open to the public.

This park, founded in 1890 by the Vyšehrad Chapter, is an
eclectic conception uniting elements of Romanticism and
Classicism. It was founded on the initiative of the then
provost, Mikuláš Karlach, where once there had been fields
and a police post. Initially it was fenced round and probably
shorter than today, though a 1910 map of Prague shows
it as also occupying the area corresponding to its eastern
section adjacent to the former capitular court. The park's
original structure can be read in part from the rectangular
plots, the avenues and the position of the statue of St John
Nepomucene on the transverse axis and the Neo-Gothic well
on the longitudinal axis. Where the police post once stood
there is now the group of three "Devil's Pillars", allegedly
remnants of a monolith used to determine the solstice. The
ultimate impression of the space is largely determined by
its trees: the avenues lining the footpaths are chiefly made
up of silver-, small- and broad-leaved limes, also to be seen
among the stands round the edges. In the vicinity of the
well limes feature also as solitaires, along with some pear
trees. In the stand parallel to V Pevnosti Street there are
Norway and field maples, false acacias and ashes.

38/ ŠTULC GARDENS
The park between Štulc Street and the north-west bastion of the old fortress. Open to the public.

The park on the north-west bastion of the Vyšehrad fortress is of a simple, but ideologically powerful, romanticising composition, whose centre point is an equestrian statue of St Wenceslas situated on the north-south axis together with the Neo-Gothic building of the New Provost's House. The optical projection of this axis affords a connection through space to the church of the Emmaus Monastery. The Vyšehrad provost and dedicated patriot Václav Štulc spent much time and effort on conserving the early Baroque statue of St Wenceslas, which had been created in 1678–80 by the Prague sculptor Jan Jiří Bendl. Štulc collected it from the municipal store at Na Františku, where it had been placed, along with its secondary plinth by Kranner, in 1879 following its removal from Wenceslas Square, and had it transported to Vyšehrad at his own expense (replaced by a copy in 1959).

Initially, the park was fenced in and its extent, as evinced by a map of Prague of *c.* 1890, roughly matched today's more elevated section. Now it stretches as far as the scenic path alongside the bastion wall, from which there are wide panoramic views across the city. The tree species represented in the main area of the park are false acacia, small- and broad-leaved lime and ash, while a row of horse chestnuts lines the eastern fringe. By the rampart wall there is, pressed in among the ash trees, a Mahaleb cherry (generally characteristic of Vyšehrad), backed up by a young specimen of bird cherry. The façade of the New Provost's House has before it a nicely contrasting Weymouth pine.

39/ VILLA KOVAŘOVIČ

The house at 3/49-VI Libuše Street occupies the corner of Rašín Embankment and Vnislav Street. It is privately owned and not normally accessible.

A view of it from above can be had from the railway bridge that crosses the river, and it can also been seen through its own railings. The Kovařovič garden is outstanding for its Cubist morphology, typical of its origins in an age obsessed with speed and dynamism. The house and garden, in a matching Cubist conception, were designed by the architect Josef Chochol for his client, Bedřich Kovařovič. Construction took place in 1912–13, and the garden's morphology has survived thanks to the renovation of it and the house carried out in 1995 (following an initial study by Lukáš Matějovský, the project was finalised by another architect, Rudolf Martínek, and other specialists). The house and garden are set on a common axis on a spatial projection looking towards Hradčany. The garden is conceived as a prestigious foreground to the house, which constitutes the dominant furthermost point of the overall composition. The five entrances in the projection of the front, garden-facing, façade are matched by the five sets of steps between the terrace and the lower part of the garden. By their means, the prevailing angularity is transferred into the layout of the garden, where opposed fans of paths mark out triangular plots, the latter further highlighted by edging formed of trimmed box. Set into the triangles there is a total of five Japanese cherries, two and one below the terrace and another two laterally in the corners. The finer detailing is brought home by the characteristic openwork railings.

VINOHRADY

Vinohrady (the name of this quarter of the city means 'vineyards') is spread out along a flat-topped ridge and down the slopes that drop towards the valley of the Botič stream. The area used to be one of the most important sections of the city's outer wreath of vineyards and orchards that came into being back in the second half of the 14th century and survived fairly intact up to the middle of the 19th century. The original farmsteads may be gone, but are not forgotten, their names surviving as those of various localities, streets or houses. The 18th- and early 19th-century era of summer retreats manifested itself in the merger of farm and out-of-town summer seat. A fine, rare example of this symbiosis is the renowned Kanálka garden, founded in the years following 1785 and far exceeding any normal idea of 'garden'. A similar case was the Wimmer Promenades or Gardens, set up in the late 18th century adjacent to the Rye (Žitná) Gate. Industrial development passed Vinohrady by, but it was largely swallowed up by housing developments instead. After it was made a municipality in 1849, construction intensified, culminating in the late 19th and early 20th centuries in a compact network of new streets lined with tenement blocks. The odd patches of land successfully saved from overbuilding are where we today find Rieger Gardens, Svatopluk Čech Gardens and Bezruč Gardens. On the hillsides above the Botič, originally called Grape Brook (Vinný potok), spacious detached houses and tenement blocks were constructed, each with their own garden. And at the end of the 19th century, the Gröbovka villa site was formed, its extensive garden containing echoes of the traditional vineyards hereabouts.

The park surrounded by Poland (Polská), Italy (Italská), Waggon (Vozová) and Chopin Streets. It is open to the public.

The largest municipal park in Vinohrady, the Rieger Gardens were created in the period 1904–08 to a design prepared by the then Vinohrady Parks Manager, Leopold Batěk. Their neo-landscapist conception is arresting for the combination of historicising treatments of macro and micro forms. Inspiration springing from the grand formations of Classicism and Romanticism is attested by the pictorial composition, framed by plantings along the fall lines and opening up a panorama of the city, dominated by the Castle and producing an effect of optical transmission. The modelling of the sightline is attributable to the tree species selected, attractive for their shapes and colours and here and there running in from the fringes as solitaires. They include weeping hornbeam, the one-leaved 'Diversifolia' and golden-leaved 'Zlatia' forms of ash, the fastigiate form of maidenhair tree (ginkgo), silver-leaved and common lime, the 'Nobilis' form of yew, and copper beech. Numerous trees of interest for their size, shape or colour are to be found in other parts of the park as well. These include London plane, pyramidal white poplar, weeping willow and pear-whitebeam.

The area by the entrance and the promenade area, embellished with Sezessionist motifs conveyed by flowerbeds, vanished with the construction of the Vinohrady Sokol Gymnasium in 1938. In the remaining parts, the morphology is small-scale, as captured by the period term "little-landscape style", where the 'little' idea may well have contained a hint of contempt. This morphology manifests itself in the way the park is parcelled up into smaller 'closet' spaces separated by different-sized 'islets' between the network of footpaths. Above them, and by contrast, the stands of vegetation merge and flow smoothly from one space to the next. Similar formations can be seen in plans and pictures dating from the first half of the 19th century, especially in the regularly shaped gardens that were undergoing change in the manner of Romantic imitations of landscapes. Given the density of the islets between the footpaths, the fragmentation must have been quite costly, yet it covered practically the entire park. The adaptation of the terrain was also costly,

especially where the original Pštroska farmstead had had a sandpit and quarry. Also needing adaptation were the changes in the terrain between the parts of the lands previously belonging to the Švihanka and Kuchyňka farms and to the Saračinka summer residence, previously the Vozová farmstead, of which certain survivals – the gateway, Classicist lookout tower and a three-sided obelisk – were integrated into the park. A map of Prague of *c.* 1910 does not yet show the approach area at the corner of Polská and Italská streets. This was not completed until *c.* 1913, when Josef Václav Myslbek sculpted the statue of the politician František Ladislav Rieger that stands above the steps leading into the park.

The renovations undertaken in 2000 were carried out to a project by the architect Dáša Tůmová and garden designer Jana Stejskalová.

The Svatopluk Čech Gardens lie between Vinohradská, U Vodárny, Slezská
and Šumavská streets, the Bezruč Gardens between Kladská, Korunní,
U Vodárny, Francouzská and Slovenská streets. Both are open to the public.

The municipal parks, Svatopluk Čech Gardens and Bezruč Gardens,
originally constituted a single entity referred to as the Municipal
Gardens. The former emerged in 1893 on one part of what had been,
before it was broken up, the Nigrinka farm, and it was conceived
along Sezession lines. Here, however, we do not find the usual
analogy with a Sezession façade; instead, we can see an analogy in
how space and ground plan are composed, each section exhibiting a
merger of this or that historicising form and Sezession morphology.
The core layout of the footpaths is formed of a Neo-Classicist circuit
that switches into a Sezession teardrop. The composition of the
sightlines, derived essentially from Classicist Romanticism, is framed
and modelled by the stands of vegetation, dominated statistically by
broad-leaved limes, Norway maples and – typically for the period –
pagoda trees. The fringes of the vegetal compositions were worked
out in fine detail à la Sezession, using trees that are attractive for
their shape, colour or especially their appearance in full bloom. And
there is a stunning copper beech near the children's playground.
A major role is played throughout by the shrubberies, enhanced
in particular along the Slezská Street side by fontanesias. In 1924
the park saw the arrival of the monument to poet and prose-writer
Svatopluk Čech, whose statue was sculpted by Jan Štursa, the plinth
being to a design by the architect Pavel Janák.

Bezruč Gardens were founded in 1895 (some say 1903), possibly on remnants of land left after the Šafránka farm was broken up into plots. They consist of two parts set corner-to-corner, though streets split the whole into four sections. A monument bearing the bust of the poet Petr Bezruč is situated within the sunken parterre in the section opposite the Vinohrady Waterworks and the Czechoslovak Hussite Church. Viewed from Kladská and Lužická streets the park works as a counterpoint to the waterworks tower, and that is its chief attribute as things are today. It is also home to a surprising range of trees, including a yellow catalpa, one of the three most important catalpas in Prague, the other two being in the Royal Game Preserve and the Gröbovka garden. Then there is a showy 'Spaethii' purple sycamore, a copper beech, a pagoda tree – much in vogue when the park was created, a hornbeam and, among the conifers, a Weymouth pine. Striking for its masses of yellow blossom that comes out before the leaves are some fine examples of Cornelian cherry.

The garden of the Villa Gröbovka is framed by U Havlíčkových sadů and
Rybalkova streets and, at the lower point, the Botič stream. The house is used
as a study centre, but the garden has regular opening times for the public.
The main entrance is from Rybalkova Street.

The Gröbovka Garden, also known as Havlíček Gardens, is a period
piece remarkable for its extent and conception. It started as part of
the family seat of a businessman, Moritz Gröbe, and was created
over the period 1871–88, a time when historical styles were prevalent.
This shows in the conception, which is based on Neo-Renaissance,
Neo-Romantic and Neo-Classicist principles. The application of
the latter typified the work of all the people involved, namely the
main architect of the house, Antonín Barvitius, the sculptor Josef
Vorlíček, who designed the grotto and oversaw its construction, and
the sculptor Bohuslav Schnirch, who did the statue of Neptune for
the fountain pool in front of the grotto. The architect Josef Schulz
was only at the start of his career. He began with work on the
interiors and had a final share in the completion of the project. For
the purposes of building his home and garden, Gröbe had bought
two Vinohrady farms, first Upper and then Lower Landhauska. As
the site evolved, full use was made of its natural dispositions, most
notably the difference in elevation between the upper plateau and the
Botič-side water meadow.

The Neo-Renaissance heart of the garden is the house, its
Italianate atmosphere amplified by a vineyard. Three factors
contribute to the final effect: the siting of the house on the borderline
between the upper plateau and the downward slope, the layout

of the vineyard below the terrace, and the connection established between the vineyard and terrace by a double flight of steps. The presence of the vineyard recalls the tradition of viticulture here on the slopes above the Botič, once called Vine Stream, and with that the glorious age of the expansion of viticulture begun under Charles IV in the 14th century. Another Neo-Renaissance section lies by the Lower Landhauska building, itself reconstructed in like vein. Here the terrace is above the house and the retaining wall is set between arched stairways. A unique period feature of the garden is the grotto, its conception inspired by late-Renaissance paradigms, but also by Classicist and Romantic templates. In front of the grotto there is a fountain pool with a statue of Neptune.

The inspiration for the remaining parts of the garden sprang from the Classicist-Romantic principles that underlie the English landscape style. Given the time when the garden was made, these, too, must be seen as historicising (Neo-Classicist and Neo-Romantic). The same spirit fired the conception of the parterre adjacent to the northern façade of the house, from which systems of pathways arc away on both sides in the direction of the vineyard and determine how the sightlines are composed through the stands of vegetation and tie together the section next to Rybalkova Street and the western part of the garden.

The main contributors to the park's vegetation are oaks, limes and beeches supplemented by maples and horse chestnuts. The ultimate range of trees is surprisingly rich, for it includes, for instance, a yellow catalpa, one of the three most important specimens to be found in Prague (the other two are in Bezruč Gardens and the Royal Game Preserve). There are also ginkgos, including the columnar form, a weeping ash, a common hackberry (nettletree), an Amur cork tree, a balsam poplar, a sweet chestnut and numerous other broad-leaved species, and among the many conifers an eastern hemlock, Nootka cypress, yew, limber pine and Schwerin pine.

Making the garden was a costly enterprise and quite a tour de force. The quarries on the site of the vineyard were filled in with diggings from the Vinohrady tunnel that was being constructed at the time, and for the banks of the pond and the rocky backdrop of the waterfall stone was brought all the way from Ďáblice in the north and Třebonice beyond the western edge of the city. Gröbe is said to have redone some of the plans himself, as well as overseeing the works; allegedly he even whacked those parts that he thought badly done with his stick.

The garden as we know it today was split into four parts in the period 2005–13: the upper playground and facilities in 2005 (designed by Pavel Joba), the vineyard and its pavilion in 2007–09 (Jiří Javůrek), the grotto in 2009–11 (Jiří Javůrek), and the garden proper in 2009–13 (Hedvika Hronová and Radka Fingerová).

VRŠOVICE

The name of this part of the city captures its up-and-down terrain (Cz. *vrch* = 'hill(top)'), owing in large measure to the slopes of the Botič valley. Vršovice survived quite long as a village, which went well with the silk-weaving mill built in 1843–44 by Jindřich Rangheri, who two years previously had planted a mulberry orchard for breeding silkworms. After Vršovice was elevated to the status of township, the former Rangheri residence was reconstructed at the turn of the 20th century as a Neo-Renaissance town hall with a municipal park (more or less lost during the Second World War). The development of industry in the second half of the 19th century brought with it a rise in tenement housing, which burgeoned in the 1930s and in turn triggered the construction of a modern church on Svatopluk Čech Square; the plan included setting up a park within the church project.

43/ SVATOPLUK ČECH SQUARE
The park on Svatopluk Čech Square is open to the public.

Matching the visual order of the Constructivist church of St Wenceslas, the unique lineaments of the 1930s park make it an assembly area of a distinctive quality. The church and park are conceived on a common north-south axis, though within the park it is an optical axis only, given that in physical terms it is articulated by a fan-shaped pattern of footpaths. The backdrop function is performed by groups of trees down the sides distinguished by their particular bulk and contrasting colours and made up of London planes and copper beeches. The upper part of the park constitutes the base on which the church stands and the trees along its edges form an extension of the vegetative framework. The design for the church and the park was by Josef Gočár, who supplemented it with drawings of the surrounding scenery. The church was built in 1929–30, the park being completed a year later, though as yet without the system of steps in front of and stretching the width of the church's frontage. These were added in the 1980s in line with one of two variants of the Gočár design.

NUSLE

The neighbourhood of Nusle spreads across what was the level water meadow in the valley of the Botič stream and up the valley sides that rise towards the flatland of Pankrác. The area was originally typified by vineyards and orchards and has had a complex evolution. During the Baroque period it fell partly within the Nusle lordly estate, with the stately home and its garden as its administrative heart. Also within Nusle there was a frequently changing pattern of farmsteads and summer seats. The idyllic environment of a suburban community began to break down at the end of the 19th century, the character of Nusle being altered beyond recognition by the construction of industrial premises and, after 1910, by an upsurge in housing development. Fidlovačka Meadow, where the shoemakers' guild used to hold its annual revels on the Wednesday of Easter Week, was broken up at the turn of the 20th century, the name surviving as that of the first municipal park in Nusle. An ancient, legendary spring is recalled by the name of the post-war municipal park called Jezerka.

44/ FIDLOVAČKA PARK
Fidlovačka Park lies between Křesomyslova, Na Fidlovačce, Boleslavova
and Ctiborova streets. It is open to the public.

The first municipal park in Nusle was founded in 1902, following a
design by the landscape gardener Karel Skalák, on a meadow named
after the tool used by shoemakers to burnish leather. Given the date
of its origins, this is an historicising Classicist-Romantic composition
with a sightline defined by its green backdrops. Their inner edge is
modelled and given its colour scheme by the trees that jut out as far
as the outer circuit of footpaths, which are looped at one end into
a Sezession teardrop. Standing out among the trees are a copper
beech, horse chestnut, English oak and a variegated 'Leopoldii'
sycamore. The sightline connects to the Fidlovačka Theatre, but in
the early days what stood here was a wooden arena.

45/ JEZERKA PARK

The Jezerka park between Jaurisova and Družstevní ochoz streets is open to the public.

In the valley called Jezerka, a municipal park was gradually created after 1949 as one of the first post-war initiatives of the kind; it is notable for how it harmonises with the terrain. The principles applied in shaping the park derive from the Romanticism and landscape style redolent of the age of historicising styles. The plan of the park was designed by the garden architect Jiří Novotný with the cooperation of Jaroslav Schollar on the engineering side.

The main footpath follows the line of the valley, branching off left and right to various scenic spots. The most picturesque of these include the area round the little lake that is fed by the Jezerka

spring, associated by legend with the Princess Libussa. The lake has the typical complement of a weeping willow. Neatly inserted into the same spot is a venerable, huge London plane, probably a survival from the earlier garden of the Šustrovka farmstead. It is one of the five largest planes in Prague, the others being in the Kinský Garden, on Kampa Island, in the Maltese Garden and on Charles Square. The core vegetation consists of English oaks, with such major secondary species as horse chestnut and honey locust.

Also incorporated into the valley park was a restaurant standing on the site of the erstwhile Šustrovka homestead. It was rebuilt, still as a restaurant, concurrently with the foundation of the park. Later it contained a TV studio and today the Jezerka Theatre.

CHODOV

The originally independent parishes of Chodov and Háje, absorbed into Prague in 1968, were, from 1971 onwards, gradually overbuilt with the largest high-rise housing estate in the Czech Republic, called Jižní Město (South City). The development proceeded from Háje towards Chodov, where the slip road to the D1 motorway was being constructed simultaneously. The construction of the latter caused the disappearance of the farm of the erstwhile Kunratice estate, including three fish ponds and the gardens. All that survived was Chodov Fort, reconstructed in the Baroque era as a dwelling, and in 1984–89 adapted to suit the ends of an arts centre for the housing estate and complemented with the surrounding park.

46/ CHODOV FORT

The park envelops the fort, which functions as an arts and culture amenity run by a not-for-profit civic association. It lies between Ledvinova and Türkova streets and is open to the public.

It is treated as an urban park that acts as a mediator between the agglomeration of the housing development and an historic building that has lost its original ambience. Between 1676 and 1728 the original mediaeval fortress gradually underwent a Baroque transformation as a dwelling, complemented after 1812 with its own Classicist interior peristyle. The renovation and adaptation of the building took place in 1984–89 to a design by Miroslav Burian. The park itself was inaugurated in 1989 following a project by garden designer Jiří Mareček.

Within the park, the contemporary resonance of Classicist-Romantic forms is concentrated in a new quality that with discipline and noblesse underlines the dominant position and shape of the Chodov Fort while cleverly exploiting it as the focal point of the park's composition. The layout of the footpaths is developed into two outer circuits linked to the central circular path that follows the circumference formed by the original moat. The plantings are located round the perimeter and modelled in such a way as to frame the areas of grass along the sightline, direct the axial optical link to Prague Castle, bolster the inner compositional connections and serve as an acoustic and visual shield against the adjacent motorway slip road and the built-up area of the housing estates.

The trees and shrubs present were consciously selected with a mind to the landscape of Central Bohemia, their blossom, but also to their capacity to offer acoustic and visual insulation, which applies pre-eminently to those along the earth wall next to the slip road and to the line of London planes at the wall's foot, that is, along Türkova Street. In the western part of the park there are significant numbers of English oak, field and Norway maple, white poplar, several species of willow, but especially white, creeping and rosemary-leaved willow, and with them rowans and wild service trees. The shrubberies are made up largely of alpine currant, common dogwood, guelder rose and wayfaring tree. Among the conifers we find larches, Scots pines and yews. In the part of the park lying to the east of the fort the assortment of trees reflects the range that typifies the age of urban parks, notably through the inclusion of pagoda trees and Norway maples and such shrubs as Thunberg's, Japanese and two varieties of bridle-wreath spiraea, flowering quince, mock orange, forsythia and Cornelian cherry.

SMÍCHOV AND KOŠÍŘE

The Prague boroughs of Smíchov and Košíře were once part of the city's rural hinterland. The mid-18th century saw the rise of mills of various kinds and its overall aspect was altered completely by 19th-century industrialisation. Because of the number of factory chimneys Smíchov allegedly earned the nickname "Prague's Manchester". From the mid-19th century Košíře began to be overtaken by residential developments, much needed to house the workforce of Smíchov's industries.

The farmsteads and summer seats with vineyard huts and wine presses, which had burgeoned during the 18th century, are still recalled in street names and other toponyms. Out-of-town summer residences essentially consisted of vast tracts of gardens, and later parks, which took over the fields and vineyards of small farmsteads, and other lands as well. In Smíchov we find the renowned Kinský Garden, the Bertramka garden with its Mozartian associations, the Na Skalce park and the Santoška and Klamovka gardens. Within Košíře there is the Cibulka park.

47A–F/ THE KINSKÝ GARDEN

The garden lies to the north of Holečkova Street and is open to the public.
The main access point is from Kinský Square, with another from Na Hřebenkách
Street, while there are more entry points from Šermířská Street or through
gateways in the Hunger Wall leading from the Nebozízek garden. The Kinský
family's summer house is home to the Ethnographical Museum, the Musaion.

The hill slopes on the Smíchov side of the Hunger Wall are steep and
south-facing. The vineyards on them survived only up to the Thirty
Years' War; in the late 18th and early 19th century they were quite
barren and were called Vrabcovna (place of sparrows). At the foot of
the hillsides there used to be small vegetable plots and in the centre
section there was a habitation with some kilns attached for making

kitchenware. The top areas of bare sandstone rock were partly covered in heather.

In 1826, Prince Rudolf Kinský commenced the construction of his summer residence on these slopes. It took the form of a vast Classicist-Romantic garden, typified by its symbiosis with an Empire-style summer house and other Classicist buildings. Kinský entrusted the design of the garden and supervision of the works to his business manager, František Höhnel. However, the basic disposition and layout of the level part of the garden seem likely to have been set by the Czech architect of the summer house, Jindřich Koch, then active in Vienna. The adaptation of this part of the garden required some major adjustments to the terrain on the lower slopes of Petřín Hill.

The summer house was built to dominate the parterre and the sightline from it. This arrangement was linked by a common central line through space which extended beyond the bounds of the garden towards the towers of Our Lady Before Týn. Not far from that church, on the Old Town Square, stands the Kinský Palace, which was once the family's main city residence. In this way, indeed twice over, the tried and tested idea of the togetherness of home and garden was brought to bear, an idea suggested and promoted by the English landscape designer Humphry Repton. Jindřich Koch had applied a similar principle in the manor park at Kostelec nad Orlicí, where he had worked for Rudolf Kinský's brother Josef. There, too, the manor house, in appearance not unlike the summer house in the Kinskýs Prague garden, and the main sightline through the park are set on a common axis and likewise this continues beyond the park boundary as an imaginary connection through space to the hills atop which stand the ruins of Potštejn Castle.

In the Kinskýs' Smíchov garden there is a brilliant application of contrast between the two separately handled parts, that is, between the garden parterre with the summer house and sightline and the downhill sections stylised as in nature. The masses of vegetation and the sightlines were organised in an uphill direction approximately at right-angles to the spatial axis of the composition that takes in the parterre, the summer house and the sightline. The way the range of trees was handled was masterly and imaginative. The core of the composition was made up of native species, primarily English oak, small-leaved, large-leaved and silver-leaved limes, hornbeam, beech and assorted species of Sorbus – wild service tree, common and broad-leaved whitebeam and rowan. In the flat part of the garden, domestic species were used to create a 'backing' to alien species and cultivars, as can be seen in, for example, how the parterre is framed: there groups of silver maples and 'Leopoldii' sycamores rely on a

backing of Norway maples. Some robust box elders (ash-leaved maples) serve to frame the parterre without the support of native species. The same obviously applies to the impressive London plane that stands proud, like a butler, by the entrance from Kinský Square and is one of the five largest specimens in Prague (the other four are in the Maltese Garden and the parks on Kampa Island, Charles Square and Jezerka). The plane is eloquent evidence of how the introduction of alien species was evolving, along with the specimens of pagoda tree, honey locust, silver maple, the 'Unifolia' form of false acacia and other species that feature in the Kinský garden in a range of forms and functions. In the sloping parts of the garden alien species and cultivars were used only to a limited extent, and in the topmost sections barely at all. One highly effective detail is the refinement of the fringes of the sightline from the Kinský Square entrance by the use of copper beeches. Domestic species used as solitaires or in clusters of solitaires are chiefly English oak, broad-leaved lime, Swedish whitebeam and wild service tree. The arrangement of the more elevated parts of the garden was designed and overseen by Bedřich Wünscher, who succeeded František Höhnel as business manager. In 1855 it was also Wünscher who drew a plan of the finished garden, though all that survives is a copy. The original was destroyed in 1945 during a fire at the Old Town town hall.

The Kinský Garden was threatened with being broken up, but this was prevented by the Smíchov municipality, which bought it and opened it to the public in May, 1903. They later meant to turn it into an ethnographic garden, an idea that, happily, failed to be brought to full fruition because of the cost.

Items that did get installed here under that plan include the sandstone wayside shrine from the Žižkov church of St Procopius, the wooden belfry and cross from Dolní Bojanovice in Moravian Slovakia and the tiny wooden Orthodox church of St Michael, relocated from Medvedovce near Mukačevo in Sub-Carpathian Ruthenia. In 1914, a statue of Hana Kvapilová by Jan Štursa was installed close to the summer house.

In 1948–49 a strip along the southern boundary of the garden was detached for the purpose of widening Holečkova Street and the construction of a new retaining wall. This inevitably disrupted the proportions of the core composition of the parterre with the summer house and the associated sightline. In part this was remedied during the garden's renovation as carried out gradually since 1999 (to a design by Magdalena Dandová and Jaromír Kosnar with the collaboration of others).

48A–C/ BERTRAMKA

The garden of a farmstead at 2/169 Mozartova Street, is accessible during the opening times of the Wolfgang Amadeus Mozart Memorial Museum.

The Bertramka garden preserves the memory of Wolfgang Amadeus Mozart, a bust of whom is incorporated into the slope to the south of what was once a dwelling. Bertramka was originally a farmstead largely given over to viticulture, but converted to a summer residence after 1743, when it was bought at auction by František z Bertramu. In 1784 it became the property of the opera singer Josefína Dušková, who often received Mozart here together with her husband, the composer František Xaver Dušek, who was also a brilliant harpist and pianist.

The Classicist-Romantic arrangement of the garden, together with the buildings that had been part of the farmstead, then summer house, was renovated in 1955 to a design by Adolf Benš. The Baroque garden of the original farmstead is recalled by the *c.* 1700 sala terrena, to which additions were made after 1784. The garden is set in a hollow beneath the Mrázovka hill and is on two elevations separated by the terrace wall and fountain. The wide sightline goes upwards and is encircled by a path, framed in vegetation and modelled using trees planted forward, out of line. The assortment of trees includes English and sessile oak, beech, small- and large-leaved lime, Norway and field maple, horse chestnut, Turkish hazel, silver birch and yew.

49/ THE NA SKALCE GARDENS
These gardens lie between Na Skalce, Ostrovského, Kováků and Bieblova streets and are open to the public.

The Na Skalce gardens are a period sample of a place deliberately conceived as a public municipal park. The land for the park was donated to the Smíchov municipality by Sir Eduard Daubek, who also part-financed the park's creation and enlisted František Thomayer to prepare the design, which was materialised in the years 1891–94. Thomayer had given evidence of his inventiveness and experience particularly in the course of setting up or adapting both public parks and the gardens of various private houses. He had gained many insights from the time he had spent in Vienna, where he played a part in setting up gardens for the Rothschilds, and later from his period working in Paris, where he was taken on by Édouard André. In his modelling of the Na Skalce park, Thomayer exploited to brilliant effect the potential of the site presented by the comb-like tongue of land and the rocky face of what had once been a quartzite quarry. In his organisation of both space and layout he went for a characteristically combined morphology. The vegetative foundation was treated in landscape terms, the end effect enhanced by the surface of a lake and the dynamism of waterfalls, and he inserted a system of paths based on the principle of circles and arcs linked into a horizontal version of Sezession drapery. He took the highest point of the terrain as its Neo-Classicist focal point and so could draw from it an eclectic star shape of sightlines. As contributors to the net effect of this dramatic composition there is a wide range of interesting tree species, such as copper beeches and fastigiate oaks, but also Turkish hazel, a mighty white poplar, yellow and red buckeye, shagbark hickory and eastern hemlock.

(221)

50/ SANTOŠKA GARDEN

This garden lies between Nad Santoškou and Na Doubkové streets and is open to the public.

This early-Baroque vineyard and farmstead, which after 1719 belonged to František Vilém Sonntag, later grew in extent, having taken in the neighbouring Klavírka, Březinka and Václavka farmsteads, and changed into a summer retreat. Its general aspect changed radically after 1883, when Sir Eduard Daubek set about reconstructing the buildings in Neo-Gothic and the gardens in a Classicist-Romantic vein. The garden's transformation into a municipal landscaped park came about after 1907, when Santoška was purchased by the Smíchov municipality. Reminders of the erstwhile Baroque farm are the gateway and its pillars adorned with putti, the sculptural group of the goddess Flora and the path leading along an east-west axis from the original farm buildings (later a restaurant, today a private dwelling), to the look-out point and dividing the park into two parts threaded by circuits of footpaths, with the vegetation landscaped.

The trees here are predominantly maples, ashes, horse chestnuts and hazels. More variety can be found near the entrance from U Santošky Street in the form of a swamp white oak, a variegated English oak, and some columnar ginkgos. And not far from the house there is a striking horse chestnut with a girth of 315 cm, a copper beech and even a thornless 'Sunburst' honey locust. Some of the trees in the upper part of the park have also reached impressive proportions: there is a huge fastigiate oak, a London plane, a Turkish hazel with a girth of 284 cm and a swamp Spanish or pin oak with a girth of 220 cm. In the parts below the house there are some robust ashes and English oaks and with them a group of conifers, specifically Weymouth pines.

51/ KLAMOVKA GARDEN

The garden lies to the north of the arterial road to Pilsen (Plzeňská ulice). From the west, north and east it is bounded by the streets U Demartinky and Podbělohorská. It is open to the public.

At the start of the park, the point to which the access from the main road brings you, there is, standing to the left, a neo-Gothic gazebo, and along the path to the right a little Classicist Temple of the Night, and a little way above that a rococo pavilion with a greenhouse. They have seen better days, days when the garden flourished and constituted the core of the summer retreat of the Clam branch of the post-1759 hyphenated Clam-Gallas family.

Originally the grounds were vineyards, brought together as a single viticultural farmstead known, after being baroquised by 1713, as the Schönfeldka winery. There are later references to a late-Baroque or rococo summer seat, but it is not inconceivable that its transformation into a summer retreat had come about during the early or high Baroque. This assumption is permitted on the basis that one record refers to Baroque statues by Matyáš Bernard Braun, or from his workshop, on the terrace of the summer house within the garden of the rococo summer seat. Surviving from the late-Baroque phase is the rococo pavilion-cum-greenhouse. The actual summer house once stood where the Sokol gymnasium stands today.

Views that promoted qualitative change in the art of the garden already began to make themselves felt at Klamovka at the end of the 18th century. This garden's post-1787 landscaping was initiated by Kristián Filip Clam-Gallas, the first to bear the hyphenated name of the two families, the Clams and the Gallases. In its Romantic, not to say sentimental-romantic conception, a use was found even for the older rococo pavilion-cum-greenhouse. By 1790 the Classicist Temple of the Night and its grotto had been built, though the Neo-Gothic gazebo did not arrive until 1820. The personal influence of Kristián Filip on how the garden took shape is evinced by his foundation of an arboretum, which his son, Eduard, then developed further. Thanks to them, Klamovka still exhibits a fairly rich variety of vegetation, exemplified by the columnar ginkgo cultivar with a girth of 235cm growing opposite the entrance from the Pilsen road; it is one of the three most important of its kind in Prague, the others being one in the Royal Game Preserve and the 'Praga' ginkgo cultivar in the Botanical Gardens at Na Slupi. The richness of the collection is also confirmed by the presence of a Kentucky coffeetree, a green ash and a one-leaved 'Diversifolia' ash, copper beech, Swedish whitebeam, Finnish whitebeam and wild service tree, common hackberry and many other species rising to a total of forty taxons. Indispensible to the collection are also such native species as English oak, ash, sycamore and Norway and field maple.

In 1895 Klamovka was bought by the mayor of Košíře, Matěj Hlaváček, who had the summer house replaced with a spacious restaurant and opened up the park to the public, who could easily reach it by the tramline that began to operate from the Anděl crossroads in 1897. In 1932 the restaurant was replaced by the Sokol gymnasium.

52/ CIBULKA PARK

The park on the site of a former farmstead stretches away from the buildings in a westerly direction towards Nad Hliníkem street and southwards towards the railway line. Most of it is open to the public, and the main entry point is from Nad Hliníkem street.

The lost lustre of the Cibulka park symbolically winds up the woes out of which Leopold Leonard Thun von Hohenstein set about building his new permanent seat in Košíře. The farmstead's homely milieu became a place of refuge for him when, still going strong at the age of fifty-five, he was forced to give up the high office of Auxiliary Bishop of Passau. Thun bought the Cibulka lands in 1815 and three years later set about reconstructing the homestead as an Empire manor house and reshaping the adjacent areas as a romantic park. In the process, after 1818, there was a merging of the principle of the ferme ornée (ornamented farm) with the sentimentalising and Anglo-Chinese currents that revealed themselves in the use of trees in areas containing buildings or statues; this applies both to the horse chestnuts and yellow buckeyes standing in the courtyard surrounded

(226)

by farm buildings, and to the *Tilia dasystylla* to be found next to the pond in front of the sculptural group of Diana and her dogs.

The Classicist-Romantic core is long past its best but, though widely disfigured, it can still be detected and remains a precious survival. It is recalled in particular by the look-out tower built at the highest point as a folly, the neo-Gothic gamekeeper's lodge nearby and the Dante's Inferno cave with its statue of Saturn, set into the hillside below the look-out. The way the view of the look-out and hermitage were interlocked has unfortunately been obliterated by vegetation, as has the painterly composition of the scene with the pond that culminated in the quasi-Classical temple with the statue of Diana; only the latter has survived. Also surviving, on an elevation a few steps from the farmstead buildings, is the Chinese pavilion, which is approached along a path lined with sessile oaks. In among the stands below the Chinese pavilion there is a statue of Jupiter and by the main entrance from Nad Hliníkem Street a statue of St John Nepomucene. Next to the western side of the farm there are residual traces of a rose garden and from the northern side of the manor house the remnants of a giardino segreto with a Tuscan column and terrace, once adorned with statues of four little Chinese boys. In the eastern garden two lodges have survived. A stele bearing a relief by Václav Prachner and showing a man seated, turning to face an angel, which was meant to remind Thun of the transience of human life, has been removed to the cemetery in Malá Strana. The process of constructing the park lasted until 1824, and in the formation of continuous stands of vegetation the bulk of the trees employed consisted of English and sessile oaks, sycamores, Norway and field maples, ashes, small- and large-leaved limes and hornbeams. Their very size speaks of the true age of some of the trees, older, then, than the actual park. Most notable are some of the English oaks, the largest of which has an unbelievable girth of 527 cm; it stands next to the woodland track that is an extension of U Cibulky Street. Along this track there are a further four impressive specimens, including one with a girth approaching four metres. Other huge trees grow near the statue of Jupiter below the Chinese pavilion, including one of the largest ashes. Here too there is a pair of horse chestnuts, one with a girth of 375 cm.

BŘEVNOV AND LIBOC

The earliest days of Břevnov and Liboc followed the establishment of the first monastery in Bohemia in 993 A.D., seen therefore as one of the oldest foci from which settlement of the area of Greater Prague proceeded. It was founded, hard by the source of the Brusnice stream, by Duke Boleslav II and the Bishop of Prague, Vojtěch (Adalbert) of the Slavník clan and, still in the 10th century, the hamlet of Břevnov began to grow around it. The monastery was called upon to colonise an area that reached as far as Liboc, where another separate settlement began to evolve. The Order of St Benedict (OSB, Ordo Sancti Benedicti) went on to make a significant mark on Bohemian (Czech) history and culture. For centuries now the Order has been governed by the Rule of St Benedict and its device, "Pray and Work" (Ora et labora). In the earliest stages of the colonisation of Břevnov and Liboc, which saw the clearing of forests to provide land for cultivation and create a safe refuge for the monks and new settlers, this motto served as a literal imperative.

The inclusion of gardens in the mediaeval structure of the monastery is confirmed by a document dating from the turn of the 14th century, when the Abbot was one Pavel Bavor of Nečtiny. According to this document, the monastery was surrounded by gardens on three sides, being partly small hop gardens and vineyards. Their subsequent development was disrupted by the near-destruction of the monastery by the Hussites in 1420, after which only a small body of monks remained, the majority of the survivors having relocated to the monastery at Broumov. The renewal of the thus depleted Břevnov monastery was a long drawn-out process, and it was not until it underwent its Baroque reconstruction that a garden emerged with a clearly defined layout and its characteristic plots and structural features.

After the Hussite Wars, Liboc was held by burghers, said to have been from Prague's Old Town, while later it became the property of the supreme burgraviate of Prague. The Liboc forest of Malejov was fenced round in the 1530s and adapted as a Renaissance game preserve, later to be known, along with its summer house, as Hvězda (Star).

After Břevnov was absorbed into Prague in 1922, its territory was expanded by a new residential area, Baterie, as an overspill from neighbouring Střešovice. One item in particular, the house and garden of the Rothmayer family, was built here in the late 1920s. In light of its territorial and evolutionary context, the garden of the Villa Rothmayer will be included in the next section after the description of the Villa Müller in Střešovice.

The garden of the Benedictine Archabbey at 23/1 Markétská Street is open
to the public at set times. There are entrances from the south and east from
Markétská Street, with other access points from the cemetery and from Větrník.

The founding of the garden, in its Baroque conception, took place
during a great surge of activity that meant a new, spiritually and
artistically fertile age in the monastery's history. This entailed the
Baroque reconstruction of the entire monastery complex, which
began in 1700 and was spread over two distinct phases, the first up
to 1721, the second to 1738. The first stage involved surveying and
reshaping the land, erecting the stone perimeter wall and planting
the first 319 saplings. The garden acquired its final form during
1737–38, the very end of the second Baroque phase.

Throughout both phases, the Abbot of Břevnov Monastery
was Otmar Zinck, who was one of the most erudite and refined
Church leaders of the Baroque era. The reconstruction was initially
overseen by the New Town master builder Paul Ignaz Bayer, with
whom Abbot Otmar parted company in 1709 to replace him with
the Dientzenhofers, father and son, as architects of his enterprise.
The conception of how the garden should be organised and what it
should contain is attributed to the son, Kilián Ignác Dientzenhofer,
but it is conceivable that the basic outlines and initial premises
had been worked up by his father Kryštof and that Kilián Ignác

tightened them up, worked out the detail and readied them for execution, which, following his father's death in 1722, he also oversaw as architect in chief and master builder. As part of the process he also designed the orangery. At the completion of the second Baroque phase in 1738, the new Abbot was Bennon Löbl, who kept Kilián Ignác Dientzenhofer on as his artistic adviser.

The main part of the garden lies to the north of the monastery buildings, rising in that direction in four terraced levels. The basic division is developed along north-south and east-west axes according to the cardo and decumanus principle, which has the two axes crossing in the middle. The underlying message and the emphasis on the garden's integrity is expressed by the double, patriarchal cross, the main beam of which lies along the north-south axis and is formed from the line joining the main altar of St Margaret's church through the garth and summer refectory to the orangery. The cross beam is symbolised by sectors of the east-west axis in such a manner that the lower beam lies on the line connecting the Lazarka chapel, the Vojtěška pavilion and the Josefka gloriette, while the upper one is made by the common longitudinal axis of the uppermost terrace and the orangery. Condensed in the symbolism of the cross as developed in the garden is the ideological relationship to the patron saint of Bohemia, St Wenceslas, and the co-founder of the monastery,

St Adalbert, expressed in the projection of the east-west line joining the Lazarka chapel, the Vojtěška pavilion and the Josefka gloriette on towards St Vitus' Cathedral, where their relics are kept. With the prolongation of the main beam of the cross on the north-south axis, towards the altar in St Margaret's church, a similar principle successfully permitted the expression of the relationship between the original monastery and the one that had been newly constructed. The cross symbolism was probably also meant to convey the powerful message of the Benedictine motto, for where else but in a garden might one learn humility, patience and diligence.

The way in which the monastery garden was shaped was largely governed by the principle of grid and modules, derived, as in the case of mediaeval gardens, from the garth and applied in particular to the layout of the terraces. Great stress was placed on the integrity of expression of the various parts of the garden, including the not insignificant orchard and the smaller plots adjacent to the buildings. Some were fenced round and may be seen as accessories to, respectively, the church, the kitchen, the pharmacy and the wash-house, given that within them flowers for the altar, vegetables and medicinal herbs were grown and the washing was hung out.

The garden's renovation in 2009–12 covered the unique system of terraces, the orangery and the orchard. A particularly noteworthy task was the reconstruction of the orangery, which had become more and more dilapidated since the 1950s with only its central section and the odd fragment surviving by the time reconstruction commenced. The renovation called for the gradual regeneration of the original hornbeam espaliers lining the ideologically significant axial pathway in the section between the Vojtěška pavilion and the Josefka gloriette. Also conserved was the monumental pair of copper beeches alongside the length of path extending the north-south approach that starts from the main courtyard of the monastery. Dozens of old and ailing fruit trees were replaced in the orchard, the original range of species being preserved: cherries, pears, apples, mulberries, medlars and others. The collaborative plans for the renovation were drawn up three architects, Pavel Joba, Jakub Havlas and Jan Hájek, the garden architect Tomáš Jiránek and others.

54A–B/ THE HVĚZDA GAME PARK AND SUMMER HOUSE

This lies between Ruzyňská, Na Vypichu and Moravanů streets and is subject to fixed opening times. The main entrance is from Na Vypichu, with other approaches from U Světličky and Libocká streets. The summer house is administered by the National Literary Museum and Archive and is also open at set times.

The sovereign's game preserve at Liboc was founded in 1534 as part of the courtly activities of Ferdinanda I of the Austrian Habsburg dynasty and also as one of the first Renaissance undertakings in Bohemia. It came into being with the fencing-off of the Malejov forest, which had belonged to the Břevnov monastery. It was first known as the New Game Park to distinguish it from the older royal park at Bubeneč. It acquired the name 'Hvězda' (Star) following construction of the summer house in 1555–58 to a design by the Archduke Ferdinand of Tyrol, at the time governor of the Lands of the Bohemian Crown. The Archduke is said to have built it for his mistress, Philippine Welser, whom he married a year before the building was completed, but under condition of secrecy because she was a commoner. A year later they had a son, Andreas, later the Cardinal Andréa d'Austria.

The Archduke, well known as a patron of the arts, conceived the summer house in philosophical terms, choosing a ground plan of two equilateral triangles to symbolise fire and masculine energy and water and feminine energy, conjoined to form the hexagram known as the Seal of Solomon and a fundamental symbol of life. Its basement was hewn from the rock and the interior was decorated with stucco reliefs. The star symbol was repeated in the arrangement of the main tracks through the game park and of the sightlines between the summer house and the three gateways – the White Mountain (Bělohorská), Liboc and Břevnov (or Prague) Gates.

The park was used for hunting up until the early 18th century. Over the same period, and indeed later, it was also the setting for countless celebrations, and it was touched by war. One of the most tragic of such events was the Battle of the White Mountain, which took place on 8 November, 1620.

Of the original, striking star-shaped design, documented as late as 1723 on František Antonín Leopold Kloss's map of the Castle water-supply system, only the main cross has survived, though its cross beam has been largely blotted out; also surviving are the lateral rays extending from the summer house to the Liboc Gate and the White Mountain Gate. The disappearance of the stellar disposition is probably due in part to the changes wrought in the first half of the 19th century, when quite large tracts of the game park were reafforested. This trend was subsequently reinforced by the expansion and opening-up of the vistas after 1923, when the Castle architect, Josip Plečnik, was active on the site. The chief concern was the routing of the main triple ray, whose character was that of a Classicist patte d'oie ('goose-foot'). Its dominance was further bolstered in 1937 with new alterations to the space in front of the summer house designed by Jan Sokol and the reconstruction of the summer house itself in 1948–51 to a design by Pavel Janák.

To this day the game preserve retains its woodland character, hence its scenic qualities change with the seasons. At the tail-end of winter it has a pinky-grey hue arising from the budding beech trees; this is best appreciated from the directions of Liboc and Ruzyně. The largest beech has a girth of 476 cm and is to be found close to the Vypich Gate. Three other impressive specimens, with girths of 350, 306 and 375 cm, grow beside the main path from that gate, at the foot of the slope towards the Ruzyně Gate and in the area between the Liboc Gate and the summer house. Also here there is a voluminous English oak with a girth of 345 cm. Beeches and English oaks, but also sessile oaks, hornbeams, sycamores and Norway maples are the most widely represented species. Less numerous are small-leaved lime, silver birch, wych elm and among the conifers Scots pine, yew and Norway spruce. The path from the Liboc Gate to the summer house is lined with small-leaved and Caucasian limes.

STŘEŠOVICE (with part of the area belonging to Břevnov)
The community of Střešovice initially belonged to Strahov
Monastery, and at the start of the 20th century it was one of the
villages lying within the district of Smíchov. Immediately following
its absorption into Prague in 1922, the residential suburb of
Ořechovka sprang into life, conceived along the lines of a garden
city. Numerous famous architects were involved in its further
development, including among others Jaroslav Vondrák, Bohumil
Hypšman, Pavel Janák, Bohumír Kozák, Ladislav Machoň, František
Roith and František Vahala. On the very edge of Ořechovka, the Villa
Müller with its garden came into being at the turn of the 1920s and
1930s.

In addition to Ořechovka, Střešovice saw the emergence of
Baterie, a residential area whose name recalls a Prussian artillery
position held during the 1757 siege of Prague. Several major
architects played a part in the area's development, notably Bohumír
Kozák, Antonín Moudrý, Ella and Oskar Oehler, Jan Gillar and
Otto Rothmayer. As early as the late 1920s, in a part of Baterie that
spills over from Střešovice into the area covered by the Břevnov land
registry, the Villa Rothmayer and its garden came into being.

No. 64 in the Střešovice land registry, located at 14 Nad Hradním vodojemem Street, the garden of Villa Müller is in the care of the City of Prague Museum, which organises guided tours of it within set opening times.

The garden of the home of engineer and Doctor of Civil Engineering František Müller, co-proprietor of the construction firm Kapsa and Müller, was set up in 1929–31 in striking harmony with the Functionalist residence. The head architect, Adolf Loos, designed the house in collaboration with Karel Lhota, enlisting the cooperation of garden architect and dendrologist Camillo Schneider to create the garden; Schneider is best known for his involvement in shaping the parks at the châteaux of Průhonice and Vrchotovy Janovice. Following an elevation survey to refine the changes to the terrain, the retaining wall, the steps at the entrance and the fencing round the garden in Loos' workshop, the overall plan of the future garden was drawn up by the essayist, breeder of rockery plants and Potsdam garden architect Karl Foerster and Hermann Mattern of the Berlin Academy. The garden was renovated in 1998–2000, to a design by architects Václav Girsa and Miloslav Hanzl and the garden architect Vítězslava Ondřejová and others.

The social and private garden space is delimited by a yew hedge and narrow border which simultaneously create an ingenious barrier between the flat and sloping areas. The space clearly mattered greatly to Loos, and so he appreciated the fact that, like him, Schneider enjoyed creating and modelling in situ. The colours of the hedge and border went far in echoing the expression of the interior: the green of the yew hedge matched the green marble of the main hall, while the mix of flowers in the border matched the florid Caucasian, Persian and Afghan carpets indoors. The purple colour of the settee is shared in the garden by irises and phloxes, the red brocade of a snuggler is recalled by peonies, the pink of one armchair by asters, and the grey-green of another by the fleshy leaves of stonecrops. A third armchair is upholstered with a floral motif on a pale background as if an embodiment of the overall gaiety of the flowerbed. It is hard to say whether the content of the flowerbed was influenced by the colour scheme in the hall or vice versa. The steep slope towards Střešovická Street is stabilised by its characteristic grid

pattern of stones and by plantings of alpines such as stonecrops and whitlow-wort and low-growing shrubs – cotoneasters, procumbent roses and junipers. Among the trees in the garden mention should be made of the two black pines and a fastigiate oak surviving on the northern slope. By the steps adjacent to the entrance next to Nad Hradním vodojemem Street there is a Chinese juniper and level with the bottom of the steps, but next to the fence, a yew. The house's being set in the south-west part of the garden and its oblique angling to the main points of the compass makes the most of its scenic connections, notably with the stately home at Troja and with Prague Castle. A broad panorama of Hradčany, dominated by the Castle, opens up from the terrace of the house's second floor.

No. 896 in the Břevnov land registry, at 50 U Páté baterie Street. Together with the house, the garden is available for guided tours. Tours can be booked on the advertised days and opening times through the City of Prague Museum.

In terms of expression and function, the garden was designed as one with the house, the project for both originating with the architect Otto Rothmayer himself, though his wife Božena, a textile designer and promoter of the modern life-style, also had some say in the final outcome. The house and garden were constructed during 1928–29. Otto Rothmayer was a pupil of Josip Plečnik and ultimately collaborated with him on the changes made at Prague Castle and on other commissions.

The ground plan of the house is based on a rectangle and a circle and is set on an east-west axis; above ground it is in the shape of a rectangular block and a cylinder. The backbone of the rectangular garden is its north-south axis, the axes crossing at the centre of the house. The exterior directional anchorage of the axis is provided by the entrance to the house and, in the garden, the projection of the square trough lying at the far end. This projection hides the water supply mechanism and looks like two cubes let one into the other. The conception of the house and garden as a *villa suburbana* evokes associations with the Mediterranean, the effect of which is supported by the plants present along with a medley of small-scale artefacts. The ground-level woody plants that catch the eye are mostly shrubs, for instance box, holly, Oregon grape (mahonia), quince, twisted

willow, climbing hydrangea, lilac, roses and among the conifers,
savin juniper and yew. In the strip between the house and the fence
along the U Páté baterie Street side grape vines are draped over
a supporting construction. At canopy height there are the tops of
such trees as small-leaved lime, walnut, maidenhair tree (ginkgo),
pyramidal black poplar, mountain ash and others.

In the 1950s the garden's aura was captured by the photographer
Josef Sudek, who brought his photos together in the book
Procházky – Kouzelná zahrádka (Walks – The Magic Garden).

The renovation of the villa during 2011–15 was accompanied by a
renovation of the garden to a design by the architect Jiří Novák and
garden designer Josef Krause. The renovation made it possible for
the garden to be included in the Museum's presentation called "The
story of one house and one family".

BUBENEČ AND TROJA

The neighbourhoods of Bubeneč and Troja are separated by the Vltava and united by history. Originally they were the communities of Přední and Zadní (Near and Rear) Ovenec, on opposite sides of a ford. All the land within the great meander of the Vltava, part of which was the village of Přední Ovenec, later Bubeneč, was held by the king. Between the river and the Letná plateau there used to be a forest, out of which grew, after being fenced, the Royal Game Preserve. The village of Zadní Ovenec was swallowed up at the end of the 17th century by the Šternberk family seat and manor farm while the vast surrounding area of vineyards changed into small viticultural homesteads and summer residences. The new Baroque planned urbanisation of Zadní Ovenec, from which sprang today's Troja, developed from the ingenious compositional layout of the house, garden and orchard of the grandiose summer seat of the Šternberks, commonly called the "château".

57A–D/ THE ROYAL GAME PRESERVE – STROMOVKA

The Royal Game Preserve between the streets Za Elektrárnou, U Výstaviště and Nad Královskou oborou and the Malá říčka arm of the Vltava is open to the public. The main entry points are by the Exhibition Ground, from Pod kaštany Square, Gothardská Street, Bubeneč railway station and the road that carries on southward from the Troja footbridge.

The Royal Game Preserve is a municipal park that came into being as a transformation of the sovereign's original immense game park and orchard after they had been handed over to the public in 1004. It is called a game park or preserve, but is also called Stromovka ('place of trees', after that orchard). It is first mentioned in 1319, though it had probably been initiated by Přemysl Otakar II in 1268. It served as a place for breeding game and for kings to hunt in right up to the 1740s, before it suffered considerable damage during the War of the Austrian Succession. Public access to it was granted by an imperial decree of Francis I in 1804.

The park's constitution as a public park began in 1805 and proceeded with varying intensity throughout the 19th century. Its conception combined the desire to create something new with the impulse to keep alive the game preserve tradition going back half a millennium. In the parts completed by 1840 the treatment of the landscape was in a Classicist and Romantic spirit. This applies to the summer house, the systems of avenues and the site of the pheasantry and beyond that the orchard which lay to the west of where Rudolph's fish pond had been. In the final phases, it was the late and then revivalist version of the landscape design movement

that prevailed, while the fashion for collecting trees was in evidence on the floor of what had been Rudolph's fish pond. At the end of the 19th century there were localised creations in the spirit of the Sezession or eclecticism. Very happily contributing to the park's scenery and subordinate formations are two surviving summer houses, a fish pond and the Rudolph Tunnel. The dominant role of the summer house, which was reconstructed during 1805–11 in Romantic and Neo-Gothic idioms, is best appreciated as part of the broader vista, and its position is fully exploited whether the composition is viewed from above or below and ties in with how the area of the former pheasantry has been modelled. The lower summer house, following its Neo-Gothic reconstruction in 1855–58, is incorporated into the promenade. The former fish pond, enlarged at the end of the 16th century under Rudolph II to an area of 20 ha and then drained at the end of the 18th century, can still be made out from its retaining dykes, while an island rises from its floor, crowned with oak trees. The expanse of the pond shifts the observer's attention onwards to the portal of the Rudolph Tunnel, excavated between 1582 and 1593 by miners from the royal mines at Kutná Hora (Kuttenberg) to provide a feed to the pond from the Vltava.

The conversion to a park respected the character of the individual sections as stabilised during the Rudolphine age of Mannerism. The ground plan of the tent meadows and the way the plantings in the western salient of the park form a basket or bowl shape are symbolic reminders of the former orchard. When viewed from the summer house, the pattern of paths combined with how the vegetation was distributed on the pheasantry site west of the former fish pond used to suggest wings, but this effect is no longer so apparent today. The wooded nature of the section meant for breeding game, which lies in a horseshoe shape embracing the pond and used to be called the Thirgarten, is recalled in the scattered structure of the vegetation.

The game preserve used to reach as far as the Vltava, but contact with the river was lost in 1847, along with a slice of land, owing to the construction of the Podmokly Railway in its northern arc. A similar situation arose, though with less land lost, in 1867, when the Buštěhrad Railway was built along its southern edge. The eastern part of the game park was set aside for the 1891 Jubilee Exhibition and has been a separate entity ever since, as the Výstaviště or Exhibition Grounds.

The contemporary renovation of the park to a design by Pavel Šimek and others has been ongoing since 2002, following serious flood damage. An important part is played in the Royal Game Preserve by backbone species of trees, most notably English oak, small- and large-leaved lime, Norway maple and sycamore. English oaks survive piecemeal or are being left to die naturally on the floor of the former Rudolph Pond; they are the last remnants of the only trees to survive the devastation caused by the War of the Austrian Succession in the 1740s. The range of trees here is interesting for a number of reasons. For example, next to the ponds there are some swamp cypresses with their distinctive woody projections above the roots, known as "cypress knees" or pneumatophores. In the nursery close by the Vicegerent's Summer House there is a ginkgo with a girth of 346 cm, which is, with the columnar specimen in the Klamovka park and the 'Praga' ginkgo cultivar in the university Botanical Gardens, one of the three most important ginkgos in Prague. Other interesting conifers are a Douglas fir, an eastern hemlock and a golden larch. Among the noteworthy broad-leaved species there is a paulownia and a yellow-wood, both planted in 1844. The paulownia here in the Royal Game Preserve is second only in size and importance to the one in the Rampart Garden at the Castle, probably the largest in the entire republic. There is also a yellow catalpa, which, again, is one of three remarkable

representatives of its species in Prague, the other two being in the
garden of the Gröbovka villa and in Bezruč Gardens. The Royal
Game Preserve is also one of the few places in Prague that are home
to sweet chestnuts. Hugely prized as a collection is the range of oaks
to be found here: they include among others burr oak, the unusual
'Fürst Schwarzenberg' form of English oak, Turkey oak and its cut-
leaf 'Laciniata' form, and Hungarian oak. Among the beeches there
are some fine examples of copper beech and oak-leaved beech. The
core species that make up the avenues are small-leaved lime and
horse chestnut.

58A–C/ TROJA HOUSE (OR VILLA ŠTERNBERK)

The garden and orchard at 4/1 U Trojského zámku Street lies between the streets U Trojského zámku, Trojská, Pod Havránkou and Povltavská. The complex is in the care of the City of Prague Art Gallery and is open at set times.

The composition of the terraced garden of the Šternberk summer residence, crowned by the stately home itself, speaks of an allegiance to the late-Renaissance and Baroque villas of the summer seats of Rome, in essence summer houses with a garden. This grand Baroque complex rose up on the right bank of the Vltava from 1678 on and included not only a garden and orchard, but also a vineyard and game park. It was commissioned by Count Václav Vojtěch Šternberk and designed for him by Jean Baptiste Mathey, a Frenchman schooled in Rome. The setting out of the garden and orchard was overseen by the landscape gardener Jiří Seeman.

The conception of the villa, garden and orchard is based on an ingenious compositional framework that was developed even further in the Baroque replanning of the territory that had been Zadní Ovenec. The basic north-south direction of the layout is determined by the main, cardo, compositional axis on which lie both house and garden and which continues beyond the garden boundary as an imaginary connecting line through space to Prague Castle. The lengthwise east-west orientation of the villa and its link to the orchard are set by the transverse, decumanus, axis. The internal partitioning of the garden is then derived from this basic framework, which also underpins the star shape in which the orchard is organised. Originally, there was a connection from this framework to the game park, which was where the zoo now lies.

The garden frontage of the house, which stands on the top terrace of the garden, has built into it a massive double flight of steps. Within it, there is a grotto with a sculptural group of the gods of Olympus battling the Titans, created over the period 1685–1703 by Jan Jiří and Pavel Heerman, with additions up to 1707 attributed to Jan Josef and Ferdinand Maxmilián Brokof. The terrace where the house stands is linked to the lower level of the garden by a ramp, with terracotta vases adorning its side walls. The plan of the lower level of the garden is based on paths that form a cross, with a pond and fountain at the intersection; its square shape has another square superimposed rhombically upon it. The original flame-patterned décor of the inner plots has been replaced by spirals of box broderie, while the outer plots have been filled with purple-flowering hybrid crabapples in a regular pattern. At the centre of the orchard is a striking hornbeam labyrinth, while the spaces between the points of its star pattern are lined with hornbeam hedging. The fruit trees are set out in concentric circles and are all of old-fashioned varieties, especially of apples, pears, cherries and plums.

The present look of the garden and orchard is down to its creative renovation during 1983–89 to a design by Otakar Kuča and others. At that time, trees of distinction planted in the first half of the 19th century under the influence of the English school of landscape gardening were left in place. Still standing today are a Turkey oak and a Veitch's silver fir.

59/ ST CLARE'S VINEYARD

This lies on the slopes above Trojská Street. It is currently an adjunct to the Prague Botanical Garden, hence access is subject to the latter's opening times. The entrance is from 134 Nádvorní Street.

St Clare's vineyard was once part of the complex that made up the summer seat of the Šternberks. The vineyard, indeed the wider environs, are dominated by the little chapel of St Clare, which Count Václav Vojtěch Šternberk had built in 1678. Also within the site is an unostentatious vineyard hut. Originally the vineyard was attached to the working end of the Šternberk residence and was approached from the courtyard of the villa, as is still called to mind by the surviving pylon-topped gateway. At the present time the vineyard is split into an education section, where an assortment of vine varieties is grown, and a production section, where the grapes are picked for wine-making.

60A–E/ PRAGUE BOTANICAL GARDENS

They stretch from Pod Havránkou and Trojská streets as far as K Pazderkám Street. There are set opening times and the main entrance is from 134 Nádvorní Street.

The first moves towards setting up a national botanical garden followed close on the heels of the creation of the Charles University Botanical Garden at Na Slupi in 1897–98, but it only came to fruition in the 1960s. The first outdoor displays, the Oriental and Japanese Gardens, were opened in 1992 and 1997, respectively. Other units followed gradually, notably The Hillside, Peony Meadow, the Lake and Wetlands, Forest Biotopes of Asia and America, the North-American Desert, Evergreen Trees and Shade-loving Perennials.
A noteworthy display devoted to the vegetation of the tropics and sub-tropics is to be found in the tropical greenhouse known as Fata Morgana.

Only a smallish part of the gardens is on the level or a slight slope; for the most part it consists of the quite rugged terrain of the Troja depression with its valleys, ravines and steep hillsides dropping down from the Bohnice plain to the bank of the Vltava. These slopes are home to some naturally occurring communities of quite rare plants. The ramparts of a Hallstatt–La Tène settlement have also been found within the area of the gardens, its location further enhanced by the presence of some special plant species, primarily meadow clary. Within the bounds of the Prague Botanical Garden there are many oddities of nature and sites subject to nature conservation legislation. In order for the public to appreciate them all, there are two trails that can be followed, one shorter, one longer.

HOLEŠOVICE: LETNÁ

Letná is an area typified by the relief of its terrain, which consists of the plateau once known as Leteň, or Letná Field, today as Letná Plain (Letenská pláň), and the slopes that fall away towards the Vltava. These slopes are part of what defines the valley of the river and together with the plain above they follow on from the silhouette of Petřín, Strahov and Prague Castle, developing it into a wide panoramic whole. The Baroque fortifications that supplemented the older defences of the different towns that made up Prague continued eastwards from the Hradčany fortified district parallel to the course of the river and separated the slopes and a strip of flat land above them from the main body of the elevated plain. In the 1860s that separate strip and the slopes below began to evolve into a municipal park and since the beginning of the 20th century this has been expanded by inclusion of some of the areas that became available following demolition of the defence works, which had begun at the end of the 19th century.

The park lies on the slopes north of Edvard Beneš Embankment and on part
of the Letná Plain. It is open to the public with entrances from Badeniho, Milady
Horákové, Kostelní and Skalecká streets and from Edvard Beneš Embankment
via the steps opposite Čech Bridge.

The founding of the park in and after 1860 chimed with the age, whence,
too, its changing names: first Belvedere Gardens, from 1871 Crown
Prince Rudoph Gardens and after the birth of Czechoslovakia Letná
Gardens. The park's conception followed the Classicist and Romantic
trends of the day and from the outset had the character of a promenade.

Its core emerged in 1861–64 following a design by Bedřich
Wünscher, the one-time director of the Kinský Gardens, and it was
elaborated further by the head gardener of the Royal Game Preserve,
Jiří Braul. The essence of Wünscher's conception resided in the delicate
use of vegetation in styling the level strip, the compact clothing of the
slopes in vegetation to act as a kind of pedestal, and in running a scenic
path along the top edge of the slope with sightlines across the city and
the river and its bridges. Grafted onto this scheme in the eastern part
of the park there was a neo-Renaissance restaurant constructed after
an 1863 project by Vojtěch Ignác Ullman on the site where the 1715
Belveder summer house had stood. The restaurant stands on a break
in the terrain and is complemented by a terrace planted with horse
chestnuts set out in a regular grid pattern.

In the period that followed, the park was added to, its appearance
tweaked and even altered. On the occasion of the 1891 Jubilee
Exhibition, held on ground that had been detached from the Royal
Game Preserve, a funicular was installed leading up from the
embankment. By the restaurant there was an interchange station with

Křížík's electric railway that went to the Exhibition Grounds in Holešovice. This technically unique set-up has not survived. In 1887-89, in parallel with the Exhibition, the landscape gardener and director of the city's parks, František Thomayer, altered the eastern part of the park to his own design. The scale and treatment of the promenade strip are testimony to the experience of handling urban public spaces that Thomayer had gained in Paris. His composition, based on sightlines and the use of vegetation at the fringes, is developed along the west-east axis on which the grand promenade was also laid, conceived as a multiple avenue of London planes. The plasticity of the composition of sightlines is in part due to small-leaved limes, but also more planes, a fastigiate oak and Turkish hazels as solitaires.

With the Jubilee Exhibition over, the Hanava Pavilion was removed from the Exhibition Grounds to the park in 1898. It had been donated to the city by the owner of the Komárov Ironworks, Prince Vilém Hanavský, is characterised by its neo-Baroque conception and cast-iron embellishments and stands at the spot where the St Thomas Bastion once stood. The character of the western part of the park changed during the period 1950–55 because of the mammoth monument to Soviet politician and Secretary General of the Communist Party of the Soviet Union, Generalissimo J. V. Stalin, set on the extension of the axis from Paris (Pařížská) Avenue and Čech Bridge. The removal of the monument in 1962 left behind the gigantic understructure, with subterranean spaces and a two-armed flight of steps from the embankment. In 1960 the eastern part of the park received the Czechoslovak pavilion on its return from the 1958 Brussels World Fair. After 1998 steps were taken to renovate the garden according to plans by Dáša Tůmová and Jana Stejskalová.

KARLÍN

The suburb of Karlín came into being on part of the land known as Spitalfield, its foundation sanctioned by an imperial decree of Francis I. The suburb was named Karolinenthal in honour of his wife, Caroline Augusta of Bavaria. The subdivision of the land was carried out according to the 1816–17 local development plan, which also laid down the rectangular system of planned development. The core consisted of three longitudinal main streets, a vast transverse square and six streets running crosswise. At the time, the Invalidovna (an institution for military invalids) was already in existence. The legendary Růžodol garden and summer house, set up by the Prague printer Jan Ferdinand Schönfeld to look like a map of Bohemia, vanished in 1799. Around the middle of the 19th century development began in earnest and in 1847 the first Prague gasworks was built in Karlín. In 1907 František Křižík launched the first electric tramline. As a reaction to the rising intensity of development the public spaces began to be made into parks; this applied in particular to Karlín Square and Lyčka Square, the open space in front of the Invalidovna, and the neighbouring Kaizl Gardens.

62/ KARLÍN SQUARE
The park on Karlín Square is open to the public.

Originally called Cyril and Methodius Square, the idea had always been to site a church and park here. Work began in 1861, took twelve years and was probably done in two stages. It is an urban park whose essence is its late or revivalist Classicist-Romantic landscaped composition on an axial sightline, crowned by a neo-Romanesque basilica. The vegetation that frames the sightline is inwardly modelled by the use of trees that stand out of line or as solitaires. The species present include pagoda tree, honey locust, copper beech, ginkgo and common hackberry. On the outer side the vegetation is edged by lines of large-leaved lime and the park in its entirety is encircled by avenues of planes. Matching this composition is the layout of the footpaths, which form three circuits, though originally there had been clear signs of an historicising semi-circular morphology that went strikingly well with the basilica. The path that goes round the main apse sketches a fascinating silhouette, drifting out sideways like the veil of the Madonna as captured in a painting. The design for the basilica was the work of Carl Rösner of Vienna and Vojtěch Ignác Ullmann of Prague, and its construction took from 1854 to 1863.

63/ LYČKA SQUARE
The park on Lyčka Square is open to the public.

This urban park is quite striking for its twin versions of Sezession
playfulness and the way it communicates with its environment on the
'borrowed scenery' principle, which is made to work both ways. It
was founded in 1905–06, possibly to a design by František Thomayer,
though more likely by one of his followers, and is developed on axial
lines and as a counterpoint to the nearby school built after a project
by Josef Sakař in 1904–06. The park's existence is documented
on period postcards published to mark the start of the school's
functioning in the academic year 1906/07. It was renovated in the
1990s to a design by Kateřina Tomanová.

In the direction of the school the layout of the footpaths looks like a beetle, while in the opposite direction it metamorphoses into two rings of different sizes which, instead of hanging, are laid out flat and split in the middle by a sunken parterre with yet more eye-catching circles filled with roses. The composition is framed longitudinally by avenues lined with wild service trees, the shorter sides having lines of mop-head maples. The view towards the school is framed by surviving specimens of Turkish hazel and wild service tree. The park is named after Břetislav Lyčka, the doctor who treated the parachutist Jan Kubiš, who had been wounded in the course of the assassination of Obergruppenführer and Reichsprotektor Reinhard Heydrich in May 1942.

64/ THE INVALIDOVNA

The park area between the Invalidovna and Sokolovská Street is open to the public. Its conversion into a park at the turn of the 20th century gave the final touch to the ambience of the Invalidovna by the application of historicising analogies. The axial interconnections, the parterre-like foreground, the arboured enclosures along the sides and the star pattern of the footpaths are all derived from traditional compositions, the star-shapes also symbolising the croix de guerre. The trees present include horse chestnuts, London planes, ashes, false acacias and silver birches. The building intended to house war invalids and veterans was built during 1731–37 to a design by Kilián Ignác Dienzenhofer and financed by a charitable foundation set up by Count Petr Strozzi, owner of the manor of Hořice, diplomat and army commander, a monument to whom stands quite close to the front of the building. By the entrance from Sokolovská Street there is an obelisk in memory of the twenty-nine Austrian soldiers who drowned in the Vltava during the floods of 1890.

(271)

65/ KAIZL GARDENS

The park is adjacent to the foreground of the Invalidovna and is open
to the public.

Kaizl Gardens are an illustration of how ideas taken from the
Sezession and the revivalist landscape movement could be adapted to
the ambience of a small-scale urban park. The footpath system shows
clear signs of the Sezessionist ring patterns that recall the ribbon
bow so characteristic of František Thomayer, and the addition of an
extra circuit created the Sezession motif of the trefoil. The influence
of the Sezession can also be detected in the revivalist landscaping,
notably in how the trees are deployed and in their assortment,
which is remarkably rich for such a small space. They include ash,
sycamore, Norway maple, black poplar, London plane, small- and
large-leaved limes, weeping willow, silver birch, hawthorn, fastigiate
oak and the thornless 'Sunburst' form of honey locust. The park is
named after the politician and promoter of Czech statehood, Josef
Kaizl, and was created during 1899–1901, simultaneously with the
Invalidovna park, probably to a design by Julius Krýsa.

PROSEK

The village of Prosek, noted for its church of St Wenceslas and the Prosek Cliffs, from which sandstone has been quarried for many years, became part of Prague in 1922. Back in the late 19th century, colonies of small houses for the workers of Vysočany and Libeň sprang up on blocks of land within its boundaries. In the 1960s, the agricultural land on part of the plateau between the valleys of Vysočany, Libeň and Střížkov were included in the programme of new housing developments to be constructed in the northern sector of Prague. The Prosek high-rise estate gradually emerged during 1965–77 as part of Prague's new North Town.

66/ FRIENDSHIP PARK
This park stretches between Vysočanská and Jablonecká roads and is open to the public.

Friendship Park on the Prosek high-rise estate is a modern rendering of the municipal park. The strip intended to become the park was earmarked on plans for the new developments and the designing of its landscape was put out to competitive tender in 1968. It came into being during 1976–83, partly in accordance with the winning design by Otakar Kuča. The park's revitalisation in 2008 was also to his design. Near the ring-shaped fountain set on a round island, a statue of the poet Jiří Wolker was installed in 1984, sculpted by Miloslav Šonka and Stanislav Hanzal. With its overall layout, structure, modelling of the spaces and its facilities the park seeks to meet the leisure needs of the people living on the estate. It extends in an oblong parallel to the spinal Vysočanská Road and along its whole length there is an extensive water feature consisting of an actual water course, ponds, fountains and cascades. It is surrounded by areas laid to grass. The lateral backdrop is made up of clumps of trees and patches of shrubbery, as are the inner sectional boundaries and highlights. The main tree species represented are small-, large- and silver-leaved limes, English, sessile and red oaks, and hornbeam. There are also horse chestnuts and a significant contingent of Norway maples, rowans and wild service trees; conifers are represented by black and Scots pines, yews and larches. As a traditional embellishment of urban parks there are also some honey locusts and tulip trees. The typical accompaniment of the water courses consists of low stands of willow, mostly creeping willow and grey willow.

CONNECTIONS THROUGH SPACE

During the long process of the formation of Prague's parks and gardens in all their variety of forms of expression a number of remarkable connections across space can be observed to have come about. They exceed the bounds of the individual sites and are the product of visual links to places of canonical significance. The range of such connections across space adds to the ways in which Prague can be viewed and magnifies the part played by parks and gardens in picking out key nodal points and creating a favourable image of the city.

Even in the Middle Ages, the visual perception of important nodal points was bolstered by otherwise strictly secluded monastic gardens, which gave added emphasis to the position of their associated churches. This applies most strikingly to the monastic gardens in the southern part of Nové Město, where imaginary lines drawn between the churches create in space the still discernible cross that expressed the blessings of the city. Its upright starts from the church of Sts Peter and Paul at Vyšehrad and leads towards the churches of the Virgin Mary 'Na Slupi', St Apollinaire and St Catherine. The cross beam, symbolised by a line drawn between the Emmaus Monastery church and the church at Karlov, intersects the upright at the church of St Apollinaire. The gardens' creation is to the credit of Charles IV, who, following the foundation of Prague's New Town (Nové Město) in 1348, donated quite large plots of land to all the newly emerging monastic houses.

The sign of the cross as a device to connect nodal points across space was also used during the Renaissance, which likewise saw continued observance of the principle whereby buildings were set on an east-west axis. Adherence to that principle was practically a matter of course in the case of, in the main, Roman Catholic churches, which would always have the presbytery on the eastern side. Places sited according to this rule are described technically as "oriented structures". The principle was also adopted in the setting up of the Renaissance Royal Garden and determined the location of the giardinetto and summer house at its eastern end. In order to create a spatial link between the garden, the Castle and the city below, the symbol of the Cross was again brought to bear; its upright stands on Malá Strana Square, where the Romanesque rotunda of St Wenceslas used to stand. The instigator of the Royal Garden, Ferdinand Habsburg, presumably meant this as a conscious expression of respect for the dearly held St Wenceslas tradition. The enlisting of gardens to assist in the creation of depth and visual contacts was masterfully developed in the terminal, mannerist, phase of the Renaissance, as can be best appreciated by looking up from the composition of the Wallenstein Garden; there, above the view from the wide sala terrena, a panorama of Prague Castle unfolds.

The age of the Baroque exhibited a unique appreciation of both visual contacts and imaginary axial projections, where linkages with external nodal points continued to be symbolised chiefly by the cross and directionality hinged chiefly on the east-west axis. For example, in the palace gardens on the northern slope of Petřín Hill and in the complex known collectively as the Palace Gardens on the Southern Slope below Prague Castle, the "theatre boxes" effect was applied, whereby ever wider vistas open up with each higher elevation. Another distinctive panoramic view across Prague is afforded from the eastern terrace of the monastery garden at Strahov, whence the city can also be glimpsed "through the keyhole" of any one of the apertures in the hornbeam hedges. In the Baroque conception of the monastery garden at Břevnov, an extension through space is provided by the east-west axis, which points eastwards beyond the garden towards the Castle. The north-south axis here gives the line that connects the monastic buildings to the garden. In the Černín Garden at Hradčany an important part is played by an ideological association with the legend-wreathed hill Říp, conveyed by an imaginary projection of the north-south axis that runs through the palace and garden.

The age of the Baroque, notably in connection with concepts of town planning, saw the axes beginning to be named after the two main streets shown on the town and city plans of ancient Rome: *cardo* for the north-south axis, and *decumanus* for that running east to west. The usage is particularly fitting in the case of Troja House (the Villa Šternberk), whose Baroque compositional framework served as the starting point for replanning the original village of Zadní Ovenec. The spatial connecting line here, directed towards the Castle, is an extension of the north-south axis on which the house and garden both stand.

Another device typically used to convey spatial links even over quite some distance was the Classicist three-pronged patte-d'oie (goose's foot). However, in Prague the spatial extensions of the parks and gardens of Classicism and Romanticism continued to be expressed mostly by the traditional east-west axis, as can be seen from the visual link between the Kinský Garden in Smíchov and the church of Our Lady Before Týn in the Old Town. Another interesting use of the extension of a space is the composition of the sightlines at the People's Garden (today's Chotek Gardens) in Hradčany; here the east-west axis is extended to take in the Royal Garden at the Castle.

Spatial connections to the city have been successfully exploited by the founders and creators of Prague's parks and gardens in every age, and traditional forms of interlinking have featured even in undertakings that sprang from the new trends of the 19th and 20th centuries. The promenade beside Prague Castle, running from the Paradise Garden the full length of the Rampart Garden, offers numerous viewpoints from which to see down into and across the city, and the line of sight that crosses it at right-angles from the Bull Staircase to the cupola atop St Nicholas' Cathedral on Malá Strana Square is anchored directionally by the pyramid in the Rampart Garden. The unique Cubist ensemble that is the Villa Kovařovic and its garden, situated beneath Vyšehrad, is angled to face the silhouette of Hradčany. Another panoramic view of Hradčany is offered from the second floor of the Functionalist Villa Müller in Střešovice, where the garden also supports a visual link to the complex of Troja House. In the envelope of trees round the park next to Chodov Fort there are gaps through which to glimpse the area round about, and from the upper floor of the fort the gaze is carried over and beyond the park towards the distant panorama of Hradčany. The church of the Emmaus Monastery is the target of the projection of the north-south axis along which the New Provostry and the equestrian statue of St Wenceslas both stand in Štulc Gardens.

Štulc Gardens are in Vyšehrad, where, with its aura of symbolism, this digression on connections across space began, and so there too does it end.

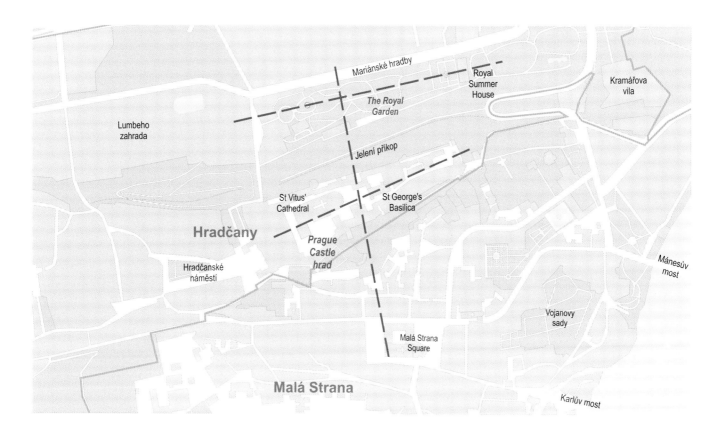

THE ROYAL GARDEN

This garden was founded during the Renaissance as an "oriented structure" as witness its directionality governed by the east-west axis and the location of the giardinetto and summer house at its eastern end, following the principle of the presbytery. Its symbolic interlinking with both the Castle and the city takes the form of a cross and the spatial relationship, expressed optically by the upright, comes as a conscious reference to the St Wenceslas tradition. The upright reaches the centre of the Royal Garden, but its foot is on the spot where once stood the Romanesque rotunda of St Wenceslas, rediscovered in 2004 on Malá Strana Square. The cross beam lies on the same east-west axis as St George's Basilica and St Vitus' Cathedral and the east-west axis of the Royal Garden runs parallel to it. However, it is also conceivable that the basic east-west line was taken to be that connecting the fountain in the second Castle courtyard with the well – today not visible above ground – between St Vitus' Cathedral and St George's Basilica. The possibility that the heart of the symbolism is the archiepiscopal or patriarchal cross of Lorraine also merits consideration.

THE BŘEVNOV MONASTERY GARDEN

The garden exudes a message of extraordinary power. In it, the Vojtěška Pavilion stands over the spring that becomes the Brusnice stream; it was this that prompted the original foundation of the monastery in 993 A.D. The garden's Baroque conception respected the primacy of the east-west axis, on which stood the Lazarka chapel, the Vojtěška pavilion and the Josefka gloriette. Beyond the garden boundary the axis carries on as an imaginary connecting line to St Vitus' Cathedral, where the relics of the patron saint of Bohemia, Wenceslas, and the co-founder of the monastery, St Adalbert (Vojtěch), are held. A line connecting the monastery buildings and the garden is given by a north-south axis leading from the high altar of St Margaret's church, across the garth and summer refectory to the orangery. The cross symbolism expresses inner integrality while at the same time recalling the principles encapsulated in the device of the Order of St Benedict: "Pray and work."

THE GARDEN AND ORCHARD OF TROJA HOUSE
(VILLA ŠTERNBERK)

Together with the villa, usually described as a château, the garden constitutes an integral compositional whole. The compatibility of their interlinking is assured by the Baroque compositional framework from which the spatial connections to points beyond the complex are also developed. The basis is formed by a north-south cardo axis and an east-west decumanus axis. Together, house and garden lie on the north-south axis, which, beyond their boundary, continues as an imaginary connecting line through space to Prague Castle. The east-west axis determines the longitudinal lie of the house and also ensures the link to the orchard, which is planned like a star. The Baroque compositional framework also gave rise to the replanning of the land formerly occupied by the village of Zadní Ovenec. In earlier times it also underpinned the link to the game park where today's Prague Zoo lies.

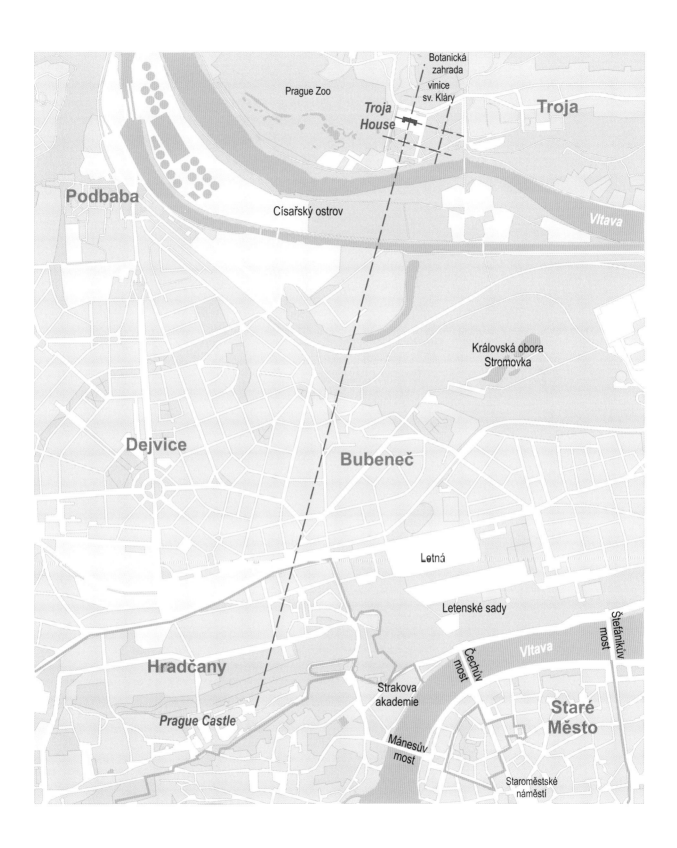

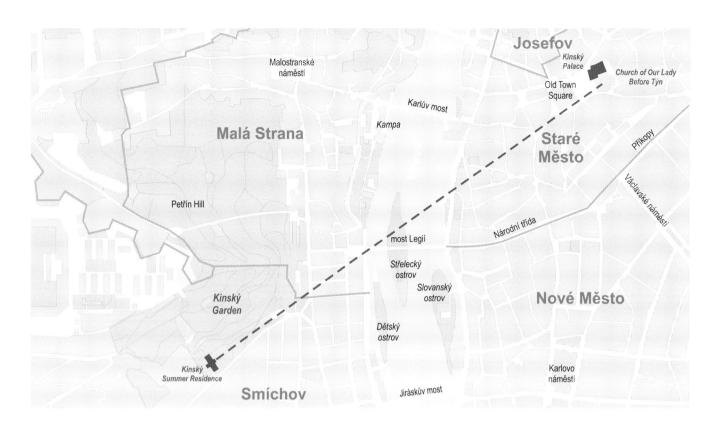

KINSKÝ GARDEN

The garden was established on the difficult terrain of the slopes of Petřín Hill in the context of an awareness of the principles of both Classicist and Romantic composition. These were successfully combined, but into this symbiosis was also projected respect for traditional values, pride in family and an emphasis on the tried and tested interdependency of house and garden. The latter is expressed first and foremost by the system that unites the summer house, the parterre and the associated sightline and is linked by a shared spinal line through space that points beyond the bounds of the garden towards the towers of the church of Our Lady Before Týn. On Old Town Square, close by the church, is the Kinský Palace. The handling of the ground plan and use of space so as to ensure that the sightlines from the summer house would actually work demanded some serious adjustments to the terrain at the foot of Petřín Hill.

GLOSSARY

Arched walkway: a pathway arched over with a supporting construction draped in climbing plants or species of woody plant that have been trained.

Avenue: a path or track lined on both sides by one or two rows of trees. The expression can be used metaphorically for an 'avenue' of statues where statues feature instead of trees.

Axial segmentation: a compositional layout governed by an axial system.

Axial system: an apparatus by which one or more axes are used to govern the compositional organisation of a park or garden. The basic direction of composition is determined by a primary axis based on points of the compass. The main axis oriented in a west-east direction is based on a cross, while a north-south orientation is derived from a pair of axes, the *cardo* and the *decumanus*, intersecting at right angles. The application of any axial system is derived from the rules and principles applicable to a particular period.

Backdrop (of vegetation): stands of vegetation located and modelled in such a way as to give definition to a sightline, draw the gaze or give a vista its lateral framework.

Bellaria: a summer house whose name, Italian in origin, expresses lightness, openness and airiness.

Belvedere: an observation area incorporated into a building as a tower, balcony or terrace. In a garden it will usually be a separate structure, most often a summer house or pavilion.

Bosquet: primarily a space tightly planted with regularly spaced trees. There are numerous permutations: until the 18th century the trees were most often shaped into a geometrical block, or trimmed individually into pyramids, cones, prisms or spirals. Later the term came to be applied to any space bounded by an espalier, i.e. a trimmed hedge, and containing within it trees, a fountain, flowerbeds, and leisure or water features.

Broderie: ornamentation created to look like a carpet or embroidery. The basis is usually a pattern made of low, trimmed box with the spaces between filled with flowers or different coloured materials such as stone chippings, crushed brick, sand, but also crushed seashells, soot, chalk etc., or it might even grassed.

Cardo: the axis setting the direction of composition as north-south according to the practice of ancient Rome.

Composition (of a garden/park): the close planar and spatial merger of the architectural and vegetational components into a single whole according to the rules and principles applicable in a given period or style.

Composition, line of (backbone): the line, straight or curved, whether present physically in the layout or optical, which either of itself connects the various elements in a composition or plays a part in how the space is organised within the development network.

Composition axis: the axis of symmetry that determines the direction of composition, whether marked physically on the ground or optical. A main axis derived from a cross runs east-west. One running north to south is derived from the *cardo* and *decumanus* (q.v.), crossing at right angles. In the quatrefoil and star the two axes count equally. The two diagonal axes in the star are secondary. In the triaxial patte d'oie (goose's foot) the middle one is main and the lateral ones secondary.

Decumanus: the axis setting the direction of composition as east-west according to the practice of ancient Rome.

Espalier: a wall of indefinite height formed of trees planted close together and trimmed to a regular pattern, the actual technique and frequency of trimming depending on the habit of the species being used.

Ferme ornée see Ornamented farm

Figgery: a structure intended primarily for growing figs, either attached as a lean-to to a wall, or free-standing, often with a sliding or detachable roof.

Fountain: an artistic stone or metal trough holding a pond, decked with statuary expressing aquatic motifs, and incorporating various kinds of water feature – jets, cascades, etc.

French garden: a label applicable to the French Baroque or Baroque-Classicist garden and others inspired by it. It is based on an axial system developed by a network of rays and a spatial framework of cross-sectional lines. Typical of the French garden is the training of trees on a grand scale and using them to replace buildings, and a wide variety of water features, including vast basins and channels.

Game preserve (Game park): a fenced-off stretch of woodland used primarily for rearing, and often hunting, game. It may contain a pheasantry, where the vegetation is adapted to raising pheasants and other game birds by allowing the understory to grow dense.

Gardens: the plural form used in the late 19th and early 20th centuries to denote a public park in a town and some private gardens after they had been made public.

Garth: the square space surrounded by a cloister (ambit). It lies at the heart of a monastic house, usually between the monks' dwelling and the church. It invariably contained a symbol of life, be it water, whether in a well or trough fountain, or a tree or rose bush as the 'tree of life'. For the practical purposes of ablutions there could be a lavatorium, set between the cloister and the well housing.

Gazebo: a light structure with its roof drawn up into a spike or turret, derived from the same kind of structure that can be found projecting above the roof level of a house.

Giardinetto: a small garden space existing either independently or as part of a larger composition.

Giardino segreto (secreto): secret garden, the intimate part of a larger garden composition.

Gloriette: a free-standing airy, open structure often standing at the highest point in a garden, or in a position with a view.

Goose's foot see **Composition axis**

Grid principle: an arrangement based on a lattice or mesh pattern.

Grotto: an artificial cave embellished with stucco stalactites and clams and other kinds of shells. It may be no more than a single wall in similar vein. Some grottos are formed from a single mass of rock or a collection of boulders.

Ha-ha or **hawhaw:** a ditch intended to act as an obstacle or barrier, being an alternative to a fence. The side further from the house slopes down and the nearer side is vertical and reinforced with a stone retaining wall. From a distance it cannot be seen and the name is usually deemed to replicate an interjection of surprised realisation.

Hermitage: a structure, sometimes little more than a shelter, in a remote part of a park.

Hide (Cz. popluží): an old unit of measurement of agricultural land, ranging – in the

Czech context – between 20 and 60 ha. in size. The expression is sometimes used as shorthand for a smallholding within a lordly estate.

Historic garden: an entity – garden or park – important in terms of history or art, created specifically as an architectural and vegetative composition in which the various components have been included and organised according to the rules in force in a particular age or style. The principles involved might be simple and modular or complex and axial, linear, transectional or dispersed, including how straight and curved lines are employed. Artworks are used as embellishments to complete the composition.

Hortus conclusus: enclosed garden.

Italianate garden: the Italian Mannerist or Baroque garden and others inspired by it. The basis of its organisation is an axial system of terraces (the Roman school) or an axial system developed on the principle of linear perspective (Florence, Tuscany). Typical of the Italianate garden is the use of water in an endless range of motifs, troughs, fountains, cascades, channels, spouts etc., and the variety of the plants used, including trees typified by their shape, such as columnar cypresses and trees amenable to being ingeniously trimmed to shape. Any artistic embellishments will be symbolic representations of parables and moral precepts. A major part in how they are deployed is played by nodal points and the hierarchy of elevations.

Labyrinth: a garden maze formed of shaped hedges, associated ideologically with the symbol found in mediaeval cathedrals.

Landscaped park: a typical product of Romanticism and its unique symbiosis with its opposite as to style, Classicism. Their coexistence is projected in how space is organised and how buildings are used as landmarks, furthermost points in a view and features to catch the eye. The Romantic tone of a park results in specific types or trends, such as the sentimentally romantic, the Anglo-Chinese, the Arcadian, the ornamented farm and others.

Lavatorium: a fountain or trough between the cloister and the well housing in a monastery, used for ablutions.

Loggetta: a loggia surmounted by an observation terrace.

Loggia: a pillared hall with arcades opening onto a garden either frontally or from both sides.

Modular principle of segmentation: an arrangement based on modules and developed on the basis of multiples of them. A module is a basic, non-subdivisible unit used to determine the dimensions of the various parts of a composition and their mutual proportions.

Municipal gardens: a type of park created and equipped for the benefit of the public. The first Czech ones were called 'people's garden'.

Orangery: A brick and glass structure meant for growing thermophilic plants, particular lemon and orange trees. Its forerunner was a sheltered spot provided with a wooden construction which would have a wooden casing fixed round it for the winter.

Ornamented farm: a type of park, so called in English, 'ferme ornée' in French. It is typified by numerous changes in its landscape suggesting different scenes on a farm. It is formed on the principle of winding and weaving, offering idealised views of the countryside and a material representation of a pastoral paradise. It may occasionally be just one section of a larger landscaped park.

Palazzetto: a grand, urban, aristocratic residence, like a palace, but smaller.

Parterre: a level area set usually on the same axis as a palace, stately home or summer house immediately adjacent to their garden frontage. In the parterres of formal gardens the ornamental plantings are often associated with a trough or fountain and statuary. An aquatic parterre is formed of a basin/pond or a water channel. The English parterre is laid to lawn.

Patte-d'oie: a triaxial shape known also as a 'goose's foot'.

Pavilion: a smallish garden structure, whether freestanding or integrated into a perimeter or retaining wall. Mostly single-storey, though they can have an upper floor, sometimes connected to the ground floor by an exterior staircase.

People's garden: in the Czech context, a garden (park) created deliberately for the benefit of the public, in the second half of the 19th century often called 'municipal gardens'.

Per purgo: a principle captured admirably by its Latin name meaning 'by purging, clearing away, levelling'. Adapting an area following this principle allows for the installation of key elements and gives any significant spatial connections the chance to stand out, uncluttered by anything undesirable, superfluous or confusing.

Physic garden: a garden reserved for growing medicinal herbs and spices, usually walled, existing as a separate entity or inserted into a larger garden or park on the principle of 'a garden within a garden'.

Pomarium: an orchard, primarily monastic.

Rosarium, Rose garden: an area devoted to a mixture of roses as shrubs, trees or ramblers. It may be freestanding or constitute one section of a larger garden or park.

Sala terrena: primarily a large room on the ground floor of a palace or stately home, opening to the garden through an arcade. There are several variants, such as examples involving two or more rooms, and various means of egress to the garden. One kind is a freestanding structure within the garden. They are usually conspicuous for their embellishments of paintings, statues and reliefs.

Sightline: a space delineated by lateral stands of vegetation and usually set on the same axis or line of composition as some landmark building.

Star (shape): a geometric formation arising from the crossing of two main – north-south and east-west axes – and two diagonal secondary axes.

Summer house: a building intended for summer or occasional use; when associated with a garden it is often used for social or hospitality purposes.

Syntactic segmentation: an arrangement arising from managed composition, whereby the various elements are used in combinations and relationships determined by the character of the composition.

Taxon: a general label used in systematic botany for a set of plants that, on the basis of common features, constitute a taxonomic unit. The naming of plants, based on their generic and specific names, and of varieties, is laid down by the Code of Botanical Nomenclature.

Theatron: a structure in a garden functioning like the backdrop on a stage. When applied as the furthermost point of a composition based on a system of terraces, its rear wall is often used as a retaining wall. Within a view conceived in planar terms it is often shifted forward of some landscape feature. It may also occur as a freestanding adjunct to a panorama.

Trellis: a light wood or metal lattice construction serving to support climbing plants.

Villa suburbana: a type of villa that is a materialisation of the socio-cultural idealisation of life in the country influenced by the urban way of living. Typically it takes the form of a luxury suburban detached house with a garden with which the spatial arrangement of the entire premises reaches its peak and which establishes a connection to the surrounding countryside.

Villa urbana: a grand urban structure usually consisting of the main building and its attached wings. A type of villa based on the notion of an urban palace.

Vivarium: an artificial environment in which live animals are kept for observation etc., but in the garden context, a tank within a pond or watercourse to hold fish for the short time between their being caught and being despatched to the kitchen.

TREES AND SHRUBS

The following overview lists important and noteworthy trees and shrubs, native and exotic, with examples of where they are to be found in the parks and gardens of Prague. The full spread of taxa is much wider, so this is only a sample listing of species and cultivars with reference to some of the parks and gardens. The stated girth (trunk circumference) of large trees is measured at 130cm above ground level.

Broad-leaved trees and shrubs

Acacia, False, or **Robinia** or **Black Locust** *(Robinia pseudoacacia)* – a tree originally from the eastern United States, but now widespread in central and southern Europe. It was named after the French botanist Jean Robin, who brought it to Europe around 1601. It rejuvenates readily and in the wild can become quite invasive. More intensive cultivation of the species in the Bohemian Lands began after 1808, the source of seedlings being the Lichtenstein nursery at Lednice, where acacias in particular, but also other tree species, were grown from seeds imported from North America. The seeds were collected by members of an expedition dispatched to North America in 1802 by the lord of the Lednice–Valtice estate, Prince Adam I von Lichtenstein. When Prague's František (today's Smetana) Embankment was being constructed in 1839-41, an avenue of acacias was planted, but it has not survived. On the other hand, the torso of an acacia can be seen in the Royal Garden that is assumed to have been planted in the mid-19th century. In the context of that early planting of acacias on the Embankment their introduction in the park surrounding the Kranner Fountain and in the park on Charles Square seems entirely felicitous. At Vyšehrad the species is to be found in the precinct of the Ducal and Royal Acropolis and in the Štulc and Karlach gardens, and there are further specimens in the Kinský Garden and the Klamovka garden. It also plays a part in the arbours that line the parterre approach to the Invalidovna, not to mention its appearance in many other parks and gardens all over the city.

Acacia, False, 'Decidens' *(Robinia pseudoacacia 'Decidens')* – a cultivar with a globoid crown to be seen in the Leslie Garden.

Acacia, False, 'Unifolia' or **Single-leaf Black Locust** *(Robinia pseudoacacia 'Unifolia')* – a narrow-crowned cultivar of False Acacia. A unique specimen stands in the Kinský Garden.

Alder, (Common or **European** or **Black)** *(Alnus glutinosa)* – a tree found growing on the banks of our watercourses, native to Europe, Asia Minor, Siberia and the Altai Mountains. It can be found in many of Prague's parks and gardens, especially wherever there is open water or a stream. It grows alongside the Čertovka in the park on Kampa Island and among the vegetation of the Royal Game Preserve, notably around the ponds.

Almond *(Amygdalus communis)* – a tree or bush originating in central Asia and naturalised in southern Europe and western Asia, now also in California, southern Africa and southern Australia. It is cultivated in some of the orchards in Prague, notably in the upper part of the Schönborn Garden and in the Seminary Garden, on the slope known as 'American'.

Almond, Flowering *(Amygdalus triloba)* – a bush or tree originally from China. It is grown on the terraces of the Great Pálffy Garden.

Apple *(Malus pumila,* frequently misnamed *M. domestica)* – one of the most widely grown fruit trees of the temperate zone. Sundry varieties are grown in pomaria, notably those in the Great Garden at Strahov, the upper section of the Schönborn Garden, in the Seminary Garden, Vojan Gardens, the monastery garden at Břevnov, and the orchard of the Villa Šternberg (country house) in Troja. Apple trees in the Franciscan Garden suggest there was an orchard there too.

Apple 'Florina' *(Malus domestica 'Florina')* – a winter variety with attractive fruit, bred in France. In Prague it is grown in the Lesser Pálffy Garden, which is essentially a pomarium.

Apple hybrid *Malus x Arnoldiana* (no common name) – a cross between *M. floribunda* (Japanese Flowering Crabapple) and *M. baccata* (Wild Apple or Siberian, Manchurian or Chinese Crabapple) and one of the six taxa that make up the range of apple types in the garden of the Villa Kramář.

Apple 'Primula' *(Malus domestica 'Primula')* – an autumn variety with more resilient fruit, grown in the Lesser Pálffy Garden and at Vojan Gardens.

Apricot, Siberian or **Tibetan** *(Prunus armeniaca)* – the commonest type of apricot cultivated, but of uncertain Oriental origins, and a member, along with peaches, cherries and plums, of the vast *Prunus* genus. It is grown in pomaria, as in the upper section of the Schönborn Garden and on the terraces of the Lesser Pálffy and Great Fürstenberg Gardens.

Aronia or **Black Chokeberry**, often called erroneously **Chokecherry** *(Aronia melanocarpa)* – a tree and shrub originally from the east of North America. It can be found growing in containers on the top terrace of the Great Pálffy Garden.

Ash, (Common or **European)** *(Fraxinus excelsior)* – a Europe-wide species, native also to the Czech Republic, that prefers moister soil. It features in stands in parks and gardens conceived in the spirit of Classicist Romantism and in conceptions derived therefrom. Typical is its appearance along the banks of the Čertovka in the park on Kampa Island, and on Slavonic Island, where it is part of the perimeter tree cover. As a particularly large tree it was included in some quite early foundations, as evinced by, for example, the Schönborn Garden. A unique solitaire specimen and one of the city's largest ash trees, with a girth of 512 cm, is to be found in the Great Garden at Strahov, next to the fishpond in the fruit tree zone beneath the Scenic Path. And there is another not far from the statue of Jupiter below the Chinese pavilion in the Cibulka park. At Vyšehrad, ashes are some of the main trees within the precinct of the Ducal and Royal Acropolis and in the Štulc and Karlach Gardens, as they are in the Santoška garden in Smíchov. Along with Horse-chestnuts, planes and birches they contribute to the tree cover in the arbours lining the parterre outside the Invalidovna, and ashes are also present in the compact Kaizl Gardens.

Ash, Green or **Red** *(Fraxinus pennsylvanica)* – native to central and eastern North America, it contributes to the tree cover within the precinct of the Ducal and Royal Acropolis – Vyšehrad, and is also to be found in the Klamovka garden.

Ash, One-leaved *(Fraxinus excelsior 'Diversifolia')* – a cultivar with simple leaves. At Rieger Gardens it features as a solitaire enhancing the monumental composition of sightlines, and it is also be to seen in the Klamovka garden.

Ash, Weeping *(Fraxinus excelsior 'Pendula')* – a cultivar with drooping branches. Examples are to be found in the Paradise Garden (Rajská zahrada), the Leslie Garden, the Gröbovka garden and within the Ducal and Royal Acropolis – Vyšehrad.

Ash 'Zlatia' *(Fraxinus excelsior 'Zlatia')* – a golden-leaved ash cultivar, it features as a solitaire enhancing the monumental composition of sightlines at Rieger Gardens.

Beech, Copper *(Fagus sylvatica 'Atropunicea')* – a red-foliaged cultivar of the Common beech often used as a solitaire, for the creation of colour contrasts and for giving shape and dynamic colour to the outline of stands, as illustrated by specimens in the Rampart (Na valech) Garden, the gardens of the Villa Kramář and at Nebozízek, and in Fidlovačka park, Rieger Gardens, Svatopluk Čech Gardens and Bezruč Gardens, on Svatopluk Čech Square in Vršovice, and in the Kinský, Santoška and Klamovka gardens, in Na Skalce park, the Royal Game Preserve and the park on Karlín Square. Under the influence of the Classicist-Romantic yen for imitation, this huge taxon also made its way into the Schönborn and Great Fürstenberg Gardens. There is an impressive specimen in Vojan Gardens and a no less impressive pair in the Monastery Garden at Břevnov.

Beech, European or **Common** *(Fagus sylvatica)* – native to Europe and an important tree in the specifically Czech context, being widespread in and a mainstay of many Prague parks and gardens conceived in Classicist-Romantic terms and in conceptions derived therefrom. Examples include Gröbovka, Kinský and Bertramka gardens and Cibulka park. Beech knows no substitute in all kinds of woodland. The Hvězda game park owes its characteristic early-spring grey-pink tints to its beeches. The largest specimen growing there, with a girth of 476 cm, is near the Vypich (Vypišská) Gate and three more, measuring 350, 306 and 375 cm, are along the main path leading from this gate. More beeches grow at the foot of the slope towards the Ruzyně (Ruzyňská) Gate and in the area that lies between the Liboc Gate and the summer house. Yet another beech is in the newer part of the Černín Garden.

Beech, Oak-leaved *(Fagus sylvatica 'Quercifolia')* – an oak-leaved cultivar of the common beech, to be found in, for example, the Royal Game Preserve.

Beech, Weeping (Purple) *(Fagus sylvatica 'Pendula')* – a drooping cultivar of the common beech. Huge specimens are to be found in the Rampart Garden and the Lobkowicz Garden.

Birch, Silver or **Warty** *(Betula pendula* syn. *B. verrucosa, B. alba)* – a tree native to Europe and Asia Minor. To be found at the Bertramka, as part of the vegetation at the Hvězda game park, in the Kaizl Gardens and as one element in the arbours lining the parterre outside the Invalidovna.

Box *(Buxus sempervirens)* – a Mediterranean evergreen shrub or small tree, naturalised in the Czech Republic. Its commonest use is as shaped into small-scale hedges, edging and eye-catching topiary work. It is so used in, for example, the gardens of the Černín Palace, Three Red Roses House (U tří červených růží) and in the Štorberg and Ledebour (Ledeburská) gardens. There is broderie ornament created from box in the Monks' (Konventní) Garden at Strahov and in the Lobkowicz, Wratislaw and Vrtba (Vrtbovská) gardens, which also have trimmed box edging round the plots and spherical and conical box topiary. More broderie edging and single items of topiary using box are also to be found in the Wallenstein (Valdštejnská) Garden, in the gardens of the Straka Academy and the Villa Šternberg (country house) in Troja. Low trimmed box hedges also line a triangular space in the garden of the Villa Kovařovic.

Box Elder or **Boxelder Maple**, **Ash-leaved (Ashleaf) Maple**, or **Maple Ash** *(Acer negundo)* – a smallish tree originally from across the United States and up into Canada. In the Kinský Garden it contributes to enhancing the inner side of the vegetational backdrop and to how the sightlines are composed.

Broom, Common or **Scotch** (*Cytisus scoparius*) – a shrub distributed Europe-wide. In the Great Pálffy Garden it shares in skirting the retaining walls.

Buckeye, Red (*Aesculus pavia* syn. *Pavia Carnea*) – a small tree or shrub from the southeast of the United States. A major contributor to the vegetation framing the sightline in Chotek Gardens and to the net impact of the composition of the Na Skalce park.

Buckeye, Yellow, Common or **Sweet** (*Aesculus octandra* syn. *A. lutea, A. flava*) – a native tree of the south-eastern United States. Specimens can be seen in, for example, the Na Skalce park and in the courtyard of the Cibulka homestead.

Catalpa or **Indian Bean Tree** (*Catalpa bignonioides*) – a tree that originates in the southeastern United States – Florida, Alabama, Georgia and Mississippi, and can be seen in the Paradise Garden and the Rampart Garden, at the approach from Valdštejnská Street to the gardens that lie beneath the Castle, and in the park on Charles Square.

Catalpa, Yellow or **Chinese** (*Catalpa ovata*) – originally from China. The three most important specimens in Prague are in Bezruč Gardens, the Royal Game Preserve and the Gröbovka garden.

Cherry, Bird or (misleadingly) **Hagberry** or **Hackberry** (*Prunus padus*) – a native bush or tree distributed throughout Europe and central Asia as far as Siberia. It is to be found in the Royal Game Preserve, the Great Strahov, Seminary and Kinský gardens, in Štulc Gardens at Vyšehrad and many other sites.

Cherry, European Dwarf, or **Mongolian** or **Steppe Cherry** (*Prunus fruticosa 'Globosa'*) – a round-headed cultivar grafted at the top of the stem. Four specimens are growing on the top terrace in the Ledebour Garden.

Cherry, Japanese, or **Hill, Oriental** or **East Asian Cherry** (*Prunus serrulata 'Kanzan'*) – a small tree with a dense crown originating in Asia. Prague has avenues of Japanese Cherry at Nebozízek, specifically in the the part known as the Dahlia Garden. Five specimens are also distributed about the garden of Villa Kovařovic below Vyšehrad.

Cherry, Mahaleb or **St Lucie Cherry** (*Prunus mahaleb*) – a bush or tree originally common in southern Europe and beyond as far as Central Asia, and later spreading to the warmer parts of central Europe. In the park around the Kranner fountain it forms part of the rearside background vegetation, and it is also to be found as one of the species that give Štulc Gardens in Vyšehrad their character. It certainly grows in many other places as well.

Cherry, Sour or **Dwarf** (*Prunus cerasus*) – a fruit tree originally from the region of the Caspian Sea, Iran and northern India. Its cultivation in pomaria is attested in the Great Garden at Strahov, the Seminary Garden and Vojan Gardens, and it is also in the orchards of the Břevnov Monastery and the Villa Šternberg (country house) in Troja.

Cherry, Sour, 'Morela pozdní' (*Prunus cerasus 'Morela pozdní'*) – an old variety of Morello Cherry bred in France. In Prague it is grown in the Lesser Pálffy Garden, which is in essence a pomarium.

Cherry, Wild, see under **Gean.**

Chestnut, Sweet (*Castanea sativa*) – originating in the Mediterranean, Asia Minor and the Caucasus, this tree does best in warmer parts of the country. In Prague we find it in the Seminary Garden, where it is scattered among other woodland trees in the parts above the scenic walk. At the restoration of the Great Fürstenberg Garden some were planted there, and it is also to be found in the Gröbovka garden and the Royal Game Preserve.

Chokeberry, Chokecherry – see **Aronia.**

Clematis, Alpine (*Clematis alpina*) – a climber originally from southern and central Europe. It can be seen in the Great Pálffy Garden.

Clematis, Himalayan or **Anemone** (*Clematis montana*) – a climber originally from central and western China and the Himalayas. It can also be seen in the Great Pálffy Garden.

Cork Tree, Amur *(Phellodendron Amurense)* – a tree that hails from north-east Asia. Its bark used to be ground down and compressed to make corks. Can be seen in the Gröbovka garden.

Cornelian Cherry, **European Cornel** or **Cornelian Cherry Dogwood** *(Cornus mas)* – a native shrub or tree to be found throughout the termperate zone of the northern hemisphere. Along with other trees it has been newly planted on the terraces of the Great Fürstenberg Garden. It is also in Bezruč Gardens and in the park beside Chodov Fort.

Cotoneasters *(Cotoneaster sp.)* – shrubs or trees originally from Eurasia and northern Africa, though in the Czech Republic it is mostly shrubby species and cultivars that are grown. In parks and gardens it is often planted in drifts to control soil erosion, as on the steep slope in the garden of Villa Müller in Střešovice.

Crabapple, Aldenham *(Malus x purpurea 'Aldenhamensis')* – a hybrid purple crabapple with the flower colour less inclined to fade, one of six taxa making up the selection of apple types in the garden of Villa Kramář.

Crabapple, Eleiy *(Malus x purpurea 'Eleiy')* – a white-flowered cultivar of purple crabapple; in the garden of Villa Kramář it was included among the mix of six apple taxa.

Crabapple, Flowering Japanese *(Malus floribunda)* – a small tree from Japan to be found all over Europe and one of six taxa making up the selection of apple types in the garden of Villa Kramář.

Crabapple, Purple *(Malus x purpurea)* – a cross between blood-red crabapple and dwarf crabapple bred at Orléans in France with dark-red leaves, crimson flowers and dark-red fruit. It occupies the outer triangular plot in the lower parterre of Villa Šternberg at Troja.

Crabapple, Red Sentinel *(Malus x robusta)* – a tree of medium height and a cross that greatly resembles familiar types of fruit-bearing apple trees. In the garden of Villa Kramář it was included among the mix of six apple taxa.

Currant, Alpine *(Ribes alpinum)* – a shrub to be found throughout Europe and Asia. It is part of the peripheral hedging that gives the park on Charles Square its character. It can also be seen in the park by Chodov Fort.

Deutzia, Fuzzy or **Fuzzy Pride of Rochester** *(Deutzia scabra)* – a tree originally from China and Japan. Specimens are to be found in the Leslie Garden, the park on Charles Square and at numerous other sites.

Dogwood, Common *(Cornus sanguinea)* – a common shrub or tree throughout Europe, grown in the Czech Republic in many cultivars and occurring, for example, in the park by Chodov Fort.

Dogwood, Red-barked or **White** or **Siberian** *(Cornus alba)* – a shrub whose origins extend from eastern Europe to as far as away as China. In the Czech Republic it is grown in numerous cultivars, the broad spectrum of which is evidenced in the gardens and parks of Prague by their appearance amongst the shrubberies in the Schönborn Garden.

Dutchman's Pipe or **Pipevine** *(Aristolochia macrophylla)* – a vine native to the south-east of North America. A well-known specimen curls about the pergola by the portico in the Bulwark Garden (Na Baště).

Dyer's Greenweed or **Dyer's Broom** *(Genista tinctoria)* – a shrub originally from the Mediterranean; it contains yellow pigments that were used in the past for dying fabrics. With other woody plants it adds to the characteristic colour palette of the Great Pálffy Garden.

Elm, Wych or **Scots** *(Ulmus glabra)* – native to central and northern Europe and an important tree in the Czech Republic. This species is fairly resistant to Dutch elm disease, the tracheomycosis caused by the fungus *Ophiostoma ulmi, syn. Ceratocystis ulmi*, that decimated populations of Smooth-leaved (or Field) Elm (*U. minor*) in this country and elsewhere. There are specimens of *U. glabra* particularly in the Hvězda game park.

Fig, (Common) *(Ficus carica)* – a fruit tree or shrub from south-east Asia, but already widespread throughout the Mediterranean in the Middle Ages. In the Czech Republic it is grown in greenhouses, orangeries, figgeries and on sheltered sites. Within Prague, figs growing outdoors can be seen especially in the Royal, Wallenstein and Great Pálffy gardens.

Firethorn, (Scarlet) *(Pyracantha coccinea)* – a naturalised evergreen shrub originally distributed from Italy to Asia Minor. Alongside other shrubs it grows in the Maltese Garden, the garden courtyard of the Wallenstein Manège and elsewhere.

Fontanesia *(Fontanesia fortunei)* – a shrub that originates in China and south-east Asia and also Sicily. It is to be found in Svatopluk Čech Gardens in Vinohrady, in among the shrubs lining the south (Slezská Street) side.

Forsythia, (Border) *(Forsythia x intermedia)* – a cross between *F. suspensa* and *F. viridissima* (Greenstem Forsythia); it is to be seen in the Leslie Garden, the park around Chodov Fort and in numerous other parks and gardens.

Forsythia, Weeping *(Forsythia suspensa)* – originally from China, this shrub has been raised in the Czech Repblic in various cultivars. It is to be found in the Leslie Garden, the park on Charles Square and elsewhere.

Gean or **Wild Cherry** *(Prunus avium)* – a tree native to Europe and the Middle East and distributed throughout the entire area. It is to be founded in the wooded parts of the Great Garden at Strahov and the Seminary Garden, while along with other trees it has been planted on the terraces of the Great Fürstenberg Garden. It doubtless occurs at countless other sites.

Golden Rain Tree or **Pride of India** *(Koelreuteria paniculata)* – a smallish species from Asia, to be found, for example in the park on Charles Square.

Grapevine, Common *(Vitis vinifera)* – a woody climber originally from southern and central Europe and the Near East and Central Asia and one of the oldest plants in cultivation in many varities across the entire temperate zone. In the St Wenceslas Vineyard the Rhine Riesling and Ruland Blue varieties of grapevine are cultivated. In the Santa Clara Vineyard in Troja one part is given over to a selection of varities, the other to actual production. Vines deck the upper retaining wall in the Lesser Pálffy Garden, which is akin to a pomarium. They also enhance the terraces of the Great Pálffy and Lesser Fürstenberg gardens, and in the Franciscan garden they share in forming the boundary of the brothers' private area. There are other small vineyards in Vyšehrad and a large one in the Gröbovka garden.

Grape(-vine), Riverbank or **Frost** *(Vitis riparia)* – a climber widespread across the east of the United States and Canada. The species is frost-hardy and resistant to fungal diseases and phylloxera and is highly adaptable to various soil types, all of which leads to its frequent use as a rootstock. In the Ledebour Garden it grows against a retaining wall with massive pillars.

Guelder Rose *(Viburnum opulus)* – a native shrub that occurs throughout Europe and western and northern Asia and can be seen in the park by Chodov Fort.

Hackberry, Common (or **Northern** or **American**, also known as **Nettletree**) *(Celtis occidentalis)* – a tree that originates in the eastern part of North America. There are specimens in, for example, the garden of the Straka Academy, the Gröbovka, Klamovka and in the park on the square in Karlín. Along with other trees it has been newly planted on the terraces of the Great Fürstenberg Garden.

Hawthorn *(Crataegus oxyacantha* syn. *C. laevigata)* – a European bush or tree grown in the Czech Republic in numerous cultivars and to be found, among others, in Kaizl Gardens.

Hazel, (Common) *(Corylus avellana)* – a European shrub whose distribution extends into adjacent areas of Asia and northern Africa. It is most commonly found in pomaria, the peripheral parts of parks and gardens conceived in the spirit of Classicist Romantism and in conceptions derived therefrom and in general woodland areas. It is found in the Seminary Garden, the Santoška garden and elsewhere.

Hazel, Turkish or **Turkish filbert** (*Corylus colurna*) – a tree of the Balkans, Caucasus and Asia Minor. Two of the species are to be found growing in the Royal Garden, with more in the Paradise and Rampart Gardens, in the garden of the Villa Kramář, the Bertramka garden, in the Na Skalce gardens, Letná Gardens and in the park on Lyčka Square. In the Santoška garden there is a specimen with a girth of 284 cm.

Hickory, Shagbark (*Carya ovata*) – from the eastern part of North America. Largely overlooked in the Czech Republic despite its interesting flaky bark, but one example is in the Na Skalce park.

Honey Locust (*Gleditsia triacanthos*) – a tree with a distinctively shaped crown that originates in the eastern part of North America. It is wreathed in legend – Christ's crown of thorns is said to have been twisted out of twigs of it. There is a young specimen in one of the bosquets in the Wallenstein garden and another in the Friendship Park at Prosek. Mature trees are to be seen in the park on Charles Square, in the Jezerka park, the Kinský Garden and the park on the square in Karlín.

Honey Locust 'Sunburst' (*Gleditsia triacanthos 'inermis'*) – a thornless form of this species, to be found, for example, in the Santoška garden and in the Kaizl Gardens.

Honeysuckle, (Common or **European)** (*Lonicera periclymenum*) – a climber originally from south-western Europe and north Africa. In the Ledebour Garden it can be seen growing on a trellis by the retaining wall.

Hornbeam, Columnar European (*Carpinus betulus 'Columnaris'*) – a pyramidal form of Common (European) Hornbeam with a columnar to egg-shaped crown. Seven of them form the divide between the Paradise Garden and the Rampart Garden within the grounds of Prague Castle, while four pairs underline the cruciform disposition of the Wratislaw Garden.

Hornbeam, Common or **European** (*Carpinus betulus*) – native to Europe as far as the Caucasus and to Asia Minor, very much a Czech tree. It makes an unrivalled contribution to how various larger spaces are shaped. In the Černín and Wallenstein (Valdštejnská) gardens there are whole walls of them, with some shaped as half-cones, and there are more hornbeam walls in the garden courtyard of the Wallenstein manège (Valdštejnská jízdárna), stepped hedges and gateways with peepholes in the Monks' Garden at Strahov monastery, and cubes and arcades in the Vrtba Garden. In the Petřín Hill Rose Garden, Hornbeams have been shaped into walls and cylinders. In the Great Fürstenberg Garden and in the garden and orchard of the Villa Šternberg (country house) in Troja there are solid hornbeam hedges. Probably the oldest hornbeam espaliers are to be found along the path between the Vojtěška pavilion and the Josefka gloriette in the monastery garden at Břevnov. In its natural form, hornbeam has been integrated into the core vegetation of parks and gardens conceived in Classicist-Romantic terms and in conceptions derived therefrom.

Hornbeam, Weeping (*Carpinus betulus 'Pendula'*) – a form of the Common (European) Hornbeam with drooping branches. In the Rieger Gardens, for example, it features as a solitaire enhancing the monumental composition of sightlines.

Horse-chestnut, also known informally as **Conker Tree** (*Aesculus hippocastanum*) – originally from Greece, but naturalised here and in many other countries. It is a core species in many of Prague's parks and gardens, both in avenues and sometimes as a solitaire. Examples can be seen in the Nebozízek garden, the park on the Kampa, the Amerika garden, or the Santoška garden, where one growing next to a dwelling has a girth of 315 cm. In the Lobkowicz Garden horse-chestnuts ensure the stability of the original Baroque composition, and its general use on older sites is further attested by the Schönborn Garden. In the Wallenstein Garden a body of horse-chestnuts helps to give the bosquets their characteristic aspect. In the Great Pálffy Garden an old specimen survives next to the massive retaining wall on the second terrace, and there is another on the lower terrace of the Kolowrat Garden. Horse-chestnuts play a substantial role within the vegetation of the Nostitz Garden and on Slavonic Island, where they also make a significant contribution to shaping the sightline, so too at the Fidlovačka park. In the Cibulka park there are two outstanding specimens, one of which has a girth of 375 cm, on the slope beneath the Chinese pavilion not far from the statue of Jupiter; some more horse-chestnuts are growing, alongside specimens of Yellow Buckeye, in the courtyard of the Cibulka homestead. Avenues of horse-chestnut can be seen in, for example, Štulc Gardens in Vyšehrad, but above all in the Royal Game Preserve. The canopy of a regularly spaced array of horse-chestnuts shades the terrace of the restaurant in Letná Gardens. The horse-chestnuts in the park adjacent to the Petřín observation tower are also arranged in a grid pattern. Along with planes, ashes and birches they constitute the vegetation enclosing the arbours on the parterre outside the Invalidovna.

Horse-chestnut, Red (*Aesculus x Carnea*) – a cross between Horse-chestnut and Red Buckeye. Alongside other trees, two of them contribute to the overall effect of the bosquets in the Wallenstein Garden. During the last renovation of the Great Fürstenberg Garden two were planted on the terraces there. A mature specimen can also be seen in the Jezerka park.

Hydrangea, Smooth or **Wild**, or **Sevenbark** (*Hydrangea arborescens*) – a shrub native to the eastern United States, unlike most hydrangeas which come from Asia. It can be found growing in, for example, the Maltese Garden.

Kentucky Coffeetree (*Gymnocladus dioicus* syn. *Gymnocladus canadensis*) – a tree originating in the Mid-West of the United States and the southern Great Lakes region of Canada. This striking tree that comes quite late into leaf grows in the Rampart Garden, the park on Charles Square, the Na Slupi Botanical Garden of Charles University, the Klamovka garden and elsewhere.

Kerria (*Kerria japonica*) – a shrub widespread in eastern Asia, China, Japan and Korea, which can be seen in the Leslie Garden and elsewhere.

Laburnum, (Common) or **Golden Chain** (*Laburnum anagyroides*) – a shrub or small tree originally from southern Europe. It is included in the perimeter shrubbery of the park on Charles Square and in numerous other parks.

Lemon (*Citrus limon*) – a small tree or bush from the sub-tropics, cultivated in the Czech Republic in greenhouses and orangeries and put out in the summer months onto areas specially set aside for summering. In particular they can found arranged in containers on the terrace section of the Ledebour Garden.

Lilac, Chinese or **Rouen** (*Syringa x chinensis*) – a cross between *S. persica* and *S. vulgaris* constituting one of the taxa making up the lilac collection in the garden of the Villa Kramář.

Lilac, Common (*Syringa vulgaris*) – a shrub native to central and south-eastern Europe and one of the taxa in the lilac collection making up the garden of the Villa Kramář. It also occurs in the Leslie Garden, among the vegetation encircling the Nostitz Garden and doubtless at many other sites.

Lilac, Nodding or **Pendulous** (*Syringa reflexa*) – a native shrub distributed throughout Europe and one of the taxa making up the lilac collection in the garden of the Villa Kramář.

Lilac, Persian (*Syringa x persica*) – a hybrid probably between *S. reflexa* (Pendulous or Nodding Lilac) and *S. vulgaris* and one of the taxa making up the lilac collection in the garden of the Villa Kramář.

Lilac, Preston *(Syringa x prestoniae)* – a cross between *Syringa x swegiflexa* (Pink Pearl Lilac) and *S. villosa* (Late or Villous Lilac) and one of the taxa making up the lilac collection in the garden of the Villa Kramář.

Lime/Linden, Caucasian or **Crimean** *(Tilia x euchlora)* – a cross between *L. cordata* and *L. dasystyla*. It is a common, but important taxon that supplements the core vegetation in parks and gardens conceived in Classicist-Romantic terms and in conceptions derived therefrom and in general woodland sites. For instance, in the Hvězda game park it grows in both stands and avenues.

Lime/Linden, Common *(Tilia x europea)* – the product of crossing *T. cordata* with *T. platyphyllos*. It is found in Rieger Gardens and in other parks. It can be hard to distinguish from its parent species.

Lime/Linden, Glenleven *(Tilia x flavescens 'Glenleven')* – a cross between *T. americana* and *T. cordata*, used for the avenue in the garden of the Straka Academy.

Lime/Linden, Broad- (or **Large-**)**Leaved** *(Tilia platyphyllos)* – widespread in central Europe and a major, centuries-old native that is a linchpin of parks and gardens conceived in Classicist-Romantic terms and in conceptions derived therefrom. In the Kinský Garden it also functions as a solitaire, in the Amerika garden it forms part of the background vegetation, and it is one of the most important trees growing within the precinct of the Ducal and Royal Acropolis – Vyšehrad and in the neighbouring Štulc and Karlach Gardens. Rows of them serve to frame the beds and lawns in the park that is Karlín Square.

Lime/Linden, Silver *(Tilia tomentosa)* – originally from sough-eastern Europe and Asia Minor, and named after the silvery underside of the leaves. It grows within the precinct of the Ducal and Royal Acropolis and in the Karlach Gardens – Vyšehrad, in Friendship Park at Prosek and at numerous other sites.

Lime/Linden, Silver-leaved *(Tilia petiolaris)* – widespread in south-east Europe, the Balkans, Asia Minor and Syria. A linchpin species in parks and gardens conceived in Classicist-Romantic terms and in conceptions derived therefrom, hence its appearance in the Kinský Garden and Chotek Gardens, where it is also part of the terminal stand at the eastern end. It also forms part of the background vegetation in the Amerika garden.

Lime, Small-leaved (US **Little-leaved** [**Littleleaf**] **Linden**) *(Tilia cordata)* – widespread in Europe as far as the Urals. A major native for many centuries and a key tree in parks and gardens conceived in Classicist-Romantic terms and in conceptions derived therefrom and in many woodland areas. It appears in many places, such as the Hvězda Game Park, but is also used formally in avenues. There is a striking solitaire at the vantage point overlooking the Upper Stag Moat (Horní Jelení příkop) at Prague Castle. In the Wallenstein Gardens it contributes to the characteristic appearance of the bosquets and along with other species has been planted on the terraces of the Great Fürstenberg Garden. In Vojan Gardens a semicircle of *S. cordata* complements the Chapel of St Theresa of Avila, and in the Franciscan Garden the species forms the perimeter in the background. In the park round the Kranner fountain it is part of the background vegetation, likewise in the Amerika garden and in Svatopluk Čech Gardens in Vinohrady. It is one of the most important tree species in the precinct of the Ducal and Royal Acropolis – Vyšehrad and in the neighbouring Štulc and Karlach Gardens Vyšehrad.

Lime, Small-leaved (US **Little-leaved** [**Littleleaf**] **Linden**) **'Rancho'** *(Tilia cordata 'Rancho')* – a smaller-statured American cultivar of Small-leaved Lime with a conical crown. Along with other species it was planted on the terraces of the Great Fürstenberg Garden at its most recent renovation.

Lime/Linden *Tilia dasystylla* (no common name in English) – a tree that originated in south-west Asia. It can be seen by the pond in front of the statue of Diana with her Dogs in Cibulka park.

Magnolia, Japanese Bigleaf or **Japanese Whitewood Magnolia** *(Magnolia obovata)* – a species from Japan to be found in the Monks' Garden at Strahov Monastery.

Magnolia, Kobushi or **Kobus** *(Magnolia kobus)* – a tree native to Japan and Korea. This interesting tree, which is covered in flowers before the leaves burst, can be seen, for example, in the Royal Garden and the Rampart Garden.

Magnolia, Saucer *(Magnolia x soulangeana)* – a bush or small tree that is a cross between *M. denudata* and *M. liliiflora* with highly conspicuous dark-pink flowers that appear before the leaves. It can be found growing in the Royal, Schönborn, Leslie, Wallenstein and Great Fürstenberg gardens.

Mallow, Rose, also **Rose of Sharon**, one of several plants that share this name *(Hibiscus syriacus)* – a shrub originating in southern Asia. In the Great Pálffy Garden shrubs of this species are cultivated on the second terrace; in the Ledebour Garden they are container-grown.

Maple, (Common) Field *(Acer campestre)* – one of our most adaptable maples, native to Europe, Asia Minor and Central Asia. A major contributor to the vegetation in many Prague parks and gardens conceived in Classicist-Romantic terms and in conceptions derived therefrom. An exceptional solitaire specimen with a girth of 278 cm is to be found in the Seminary Garden next to the small pond beneath the erstwhile summer refectory, today the restaurant on the Petřín terrace. At the restoration of the Wallenstein Garden a Common maple was planted in one of the bosquets, several young trees of the species were also used in the restoration of the Great Fürstenberg Garden.

Maple, Field, 'Schwerinii' *(Acer campestre 'Schwerinii'*, **Hedge Maple**) – a cultivar typified by its burgundy-red autumn colouring; planted in the Great Fürstenberg Garden at the most recent renovation.

Maple, Mop-head *(Acer platanoides 'Globosum')* – a round-headed cultivar of Norway Maple, grafted at the top of the stem. For example, in the Černín Garden a row of lollipop maples separates the old part from the new, and two rows of them are part of the avenue approaching the Villa Kramář.

Maple, Norway *(Acer platanoides)* – the most common maple in Prague, otherwise distributed throughout central and northern Europe. It is a substantial component of the vegetation in almost all the gardens and parks conceived in the spirit of Classicist Romantism and in conceptions derived therefrom and in other wooded areas. It also enters other compositional contexts: for example, it is an element of the eastern margin in the garden of the Straka Academy, in the Great Fürstenberg Garden it has been more recently planted on the terraces, on Slavonic Island it is part of the perimeter tree cover, in the park surrounding the Kranner Fountain it is part of the backdrop, and in Svatopluk Čech Gardens in Vinohrady it contributes to how the patches of woodland are modelled. At Vyšehrad it is one of the most important trees within the grounds of the Ducal and Royal Acropolis – Vyšehrad and in Karlach Gardens – Vyšehrad.

Maple, Silver *(Acer saccharinum)* – a tree originally from the United States and southern Canada. There are specimens in the park on Charles Square, while in the Kinský Garden it contributes to enhancing the inner side of the vegetational backdrop to how the sightlines are composed, and there are others elsewhere.

Medlar, (Common) *(Mespilus germanica)* – originally from Asia Minor, the Caucasus and northern Persia, it spread to central Europe as early as the twelfth century. Very popular in mediaeval times and grown for its round brown or brownish-green pomes, today it is largely forgotten. Along with other fruit trees it is grown on the terraces of the Kolowrat

Garden and has also been planted on the terraces of the Great Fürstenberg Garden and in the pomarium of the monastery garden in Břevnov.

Mock Orange *(Philadelphus coronarius)* – a native shrub thought to have spread from a homeland stretching from southern Europe as far as the Caucasus, cultivated in central and western Europe since the 16th century. It grows in the Leslie Garden, the park next to Chodov Fort and doubtless elsewhere.

Mulberry, Black *(Morus nigra)* – a fruit tree originally from Asia Minor. In mediaeval times it was already being cultivated in Greece and the Mediterranean, though it is rarely grown today; one of the few sites is the pomarium of the Břevnov monastery garden.

Mulberry, White *(Morus alba)* – the fruit tree whose leaves are consumed by silkworms. It reached central Europe from Japan, China and central Asia, where it had been in cultivation for millennia. In 1841 an entire orchard of White Mulberry was planted in Vršovice. Today it is barely grown at all, but it can still be found in the pomarium of the Břevnov monastery garden.

Oak, Bur(r) *(Quercus macrocarpa)* – a tree from North America, striking for its large, deep-lobed leaves. Can be seen in the Royal Game Preserve and in the park on Charles Square.

Oak, Cut-leaf Turkey, 'Wodan' *(Quercus cerris 'Laciniata')* – a cultivar with deeply lobed leaves. Like the Turkey Oak proper this cultivar can also be seen in the Royal Game Preserve.

Oak, English, 'Fürst Schwarzenberg' *(Quercus robur 'Fürst Schwarzenberg')* – a form of Pendunculate (English) Oak with a conical crown, to be found in the Royal Game Preserve.

Oak, Fastigiate *(Quercus robur 'Fastigiata')* – A form of Pedunculate Oak with a slim, columnar crown. Two pairs of pillar-like oaks play a part in how the Monks' Garden at Strahov Monastery is structured. Individual samples of this cultivar in the Bulwark Garden, Chotek Gardens, and on Kampa, in the garden of the Villa Kramář, the Leslie, Great Fürstenberg and Santoška gardens, in the Na Skalce park, the garden of the Villa Müller and Kaizl Gardens. Along with London Plane and Small-leaved Lime this cultivar contributes to the fluidity of the sightlines in the eastern part of Letná Gardens.

Oak, Hungarian or **Italian Oak** *(Quercus frainetto)* – a spreading tree originally from south-east Europe and the Balkans. Side by side with many other species of oak it can be found in the Royal Game Preserve.

Oak, Northern Red *(Quercus rubra)* – originally from North America, this tree grows faster than native European oak species. It can be found in the Friendship Park at Prosek and was also planted on the terraces of the Great Fürstenberg Garden when they were last renewed.

Oak, Pedunculate or **English Oak** *(Quercus robur)* – a tree of Europe, north Africa and east Asia. A major long-lived native species. The way the leaves are attached to their stalks recalls knickerbockers, which helps distinguish this species from Sessile Oak. The Pedunculate Oak is used as a staple element of the parks and gardens of Prague conceived in Classicist-Romantic terms and in conceptions derived therefrom. It knows no substitute in all kinds of woodland. Outstanding examples can be found in the Cibulka park. The largest of all, beside the woodland path that is an extension of U Cibulky Street, has a girth of 527 cm. Another four outstanding specimens stand along this path, one with a girth of almost four metres. Another huge pedunculate oak with a girth of 345 cm is in the Hvězda Game Park. On the little island within what was Rudolph's fish pond in the Royal Game Preserve there are remains of the oaks that, alone of all the trees there, survived its destruction in the 1740s during the War of the Austrian Sucession.

In many cases pedunculate oaks can be found in the role of solitaires or contributing to shaping the fringes of stretches of woodland. We can see this in Chotek Gardens, the garden of the Villa Kramář, the Fidlovačka and Jezerka parks and in the Kinský, Santoška and Klamovka gardens. In the Wallenstein Garden pedunculate oaks contribute alongside other species to the characteristic aspect of the bosquets.

Oak, Pin or **Swamp Spanish Oak** *(Quercus palustris)* – a tree originally from the north of the United States and up into Canada. A specimen with a girth of 220 cm grows in the Santoška garden.

Oak, Sessile or **Durmast Oak** *(Quercus petraea)* – a tree native to Europe and the Far East, long-lived and of major significance in this country. The way the leaves are attached to their stalk recalls tight-fighting ski pants and are the quickest way to tell this tree apart from the Pedunculate Oak. The Sessile (Durmast) Oak is the backbone of stands in landscaped parks, but is also used as solitaires or in groups that tailor the edges of sightlines. They can be seen in this role in Chotek Gardens, where the largest individual has a girth of 332 cm. An avenue of sessile oaks lines the path leading to the Chinese Pavilion in the Cibulka park. The species can be found in the Bertramka and Klamovka gardens and has already been planted in the Friendship Park at Prosek.

Oak, Swamp White *(Quercus bicolor)* – a long-lived deciduous or semi- to fully evergreen tree from the east of the United State and Canada. Can be seen in the Santoška garden.

Oak, Turkey or **Austrian Oak** *(Quercus cerris)* – a frost-sensitive tree from southern Europe and Asia Minor. It can be found in the Royal Game Preserve, one fine sturdy specimen has survived in the garden of the Villa Šternberg (country house) at Troja. Along with other trees it was planted on the terraces of the Great Fürstenberg Garden when they were last renewed.

Oak, Turner's *(Quercus x turneri 'Pseudoturneri')* – a cultivar of the semi-deciduous *Quercus turneri*, a cross between the native Pedunculate (English) Oak and the Holm Oak from the Mediterranean, which was raised in Essex and is named after the nurseryman Mr Turner. This cultivar is relatively smaller than its parent, but more frost-resistant and less inclined to lose its leaves in winter; the best-known specimens are in the Rampart and Bulwark gardens.

Oak, Variegated English *(Quercus robur 'Variegata')* – a form of Pedunculate (English) Oak marked out by its leaves with their creamy-white irregular fringe. Can be seen in the Santoška garden.

Pagoda Tree, (Japanese) or **Chinese Scholar Tree** *(Sophora japonica)* – originally from central China and Korea, pagoda trees grow in a number of Prague's parks and gardens. A notable example is in the Paradise Garden at Prague Castle, another in the Rampart Garden. It has an important place in parks on the Kampa, round the Kranner Fountain, on Charles Square, within the grounds of the Ducal and Royal Acropolis – Vyšehrad, and in Svatopluk Čech Gardens and Bezruč Gardens in Vinohrady, in the eastern part of the park by Chodov Fort, the Kinský Garden and in the park on the main square in Karlín.

Pagoda Tree, Weeping or **Weeping Scholar Tree** *(Sophora japonica 'Pendula')* – a cultivar with a drooping canopy, grafted on the top of the stem. It can be found in the Rampart and Bulwark gardens, and in the park on the Kampa and in Svatopluk Čech Gardens.

Paulownia (sometimes known as **Princess Tree**, **Foxglove-tree**, **Empress Tree** or **Kiri**) *(Paulownia tomentosa)* – originally from China, hence the imperial/regal element in some of its names. Probably the largest specimen in Prague, indeed in the whole country, grows in the Rampart Garden, though the oldest may be the one in the Royal Game Preserve, thought to have been planted back in 1844.

Pear 'Boscova lahvice' *(Pyrus communis 'Boscova lahvice')* – a variety originating in France and grown in Prague in the Lesser Pálffy Garden, which is basically a pomarium.

Pear, Callery *(Pyrus calleryana)* – a tree or substantial shrub with a conical to rounded crown, distributed through north-east China, Japan and Vietnam. Along with other fruit trees it is grown on the terraces of the Kolowrat Garden, the upper end of which is essentially a pomarium.

Pear, Common or **European** *(Pyrus communis)* – a fruit tree widespread throughout central Europe, the Mediterranean and western Asia. Various varieties of pear are grown in Prague in pomaria like the one in the Great Garden at Strahov, the upper part of the Schönborn garden, the monastery orchard at Břevnov, and the orchard of the Villa Šternberg (country house) at Troja. Along with other trees it has been planted on the terraces of the Great Fürstenberg Garden. It features as a solitaire in Karlach Gardens in Vyšehrad.

Pear-Whitebeam hybrid *(Sorbopyrus x aucuparius)* – numerous such hybrids exist, derived from the first French hybrid **Bollwiller Pear**; this one is a tree with edible red fruit and can be seen in Rieger Gardens.

Peony, Tree *(Paeonia suffruticosa)* – a shrub that originated in China, brought to Europe in the late 18th century. It is certainly in the Leslie Garden and may be elsewhere as well.

Pipevine, see **Dutchman's Pipe**

Plane, London or **Hybrid** *(Platanus hispanica* syn. *Platanus x acerifolia)* – a substantial tree, a cross between *P. occidentalis* and *P. orientalis*. The five largest London Planes in Prague are to be seen in the Kinský Garden, the park on the Kampa, the Maltese Garden, the park on Charles Square and the Jezerka park. At Charles Square the taxon is represented by several other specimens as well. A huge solitaire is to be found in the new part of the Černín Garden and a fine pair of the trees anchors the sightline from Chotek Gardens to Queen Anne's summer house in the neighbouring Royal Garden. Other vast London Planes are to be seen growing in the garden of the Straka Academy, in Rieger Gardens and the Santoška garden. A promising specimen is growing in a lateral bosquet in the Wallenstein Garden. In the park on Svatopluk Čech Square in Vršovice this plane is represented amid striking stands of different form and colouration, while in the park close to Chodov Fort there is an avenue of plane trees at the foot of an earthwork. Together with small-leaved limes and columnar forms of English oak they share in giving the composition of sightlines in the eastern part of Letná Gardens its plasticity, and in the form of a multilinear avenue they stand along the gardens' approach walk. The park on the square in Karlín is set between lines of plane trees. And somewhat surprisingly the species also figures in the compact Kaizl Gardens.

Plum, (Common or **European)** *(Prunus domestica)* – a fruit tree with an age-old tradition of cultivation in central Europe. In Prague plums are grown in pomaria, in the Great Garden at Strahov, in the upper level of the Schönborn Garden, the Seminary Garden, Vojan Gardens, and in the orchard of the Villa Šternberg (country house) in Troja.

Plum, Purpleleaf *(Prunus cerasifera 'Atropurpurea')* – a red-leaved cultivar of the Cherry Plum that can be seen in the Leslie Garden.

Poplar, Balsam, or **Tacamahac** *(Populus balsamifera)* – a tree that originates in Alaska, Canada and the northern fringe of the United States. On Slavonic Island it is part of the perimeter vegetation and it also grows in the Gröbovka garden.

Poplar, Black *(Populus nigra)* – a native tree distributed throughout Europe and as far as Siberia and the Altai Mountains. One massive specimen plays a major role among the easterly vegetation that helps mould the composition of sightlines from the Chotek Gardens. On Slavonic Island it is part of the perimeter vegetation and it also grows in the compact Kaizl Gardens.

Poplar, Canadian *(Populus x canadensis)* – a cross between *P. nigra* and *P. deltoides* (Eastern Cottonwood or Necklace Poplar), among huge specimens of which, close by the lake near the Zeyer memorial in Chotek Gardens, the largest has a girth of 465 cm. On Slavonic Island it is part of the perimeter vegetation.

Poplar, Lombardy *(Populus nigra 'Italica')* – a tightly columnar variety of Black Poplar. Several specimens serve to enhance the period silhouette of Slavonic Island.

Poplar, Pyramidal White *(Populus alba 'Pyramidalis')* – a pyramidal cultivar of White Polar. On Slavonic Island it is part of the perimeter vegetation and it is also to be found in Rieger Gardens.

Poplar, White *(Populus alba)* – a native tree, originating further south in Europe, but now distributed Europe-wide and in Asia as far as the Himalayas. To be found in Na Skalce Gardens and in the park adjacent to Chodov Fort.

Pride of India, see **Golden Rain Tree**.

Privet, Common or **Wild** or **European** *(Ligustrum vulgare)* – widespread throughout Europe. It features in the perimeter shrubbery round the park on Charles Square and in the shrubberies of many other parks.

Quince, Flowering *(Chaenomeles speciosa)* – a shrub from Japan which can be found in the park by Chodov Fort.

Rose *(Rosa)* – a genus of shrubby, climbing and creeping plants with a distribution throughout the northern hemisphere, of which many varieties and cultivars are grown in the Czech Republic. Roses are found in numerous Prague parks and gardens, climbing varieties in, for example, the Hartig, Lesser Fürstenberg and Ledebour gardens, where it contributes to a strikingly colourful ensemble that includes the red-flowered 'Sympathie', the pink floribunda 'Coral Dawn', the yellow-flowering 'Casino' and the white-flowered 'Schwanensee'. The Great Fürstenberg Garden has climbers and 'landscape' roses; roses in beds are found in the park on Lyčka Square. In the Maltese Garden they have both climbers and shrubby roses. Ground-cover roses feature in, for instance, the garden of the Villa Müller in Střešovice. There is an extraordinary concentration of species and forms in the Petřín Hill Rose Garden.

Rose, Red-leaved *(Rosa glauca* syn. *R. rubrifolia)* – distributed across southern and, in part, central Europe, a species whose red leaves have a purplish tinge. In the Great Pálffy Garden it adorns the tops of the retaining walls.

Rose of Sharon, see **Mallow, Rose**

Rosebay, Mountain or **Catawba**, or **Catawba Rhododendron** *(Rhododendron catawbiense)* – an evergreen shrub or small bushy tree from North America. It can be found in, for instance, the Schönborn, Leslie and Maltese gardens. A noteworthy site for rhododendrons and azaleas of a range of species and varieties is the Na Slupi Botanical Garden.

Rowan or **Mountain Ash** *(Sorbus aucuparia)* – a small tree native in the Czech Republic and widespread throughout Europe and Asia. It is to be found in the Kinský Garden, the park by Chodov Fort and Friendship Park at Prosek as well as forming part of the basic tree cover in many of Prague's parks and gardens conceived in the spirit of Classicist Romantism and in conceptions derived therefrom.

Service Tree, Wild *(Sorbus torminalis)* – native to the Czech Republic, otherwise distributed from southern to central Europe. In many of Prague's parks and gardens conceived in the spirit of Classicist Romantism and in conceptions derived therefrom it enhances the basic tree cover. It shares this role with other *Sorbus* species most notably in the Kinský Garden, where it also features as a solitaire. Likewise in the park by Chodov Fort, in the Santoška garden and in the Friendship Park at Prosek. The species also constitutes the avenue that frames the park on Lyčka Square.

Snowberry, Common *(Symphoricarpos albus)* – a shrub originally from the west of North America. It makes up part of the undergrowth in the Nostitz Garden and of the perimeter hedging round the park on Charles Square, and it figures as a matter of course in many other parks and gardens.

Spindle, European or **Common** *(Euonymus europaeus)* – a bush or small European tree. It figures in the perimeter hedging around the park on Charles Square.

Spiraea, Bridal Wreath *(Spiraea x arguta)* – a shrub, probably triply crossed, that can be found in the park by Chodov Fort and elsewhere.

Spiraea, (Common) Bridal Wreath *(Spiraea vanhouttei)* – a cross between *S. cantoniensis* (Reeves' Spiraea or Double Bridal Wreath) and *S. trilobata* (Three-lobe[d] Spiraea) and part of the perimeter shrubbery that typifies the park on Charles Square. It also grows in the park by Chodov Fort and at many other sites.

Spiraea, Japanese, 'Bumalda' *(Spiraea x bumalda)* – a cross between *S. albiflora* (Japanese White Spiraea) and *S. japonica* (Japanese spiraea) that grows, *inter alia*, in the park by Chodov Fort.

Spiraea, Scalloped *(Spirea crenata)* – a shrub very widely distributed throughout Europe and western Asia and part of the perimeter shrubbery that typifies the park on Charles Square.

Spiraea, Thunberg's or **Thunberg's Meadowsweet** or **Baby's Breath Spiraea** *(Spiraea thunbergii)* – native to Japan and China and growing, *inter alia*, in the park by Chodov Fort.

Sycamore (US **Sycamore Maple**) *(Acer pseudoplatanus)* – a native species distributed throughout central and southern Europe. In Prague parks and gardens conceived in the Classicist-Romantic spirit and others derived therefrom it is a major component of the tree cover. Sycamore knows no substitute in all kinds of woodland. It features in other compositional contexts, as in the garden of the Straka Academy, where it forms part of the eastern margin. It is one of the most important trees in the grounds of the Ducal and Royal Acropolis – Vyšehrad, and also features in the compact Kaizl Gardens.

Sycamore, Purple, 'Spaethii' *(Acer pseudoplatanus 'Spaethii')* – a cultivar with burgundy leaves, with pale veins on the underside. To be found in, for example, Bezruč Gardens in Vinohrady.

Sycamore Purpurascens *(Acer pseudoplatanus 'Purpurascens')* – a cultivar whose leaves are dark-green above and pale-green below when fresh, later speckled red and ultimately red all over. It grows, for example, in the grounds of the Ducal and Royal Acropolis at Vyšehrad.

Sycamore, Variegated *(Acer pseudoplatanus 'Leopoldii')* – a cultivar with leaves that are yellowish pink, turning to green with yellow and pink dappling, and having red petioles. In the Kinský Garden and Fidlovačka park it contributes to enhancing the inner side of the vegetational backdrop to how the sightlines are composed.

Tacamahac, see **Poplar, Balsam.**

Trumpet Vine or **Trumpet Creeper** (US **Cow Itch Vine** or **Hummingbird Vine**) *(Campsis radicans)* – a North-American vine to be found growing by a retaining wall with an illusory trellis in the Ledebour garden..

Tulip Tree *(Liriodendron tulipifera)* – originally from North America, this striking tree has an interesting habit with flowers similar to tulips. It can be seen in the Royal Game Preserve and the new part of the Černín Garden; there is a young specimen in the Friendship Park at Prosek.

Vine, Crimson Glory *(Vitis coignetiae)* – a climber originally from Korea and Japan. In the Ledebour Garden it grows by a retaining wall on a trellis.

Walnut, (Common or **English** or **Persian)** *(Juglans regia)* – originated in the western Himalaya, from where it spread within Roman times into northern and western Europe. Walnuts trees feature in numerous Prague parks and gardens, such as at the palace of the Hložeks of Žampach, and the Seminary and Great Fürstenberg Garden.

Wayfaring Tree *(Viburnum lantana)* – a native shrub whose spread stretches from the Iberian Peninsula across central Europe and Ukraine to Asia Minor and the Caucasus and which can be seen in the park by Chodov Fort.

Whitebeam, Broad-leaved *(Sorbus latifolia)* – a tree originating in south-western Europe, most likely a hybrid of *S. torminalis* and *S. aria*. It enhances the basic tree cover in many of Prague's parks and gardens conceived in the spirit of Classicist Romantism and in conceptions derived therefrom. It shares this role with other *Sorbus* species most notably in the Kinský Garden.

Whitebeam, (Common) *(Sorbus aria)* – native to the Czech Republic, otherwise distributed from southern to central Europe. In many of Prague's parks and gardens conceived in the spirit of Classicist Romantism and in conceptions derived therefrom it enhances the basic tree cover. It shares this role with other *Sorbus* species most notably in the Kinský Garden, the garden of the Villa Kramář and elsewhere.

Whitebeam 'Magnifica' *(Sorbus aria 'Magnifica')* – a cultivar with shiny leaves, silvery on the underside, that may be seen in the garden of the Villa Kramář.

Whitebeam, Finnish or **Oakleaf Mountain Ash** or **Swedish Service Tree** *(Sorbus x hybrida)* – a cross between *S. aria* and *S. aucuparia*, to be found in, for example, the Klamovka garden.

Whitebeam, Swedish *(Sorbus intermedia)* – a tree or shrub, originally from southern Sweden, Denmark, north Germany and Scotland. In many of Prague's parks and gardens conceived in the spirit of Classicist Romantism and in conceptions derived therefrom it enhances the basic tree cover. It shares this role with other *Sorbus* species most notably in the Kinský Garden, where it also features as a solitaire. Likewise in the Klamovka garden.

Willow, Creeping *(Salix repens)* – a low shrub, widespread in Europe. It can be seen in the park at Chodov Fort and in Friendship Park in Prosek.

Willow, (Golden) Weeping or **Golden White** *(Salix alba 'Tristis')* – the commonest pendulous form of the White Willow. A fine sturdy specimen of Weeping Willow is growing in the Great Garden at Strahov right by the gardener's house, others are in Vojan Gardens in the part with the lake, by the lake in the Jezerka park, in Rieger Gardens, Kaizl Gardens and numerous other locations.

Willow, Grey or **Grey-leaf** or **Glaucous** *(Salix glauca)* – a shrub originally from Iceland, Scandinavia and northern Russia. It can be seen in Friendship Park in Prosek.

Willow, Rosemary Leaf *(Salix rozmarinifolia)* – a European and Asian shrub, to be found in the park by Chodov Fort.

Willow, White *(Salix alba)* – a tree or bush distributed throughout Europe and western Asia. It is to be found in the park by Chodov Fort, in Friendship Park at Prosek and elsewhere.

Wingnut, Caucasian or **Caucasian Walnut** *(Pterocarya fraxinifolia)* – originally from south of the Caucasus – north-eastern Iran and eastern Turkey. A mighty specimen with three trunks grows in the Na Slupi Botanical Garden of Charles University.

Wisteria or **Wistaria** *(Wisteria chinensis)* – a woody climber originally from China, Korea and Japan and the eastern United States. Perhaps the best-known example is the one growing round the pergola by the portico in the Bulwark Garden. Another is to be seen in the Hartig Garden, and possible the youngest specimen is growing in the Great Pálffy Garden.

Yellow(-)wood (*Cladrastis lutea*) – a tree whose origins are in Asia and North America. In the Czech Republic it is grown only as American or Kentucky Yellowwood (*C. kentukea*). It can be seen in the Na Slupi Botanical Garden of Charles University and in the Royal Game Preserve, where it may have been planted as early as 1844; and there is also a young one in the Nostitz Garden, where it is surrounded by the decaying trunk of the original tree.

Conifers

Arborvitae, Eastern, see **Cedar, (Northern) White**

Arborvitae, Oriental, see **Thuja, Chinese**

Arborvitae, Western or **Giant**, or **Giant** or **Pacific Red Cedar**, **'Aurea'** (*Thuja plicata 'Aurea'*) – a cultivar whose branches have a golden tinge. A fine pair of specimens is set in the oval of the parterre seen as you enter the garden of the Villa Kramář.

Cedar, (Northern) White or **Eastern Arborvitae 'Malonyana'** (*Thuja occidentalis 'Malonyana'*) – a variety typified by its slender, columnar shape. It was bred at the Mlyňany arboretum in Slovakia and can be seen in the Bulwark Garden within the precinct of Prague Castle.

Cedar of Lebanon (*Cedrus libani*) – a Middle-Eastern tree highly valued since ancient times. It fragrant wood has been used for burning as incense, in shipbuilding and furniture-making. Medicinal extracts are made from it, as well as cedar oil, used in treating wood and in embalming. A rare specimen can be found growing in the garden of the Villa Kramář.

Cypress, Nootka (also known by many other names) (*Chamaecyparis nootkatensis*) – originally from the coastal regions of North America, this is hardier than other cypress species planted in the Czech Republic. In Vojan Gardens in grows in the part with a small lake. It also grows in the Gröbovka garden and elsewhere.

Fir, (Colorado) White (*Abies concolor*) – originally from the west of North America, now one of the most widely used firs in this country. In the Bulwark Garden one has been deliberately shaped by cutting, and in the garden of the Villa Kramář it has been integrated into the sytem that composes the sightlines.

Fir, Douglas (*Pseudotsuga menziesii*) – native to western North America. A fast-growing fir that reaches huge proportions in maturity and is hardier at lower altitudes than pines and spruces. It is to be found in the Royal Game Preserve.

Fir, Grand, or **Giant, Lowland White, Great Silver, Western White, Vancouver** or **Oregon Fir** (*Abies grandis*) – a tree originally from the north-west of North America conspicuous for its symmetrical conical crown. Cultivation in Europe began after it was first brought to England in 1831. Specimens can be found in the garden of the Villa Kramář.

Fir, Veitch's (Silver) (*Abies veitchii*) – originally from central Japan. It has a slender conical crown and is used in Prague parks mostly as a solitaire. A voluminous specimen survives in the garden of the Villa Šternberg (country house) in Troja.

Hemlock, Eastern or **Canadian** (*Tsuga canadensis*) – from the far east of the United States and Canada. In the Czech Republic it is hardy and highly adaptable. Its occurrence in Prague's parks and gardens is attested by a group in the Nebozízek garden, and specimens in the Flower Garden of the Petřín Hill Rose Garden, the Gröbovka garden, the Royal Game Preserve and the Na Skalce park.

Juniper, Chinese (*Juniperus chinensis*) – a tree or bush from north-east China, Manchuria, Korea and Japan. Besides the basic species, several formally distinctive cultivars are grown in this country. A robust shrubby version of the taxon grows in the garden of the Villa Müller in Střešovice.

Larch, European *(Larix decidua)* – a native tree that, unlike most conifers, is deciduous. Besides the Alps and Carpathians, its original homeland includes Slovakia and Moravia. It significantly enhances the vegetation of many of Prague's parks and gardens conceived in Classicist-Romantic terms and in conceptions derived therefrom, and its pale green colour plays a special part in compositions based on contrast. This is its role in the garden of the Villa Kramář, the Great Fürstenberg Garden, the park by the Chodov Fort and Friendship Park in Prosek.

Larch, Golden *(Pseudolarix amabilis)* – a tree that originates in eastern China, relatively frost-hardy in the Czech Republic; it is used as a solitaire or in small groups. It can be seen in the Royal Game Preserve.

Maidenhair Tree or **Ginkgo/Gingko** *(Ginkgo biloba)* – a dioecious tree probably from eastern China, which is extremely long-lived. In China and Japan it is deemed sacred. Its deciduous fan-shaped leaves representd an historic form of needles unknown in any other needle-bearing species. Clusters of leaves grow out of truncated lateral shoots called brachyblasts. Known also for its medicinal powers, the tree is grown in the Czech Republic as a curio. In the Royal Game Preserve (Stromovka) there is one with a girth of 346 cm, in Klamovka park there is a columnar cultivar, and in the Na Slupi Botanical Garden they have a special cultivar called *Praga*. These are the three most important specimens in Prague. Others are in the Royal, Leslie and Wallenstein gardens, in Vojan Gardens, the garden of the Straka Academy, the Gröbovka garden and in the park on the main square in Karlín.

Maidenhair Tree or **Ginkgo 'Fastigiata'** *(Ginkgo biloba 'Fastigiata')* – a columnar Ginkgo cultivar. As a solitaire it augments the monumental composition of sightlines in Rieger Gardens, also occurring in the Gröbovka and Santoška gardens. The largest specimen of this cultivar, with a girth of 235 cm, is in the Klamovka garden. Together with the tree in the Royal Game Preserve and the special *Praga* cultivar in the Na Slupi Botanical Garden it is one of the three most important maidenhair trees in Prague.

Maidenhair Tree or **Ginkgo 'Pendula'** *(Ginkgo biloba 'Pendula')* – a Ginkgo cultivar with a drooping crown. A distinctive, picture-postcard specimen stands in the Nostitz Garden.

Maidenhair Tree or **Ginkgo 'Praga'** *(Ginkgo biloba 'Praga')* – a curious Ginkgo cultivar with horizontal-to-drooping branches. A male specimen grows in the Charles University Botanical Garden at Na Slupi and is probably the best-known maidenhair tree in the country. This tree, the one in the Royal Game Preserve and the columnar cultivar in the Klamovka garden are the three most magnificent maidenhair trees in Prague.

Pine, Black or **Austrian** *(Pinus nigra)* – a tree found in Europe, including the Balkans, and in Asia Minor. A resilient native species typified by its grey bark, deeply fissured at maturity and its needles, bundled in twos. In the parks and gardens of Prague it figures in a variety of compositions, in the garden of the Villa Bílek, the Villa Müller, Letná Gardens, Friendship Park in Prosek and elsewhere.

Pine, Limber or **Rocky Mountain White Pine** *(Pinus flexilis)* – a tree from the west of North America. It is a slow grower and in the Czech Republic it is hardy and undemanding. Its bark is dark-grey and its needles in bundles of five. It can be seen in the Gröbovka garden.

Pine, Schwerin *(Pinus x schwerinii)* – a frost-hardy cross between *P. wallichiana* (Bhutan or Himalayan Pine) and *P. strobus*, with silky, grey needles in bundles of five. It can be seen in the Gröbovka garden.

Pine, Scots *(Pinus sylvestris)* – a tree distributed across the temperate zone of Europe and Asia. An important native conifer notable for its rusty flaking bark in maturity. Its grey-green are bundled in twos. Scots Pine grows in many of Prague's parks and gardens conceived in Classicist-Romantic terms and in woodlands. It grows in the Stag Moat, the Hvězda Game Park, the park by Chodov Fort, Friendship Park in Prosek and elsewhere.

Pine, Weymouth or (**Eastern** or **Northern**) **White**, or **Soft Pine** *(Pinus strobus)* – originally from eastern North America. It is fast-growing, with a picturesque crown and delicate silky needles in bundles of five. Weymouth pines are often planted in groups, as in the park at Chotek Gardens, where a group of five contributed to how the vegetation was modelled, though only one of them has survived. Other sites include Štulc Gardens, Bezruč Gardens and, with a very fine group, the Santoška garden.

Redwood, Dawn *(Metasequoia glyptostroboides)* – a tree that originates in central China, fast-growing and, unlike most conifers, deciduous. It was not discovered until 1941, in Szechuan Province, having been known previously only as a fossil. European botanical gardens and arboreta acquired seeds in 1948, when they were distributed worldwide. This was probably when they were also acquired by the arboretum in Průhonice. Two specimens at the Castle, in the Royal Garden and the Rampart Garden, were planted in or shortly after 1950. Two had already been planted at the Na Slupi Botanical Garden.

Spruce, Norway *(Picea abies)* – a tree originally from central and northern Europe and one of the most widespread and fast-growing conifers. It is known in the Czech Republic in numerous cultivars of distinctive habits. It grows in many of Prague's parks and gardens conceived in Classicist-Romantic terms and in different applications. In Chotek Gardens it is part of the vegetation framework. It grows in the Cibulka park, where it has been planted secondarily as an extensive monoculture, and in the Hvězda Game Park and elsewhere.

Thuja, Chinese or **Oriental**, or **Oriental Arborvitae** *(Thuja orientalis* syn. *Platycladus orientalis)* – a small tree originally from eastern Asia. A thermophilic, fairly tender species that needs sheltered locations in this country. Two specimens of the taxon survive in the Vrtba Garden.

Yew, (European or **English)** *(Taxus baccata)* – a tree or shrub widespread in western, central and southern Europe. It is dioecious, slow-growing and long-lived, with hard, heavy wood. The needles are poisonous, as are the seeds, but not the fleshy, red, cup-like false-fruit. In parks and gardens it features in both natural and shaped forms and in many cultivars that vary in shape and habit. Probably the oldest yew in Prague is in the Paradise Garden of Prague Castle, there are many in the Lobkowicz Garden, two exceptional specimens in the Lesser Fürstenberg Garden, yet more in the park on Kampa Island, in the Gröbovka garden and the garden of the Villa Müller. Promising young plants can be seen in the park by Chodov Fort and in Friendship Park in Prosek. The monumental sightline composition in Rieger Gardens finds yew in the forgotten *'nobilis'* form, though it is possibly lurking today under a different name. There are eye-catching yews in the Černín, Vrtba and Great Fürstenberg gardens, and trimmed yew edging in the Franciscan Garden.

Yew, Japanese or **Spreading** *(Taxus cuspidata)* – originally from eastern Asia, this is a frost-hardy tree or shrub that includes naturally shape-specific cultivars, notably a columnar one and a spreading one. It is paler than *T. baccata* but equally amenable to being trimmed to shape; there are certain eye-catching examples of this in the Vrtba Garden.

Cypress, Bald or **Swamp** (and many other names) *(Taxodium distichum)* – originally from the swamps of the south-eastern United States. It prospers in the Czech Republic in damp environments, but without standing water. Examples of the taxon, typified by stumps that project upwards from the roots and are known as cypress knees, grow beside the ponds in the Royal Game Preserve.

LUMINARIES IN THE HISTORY OF THE GARDENS OF PRAGUE

Alliprandi, Giovanni Battista (1665?–1720), architect of Italian origin

Aostalli de Salla, Ulrico (1525–1597), master builder and architect of Italian origin

Barvitius, Antonín (1823–1901), architect

Batěk, Leopold (1864–1928), garden architect and technician, pomologist, dendrologist and teacher

Bayer (Beyer), Paul Ignaz (1656–1733), architect and master builder

Bendl, Jan Jiří (1610–1680), sculptor from a family who hailed from Schwabia

Benš, Adolf (1894–1982), Functionalist architect

Bílek, František (1872–1941), sculptor, graphic artist and architect

Božek, Romuald (1814–1899), design engineer and inventor

Böhm, Josef Kamil (1828–1862), sculptor

Braul, Jiří (?), garden architect and technician, court gardener to Prague Castle in 1834

Braun, Antonín (1709–1742), wood carver and sculptor from a family with roots in Tyrol

Braun, Matyáš Bernard (1684–1738), wood carver and sculptor from Tyrol

Brokof, Ferdinand Maxmilián (1688–1731), sculptor and wood carver

Brokof, Jan Josef (1652–1718), sculptor

Capauli, Jan Jiří (?), artistic and practical gardener and technician from a family with Italian roots, active before and after 1700 in the Přehořovský household in Malá Strana

Caratti, Francesco (1615/1620–1677), Italian architect and master builder originally from Switzerland

Červenka, Karel (1927–2001), fruit grower, research scientist and teacher

Dientzenhofer (Dienzenhofer), Kilián Ignác (1689–1751), architect and master builder from a family with roots in Bavaria

Dientzenhofer (Dienzenhofer), Kryštof (1655–1722), architect and master builder originally from Bavaria

Dinebier, Johann Heinrich (?), master builder and clerk of works at Prague Castle, active *c.* 1720-30

Fanta, Josef (1856–1954), architect

Ferdinand I Habsburg (1503–1564), King of Bohemia and Hungary, Archduke of Austria, Holy Roman Emperor, amateur architect and urbanist

Ferdinand of Tyrol (1529–1595), Austrian Archduke, Vicegerent of Bohemia, connoisseur of art, collector and amateur architect

Fialka, Jindřich (1855–1920), architect and master builder

Fierlinger, Otokar (1888–1941), garden architect, landscape gardener and urbanist

Foerster, Karl (1874–1970), garden architect, commercial grower, devotee of alpines and essayist

Fragner, Jaroslav (1898–1967), architect and painter

Fuchs, Josef (?), garden architect and technician, court gardener at Prague Castle in 1822

Gočár, Josef (1880–1945), architect and urbanist

Gotwiek, Jiří (?), master builder active at Strahov in the 1680s and 1690s

Hanzelka, Jiří (1920–2003), commercial engineer, traveller, writer, journalist, practical gardener and fruit-grower

Heerman, Jan Jiří (?–1710), sculptor

Heerman, Pavel (1673–1732), sculptor

Holub, Josef (1870–1957), painter

Höhnel, František (?), steward to the Kinskýs *c.* 1840, garden architect and technician

Chochol, Josef (1880–1956), architect

Jaroš, Tomáš (?), bell-founder, gun-maker and metal founder, active in Prague from 1540 onwards

Jäckel, Matěj Václav (1655–1783), sculptor and woodcarver of Lusatian-Serbian origins

Kaňka, František Maxmilián (1674–1766), architect and master builder

Klouček, Celda (1855–1935), sculptor, potter and stuccoer

Koch, Jindřich (1781–1861), architect

Kranner, Josef (1801–1871), master builder and architect

Krýsa, Julius (?), garden architect and technician, active in Prague in the late 19th and early 20th centuries

Křižík, František (1847–1941), engineer, inventor and entrepreneur

Kumpán Josef (1885–1961), garden architect

Lhota, Karel (1894–1947), architect

Loos, Adolf (1870–1933), architect

Lurago, Anselmo Martino (1701–1765), master builder and architect of Italian origin

Lurago, Carlo (1615–1684), master builder and architect of Italian origin

Machek, Antonín (1775–1844), painter and lithographer

Malý, František (1810–1895), garden architect, artist and engineer

Mathey, Jean Baptiste (1630–1696), painter and architect of French origin

Mattern, Hermann (1902–1971), German garden architect, artist, landscapist, journalist and teacher

Mauder, Josef (1854–1920), sculptor and painter

Max, Emanuel (1810–1901), sculptor

Max, Josef (1804–1855), sculptor

Mocker, Svatopluk (?), garden technician, fruit grower and teacher, active in Prague during 1912–14

Myslbek, Josef Václav (1848–1922), sculptor

Novotný, Jiří (1908–1978), garden architect and technician

Ohman, Friedrich (1858–1927), Austrian architect

Orsi de Orsini, Giovanni Domenico (1634–1679), master builder and architect of Italian origin

Palliardi, Ignác Jan Nepomuk (1737–1824), master builder and architect from a family of Italian origin

Pambio, Giovanni Mario del (?), master builder of Italian origin, active in Prague after 1539

Pavliš, Jindřich (1945–2011), forester, garden technician, humanist

Pieroni de Galiano, Giovanni (1586–1654), Italian lawyer, mathematician, cosmographer, engineer and architect

Plečnik, Josip (1872–1957), Slovene architect

Pokorný, Karel (1891–1962), sculptor and teacher

Prachner, Václav (1784–1832), sculptor

Profous, Zdeněk (?), garden architect, technician and plantsman, active in Prague in the 1830s

Reinhard, Claudius (?), Alsatian landscape gardener and technician, active in Prague after 1541

Reinhard, Nicolas (?), Alsatian landscape gardener and technician, active in Prague after 1541

Reiner, Václav Vavřinec (1689–1743), painter, especially of frescoes

Ritschl, František (?), landscape and practical gardener, designer and technician, court gardener at Prague Castle during 1851–82

Rossi, Domenico Egidio (1659–1715), Italian master builder and architect

Roštlapil, Václav (1856–1930), architect

Rösner, Carl (1804–1869), Austrian architect

Rothmayer, Otto (1892–1966), cabinet-maker, architect, designer, pedagogue

Rothmayerová, Božena (1899–1984), textile artist, clothes designer, pedagogue

Šaloun, Ladislav (1878–1946), sculptor

Santini-Aichl, Jan Blažej (1677–1723), master builder and architect from a family with roots in Italy

Schneider, Camillo (1876–1951), German garden architect, artist and dendrologist

Schnirch, Bohuslav (1845–1901), sculptor

Schollar, Jaroslav (1913–?), master builder

Schulz, Josef (1840–1917), architect

Scotti, Bartolomeo (1685–1737), Italian master builder

Seeman, Jiří (?), garden architect, artist and technician, active in Prague in the late 17th and early 18th centuries

Seidan, Tomáš (1830–1890), sculptor

Spatio, Giovanni (?), Italian stuccoer and master builder, active in Prague until 1534 at the latest

Stella, Paolo della (?), Italian stonemason, master builder and architect, active in Prague after *c*. 1538

Stevens ze Steifelsu, Antonius (1618–1672), painter of pictures and murals

Štrunc, Vladimír (1903–?), sculptor

Štursa, Jan (1880–1925), sculptor

Sudek, Josef (1896–1976), photographer

Thomayer, František (1856–1938), garden architect, artist and technician, nurseryman, journalist

Terzio, Francesco (1523?–1591), Italian painter and copper engraver

Ulman, Vojtěch Ignác (1822–1897), architect

Vobišová-Žáková, Karla (1887–1961), sculptor

Vosmík, Čeněk (1860–1944), sculptor and restorer

Vredeman de Vries, Hans (1527–1604), Dutch sculptor, architect and interior decorator, practical theorist of garden art

Vries, Adriaen de (1545/1560–1626), sculptor of Dutch origin

Wachsmann, Bedřich (1820–1897), painter and lithographer

Weppel, Jan František (?), artistic and practical gardener, court gardener at Prague Castle during 1793–1822.

Weppel, Matyáš (?), artistic and practical gardener, court gardener at Prague Castle during 1772–1793

Weinfurter, Václav (1954–2004), garden architect and technician

Wiehl, Antonín (1846–1910), architect

Wohlmuth, Bonifác (?), stonemason and master builder originally from Baden, active in Prague at the latest from 1556 onwards

Wurzelbauer, Benedikt (1548–1620), German sculptor and metal founder

Wünscher, Bedřich (?), garden technician and architect, painter and graphic artist, steward to the Kinskýs from *c.* 1840

Zábranský, Adolf (1909–1981), painter, graphic artist and illustrator

Zinner, František jr. (?), artistic gardener, designer and technician, court gardener at Prague Castle during 1727–42

Zinner, František Josef sr. (?), artistic and practical gardener, court gardener at Prague Castle during 1706–27

Zoula, Gustav (1871–1951), sculptor

WHERE THE GARDENS ARE: HRADČANY AND MALÁ STRANA

(For ease of orientation on maps outside this publication,
the Czech names are given in brackets; addresses are not translated
and are given in the conventional Czech form.)

Hradčany

1. Stag Moat (Jelení příkop)
2. The Royal Garden (Královská zahrada)
3. The Paradise Garden (Rajská zahrada)
4. The Rampart Garden (zahrada Na Valech)
5. The Hartig Garden (Hartigovská zahrada)
6. The Bulwark Garden (Zahrada Na Baště)
7. St Wenceslas Vineyard (Svatováclavská vinice)
8. Chotek Gardens (Chotkovy sady)
9. The Villa Kramář (Kramářova vila): Gogolova ulice 1
10. The Villa Bílek (Bílkova vila): Mickiewiczova ulice 1
11. The Černín Garden (Černínská zahrada): Loretánské náměstí 5
12. The Monks' Garden (Konventní zahrada): Strahovské nádvoří 1
13. The Great Strahov Garden (Velká strahovská zahrada)

Malá Strana

14. The Lobkowicz Garden (Lobkovická zahrada): Vlašská ulice 19
15. The Three Red Roses Garden (Zahrada U Tří červených růží): Vlašská ulice 9
16. The Štorberg Garden (Zahrada U Štorberků): Vlašská ulice 3
17. The Wratislaw [Mitrovitz] Garden (Vratislavská [Mitrovická]) zahrada: Tržiště 13
18. The Schönborn Garden (Schönbornská zahrada): Tržiště 15
19. The Vrtba Garden (Vrtbovská zahrada): Karmelitská ulice 5
20. The Seminary Garden on Petřín Hill (Seminářská zahrada, Petřín)
21. Nebozízek garden on Petřín Hill (Nebozízek, Petřín)
22. The Petřín Hill Rose Garden (Růžový sad na Petříně)
23. The Park by the Petřín Lookout Tower (park U petřínské rozhledny)
24. The Ledebour Garden (Ledeburská zahrada): Valdštejnské náměstí 3 / Valdštejnská ulice 14
25. The Great and Lesser Pálffy Gardens (Malá a Velká Pálffyovská zahrada): Valdštejnské náměstí 3 / Valdštejnská ulice 14
26. The Kolowrat Garden (Kolovratská zahrada): Valdštejnské náměstí 3 / Valdštejnská ulice 14
27. The Lesser Fürstenberg Garden (Malá Fürstenberská zahrada): Valdštejnské náměstí 3 / Valdštejnská ulice 14
28. The Great Fürstenberg Garden (Velká Fürstenberská zahrada): Valdštejnská ulice 8
29. The Wallenstein Garden and courtyard (Valdštejnská zahrada a zahradní nádvoří): Valdštejnské náměstí 4
30. The Leslie Garden (Lesliovská zahrada): Thunovská ulice 14
31. Kampa (Island)
32. The Nostic Garden (Nosticova zahrada): Maltézské náměstí 1
33. The Maltese Garden (Maltézská zahrada): Velkopřevorské náměstí 4
34. Vojan Gardens (Vojanovy sady): U Lužického semináře 17
35. Straka Academy (Strakova akademie): nábřeží Edvarda Beneše 4

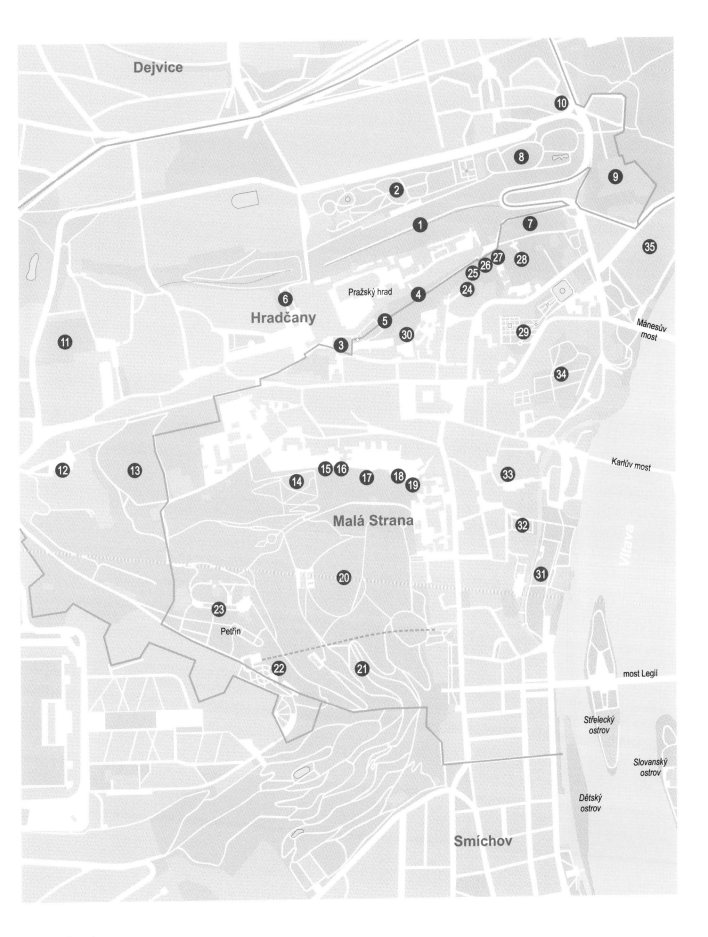

Dejvice

Hradčany

Pražský hrad

Malá Strana

Petřín

Smíchov

Vltava

Mánesův most

Karlův most

most Legií

Střelecký ostrov

Slovanský ostrov

Dětský ostrov

(311)

WHERE THEY ARE – IN THE REST OF PRAGUE

1. The Kranner Fountain (Krannerova fontána), Staré Město
2. The Franciscan Garden (Františkánská zahrada), Nové Město
3. Slavonic Island (Slovanský ostrov), Nové Město
4. Charles Square (Karlovo náměstí), Nové Město
5. The Amerika summer house (Letohrádek Amerika): ulice Ke Karlovu 20, Nové Město
6. The Botanical Garden of Charles University (Botanická zahrada Univerzity Karlovy): ulice Na Slupi 16, Nové Město
7. The Ducal and Royal Acropolis (Královská a knížecí akropole – Vyšehrad)
8. Štulc Gardens (Štulcovy sady – Vyšehrad)
9. Karlach Gardens (Karlachovy sady – Vyšehrad)
10. The Villa Kovařovič (Kovařovičova vila): Libušina ulice 3, Vyšehrad
11. Fidlovačka park, Nusle
12. Jezerka park, Nusle
13. Rieger Gardens (Riegrovy sady), Vinohrady
14. Svatopluk Čech Gardens and Bezruč Gardens (Sady Svatopluka Čecha a Bezručovy sady), Vinohrady
15. The Gröbovka garden (Gröbovka), Vinohrady
16. Svatopluk Čech Square (Náměstí Svatopluka Čecha), Vršovice
17. Chodov Fort (Chodovská tvrz), Chodov
18. The Kinský Garden (Zahrada Kinských), Smíchov
19. The Bertramka garden (Bertramka): Mozartova ulice 2, Smíchov
20. 'Na Skalce' Gardens, Smíchov
21. The Santoška garden (Santoška), Smíchov
22. The Klamovka garden (Klamovka), Smíchov
23. Cibulka park (Cibulka), Košíře
24. The Monastery Garden at Břevnov (Klášterní zahrada v Břevnově)
25. Hvězda Game Park (Obora Hvězda), Liboc
26. The Villa Müller (Müllerova vila): Nad Hradním vodojemem 14, Střešovice
27. The Villa Rothmayer (Rothmayerova vila): U páté baterie 50, Břevnov
28. The Stromovka Royal Game Preserve (Královská obora Stromovka), Bubeneč
29. Troja House or Villa Šternberg (Trojský zámek [Šternberská vila]): U Trojského zámku 4, Troja
30. Santa Clara Vineyard (Vinice sv. Kláry): Nádvorní ulice 134, Troja
31. Prague Botanical Gardens (Pražská botanická zahrada): Nádvorní ulice 134, Troja
32. Letná Gardens (Letenské sady), Holešovice
33. Karlín Square (Karlínské náměstí), Karlín
34. Lyčka Square (Lyčkovo náměstí), Karlín
35. Invalidovna and Kaizl Gardens (Kaizlovy sady), Karlín
36. Friendship Park (Park Přátelství), Prosek

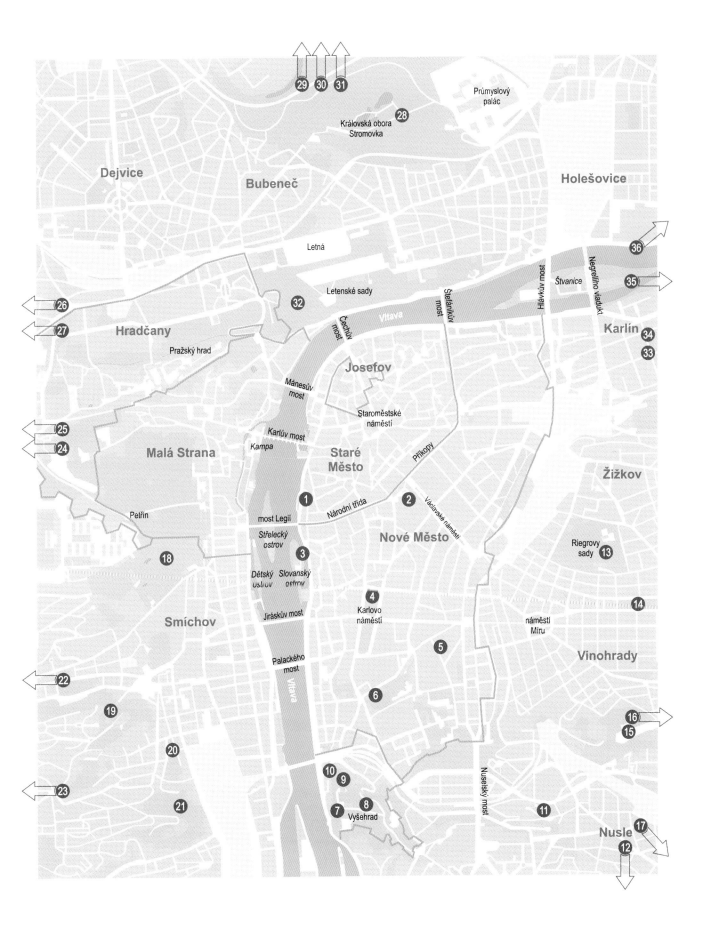

ILLUSTRATIONS

Unless otherwise stated, photographs are by Věroslav Škrabánek

Jacket: The Ledebour Garden; View from Villa Kramář
Jacket flap: Stag moat
Opening pages: View from the Seminary Garden, Lesser Fürstenberg Garden, Seminary Garden, The Singing Fountain in the Royal Garden, Vojan Gardens, Charles University Botanical Garden at Na Slupi

I. Documentary photos

Master of Vyšší Brod: 'Christ on the Mount of Olives', pre-1350, tempera on wood. After Jan Royt, *Česká středověká malba*, Karolinum 2002, p. 39 (National Gallery in Prague), p. 16

Master of the Tiburtine Sibyl: 'The Madonna in an Enclosed Garden', 1492 (1494?), tempera on wood, Gallery and Museum of the Litoměřice Diocese, Litoměřice, p. 17

'Men Working in an Orchard' – The Bible of Wenceslas IV, Vol. 1, 1390–1400. After Josef Krása, *České iluminované rukopisy 13.–16. století.* Prague, Odeon 1990. fig. 93, p. 163. (ÖNB Vienna, cod. 2759–64), p. 18

Jan Kozel – Michael Petrle: 'Veduta of Prague 1562' (the 'Wroclaw Prospect'), woodcut, City of Prague Archive, AMP-1, pp. 20–21

'The Royal Garden and Summer House', 1666, copper engraving, from the book: Lucia Barreta: *Historia Coelestis*, author's archive, p. 22

František Antonín Leopold Klosse: The Hvězda Game Park section of the 'Map of the Castle Water Supply System', 1723, Prague Castle Archive, p. 23

J. M. Ziegelmayer: Plan of the Royal Garden, 1744, Prague Castle Archive, 142/36, pp. 24–25

View of Malá Strana and Strahov, 1659–1665, colourised drawing (anon.), National Literary Archive, s. 27

Antonín Langweil: Vrtba Garden – a section of Langweil's model of Prague, paper, 1826–1837, City of Prague Museum, p. 29

Strahov Monastery and Garden, 1736, engraving, probably after a drawing by J. J. Dietzler, National Literary Archive, p. 30

Johann Georg Ringle: Černín Palace and Garden, 1740, engraving, probably after a drawing by F. B. Werner, National Gallery in Prague, p. 31

Leopold Paukert: The Powder Tower and the Old Avenues, 1790, colourised etching, City of Prague Archive, 196, p. 32

Filip and František Heger: The New Avenues, 1794, colourised etching, City of Prague Archive, 135, p. 33

Vincenc Morstadt: Prague from Chotek Road, 1832. After Božena Pacáková-Hošťálková et al., *Pražské zahrady a parky,* Společnost pro zahradní a krajinářskou tvorbu, o. s., 2000, p. 35

V. Gottman: View of the Temple of Diana in the Cibulka Park, post-1830, colourised engraving after a drawing by J. Rattay, colourised etching, City of Prague Museum, inv. no. 12662, p. 36

Antonín Langweil: The Palace Gardens of the Southern Slope of Prague Castle – a section of Langweil's model of Prague, paper, 1826–1837, City of Prague Museum, p. 38

Antonín Langweil: The Wallenstein Garden – a section of Langweil's model of Prague, paper, 1826–1837, City of Prague Museum, p. 38

Chotek Gardens, a) map, b) close-up of the pond, 1889, Archive of the National Museum of Agriculture, p. 40

Frontispiece on pp. 44– 45: View of the Great Strahov Garden

II. A guide to the parks and gardens of Prague

Hradčany: The Castle – Pohořelec – The Marian Walls
1 A–C/ Stag moat
2 A–D/ The Royal Garden
3 A–C/ The Paradise and Rampart Gardens
4/ The Hartig Garden
5/ The St Wenceslas Vineyard
6/ The Bulwark (Na Baště) Garden
7 A–B/ The Černín Garden
8/ Chotek Gardens
9/ Villa Bílek
10 A–C/ Villa Kramář

Hradčany: Strahov
1 1A–C/ The Great Strahov Garden
12/ The Monks' Garden

Malá Strana: Petřín Hill
13/ The Lobkowitz Garden
14/ The Garden at Three Red Roses House, photo by Božena Pacáková-Hošťálková
15/ The Garden of the Storberg House, photo by Božena Pacáková-Hošťálková
16/ The Schönborn Garden
17/ The Wratislaw (Mitrowitz) Garden, photo by Božena Pacáková-Hošťálková
18 A–F/ The Vrtba Garden
19 A–C/ The Seminary Garden
20 A–C/ Nebozízek Garden
21/ The Park by the Petřín Lookout Tower
22 A–C/ Petřín Rose Gardens

Malá Strana: Malá Strana Square – Klárov
23/ The Leslie Garden
24 A–C/ The Wallenstein (Valdštejnská) Garden
25/ The Palace Gardens on the Southern Slope of Prague Castle
25.1 A–B/ The Ledebour Garden

25.2 A–G/ The Lesser and Great Pálffy Gardens
25.3/ The Kolowrat Garden
25.4 A–D/ The Lesser Fürstenberg Garden
25.5 A–D/ The Great Fürstenberg Garden

Malá Strana: Kampa Island – Kosárek Embarkment
26 A–C/ Kampa Island and the Nostitz Garden
27/ The Maltese Garden
28 A–D/ Vojan Gardens
29/ The Straka Academy

Prague Old Town (Staré Město)
30/ The Kranner Fountain

Prague New Town (Nové Město)
31/ The Franciscan Garden
32/ Slavonic (Slovanský) Island
33 A–C/ Charles Square Park (Karlovo náměstí)
34/ The Amerika Summer House
35 A–C/ The Charles University Botanical Garden

Vyšehrad
36 A–E/ The Ducal and Royal Acropolis
37/ Štulc Gardens
38/ Karlach Gardens
39/ Villa Kovařovič

Vinohrady
40/ Rieger Gardens
41 A–B/ Svatopluk Čech and Bezruč Gardens
42 A–C/ Gröbovka Garden

Vršovice
43/ Svatopluk Čech Square

Nusle
44/ Fidlovačka Park
45/ Jezerka Park

Chodov
46/ Chodov Fort

Smíchov and Košíře
47 A–F/ The Kinský Garden
48 A–C/ Bertramka
49/ The Na Skalce Gardens
50/ Santoška Garden
51/ Klamovka Garden
52/ Cibulka Park

Břevnov and Liboc

53 A–D/ The Monastic Garden at Břevnov

54 A–B/ The Hvězda Game Park

Střešovice

55 A–B/ Villa Müller

56 A–B/ Villa Rothmayer

Bubeneč and Troja

57 A–D/ The Royal Game Preserve Stromovka

58 A–C/ Troja House (or Villa Šternberk)

59/ St Clare's Vineyard

60 A–E/ Prague Botanical Gardens

Holešovice: Letná

61 A–C/ Letná Gardens

Karlín

62/ Karlín Square

63/ Lyčka Square

64/ The Invalidovna

65/ Kaizl Gardens

Prosek

66/ Friendship Park

ACKNOWLEDGEMENTS

The Publisher, Karolinum, wishes to thank the curators of the various art and historical collections concerned for kindly making the original images available for the purpose of this publication and for agreeing to their being reproduced herein.

BOŽENA PACÁKOVÁ-HOŠŤÁLKOVÁ (b. 1946)

The author has devoted her professional career to the study of gardens, parks and land-scapes, mostly at the Czech National Heritage Institute (Národní památkový ústav) and its forerunners. She began in Prague in 1974, acting as specialist adviser to a number of the city's parks and gardens, a function in which she continued after moving in 1998 to the State Institute for the Care of Monuments. She has promoted with enthusiasm and erudition the proper care of parks and gardens under protection orders with respect to their history, organisation, structural engineering and botanical core, as well as to their respective ambiences. In the case of Prague's historic gardens she has been particularly able to apply her special knowledge to the drafting and execution of programmes of restoration. Gardens whose renovations have benefited from her expertise include the Černín, Vrtba, Wratislaw and Wallenstein palace gardens and the set of palace gardens beneath Prague Castle. She has also been involved in projects to restore monastic gardens (the Franciscan and Seminary gardens and at Břevnov) and the gardens of some major houses (the Kinský, Kovařovič and Müller villas among others). She also brought her experience to bear during the creation of the park adjacent to Chodov Fort and during the adaptations carried out at the Vyšehrad acropolis.

Select bibliography:
'Vývoj a pojetí přírodně krajinářské tvorby v Praze.' *Staletá Praha*, XV. Prague: Panorama, 1985, pp. 261–78.
'Zpravodaj o pražských zahradách a parcích.' *Portál*, Vol. XII, 31/1. Pražské středisko státní památkové péče a ochrany přírody, 1987.
'Kovařovičova kubistická zahrada pod Vyšehradem.' *Staletá Praha*, XXIII. Prague 1997, pp. 201–06.
'Odezva anglického krajinářského parku v Praze.' In: *Kamenná kniha, sborník k Romantickému historismu – Novogotice*. Sychrov: Zámek Sychrov, 1997, pp. 271–77.
Pacáková-Hošťálková, Božena – Petrů, Jaroslav – Riedl, Dušan – Svoboda, Antonín, M.: *Zahrady a parky v Čechách, na Moravě a ve Slezsku*. Prague: Nakladatelství Libri, 1999, 2nd edn, 2004.
Pacáková-Hošťálková, Božena et al: *Pražské zahrady a parky*. Prague: Společnost pro zahradní a krajinářskou tvorbu, občanské sdružení, 2000.
'Zahrada vily.' In: *Müllerova vila*. Prague: Argo in partnership with others, 2000, pp. 168–75.
Méně známé Pražské zahrady a parky. Prague: Společnost pro zahradní a krajinářskou tvorbu občanské sdružení, 2001.
'Petřínské zahrady a parky.' In: Zavřel, Jan et al.: *Pražský vrch Petřín*. Praha – Litomyšl: Nakladatelství Paseka, 2001, 2012, pp. 164–75.
'Péče o historické zahrady a parky, problémy a formy řešení.' In: *Tvář naší země*, conference volume, s.l., Nakl. Studio JB, 2002.